D0710378

George Alexander Stevens and *The Lecture on Heads*

Frontispiece: Rowlandson engraving published as a frontispiece to the Woodward edition of *The Lecture on Heads*, 1808. The actor is probably Lee Lewes. (University of Georgia Libraries.)

George Alexander Stevens

and

The Lecture on Heads

GERALD KAHAN

The University of Georgia Press
Athens

Set in Linotron 202 Baskerville

The paper in this book meets the guidelines for permanence
and durability of the Committee on Production Guidelines
for Book Longevity of the Council on Library Resources.

Library of Congress Cataloging in Publication Data
Kahan, Gerald.
George Alexander Stevens and the Lecture on heads.

Bibliography: p.
1. Stevens, George Alexander, 1710–1784.
2. Stevens, George Alexander, 1710–1784.   Lecture on
heads.   3. Actors—Great Britain—Biography.
4. Authors, English—18th century—Biography.
I. Title.
PN2598.S747K33   1984   822'.6   83-5054
ISBN 0-8203-0693-2

For my mother

Contents

Acknowledgments

The material for this book has been collected over a period of seven years, and I am indebted to many institutions and persons for their interest and assistance. In particular:

To the American Philosophical Society, whose two grants made it possible for me to travel to many libraries and examine their holdings; and to the University of Georgia Research Foundation, which generously provided funds to cover some of the publication costs.

To Dr. August Staub, who made available the resources of the Department of Drama at the University of Georgia.

To the efficient and courteous library staffs at the University of Georgia, the British Library at Great Russell Street and at Colindale, the Victoria and Albert Museum, the Library of Congress, the Folger Shakespeare Library, the Harvard Theatre Collection, Cornell University, the Maryland Historical Society, the Colonial Williamsburg Foundation, and the Manchester Public Libraries.

To Professors Yashdip S. Bains, Samuel N. Bogorod, John Dowling, Errol Hill, Kurt L. Garrett, Terence X. McGovern, Charles Pecor, and particularly Philip H. Highfill, Jr.

To my wife, Sara, for her continued encouragement, patience, and uncanny eye.

Introduction

GEORGE ALEXANDER STEVENS was a minor late Augustan who, although he moved at the fringes of his literary and theatrical world, was widely known and almost universally admired. Stevens pecked away at life and had one resounding success which brought him short-lived wealth but fame which lasted a century. He was a mediocre actor who performed many roles with the provincial companies and a few at the London patent houses. He wrote three novels, six theatrical entertainments, edited a magazine, and penned the lyrics for hundreds of songs, most of which were sung at the drinking clubs to which he belonged. His thrust was essentially satiric with large doses of classical allusions interspersed with comments on contemporary manners and foibles. In April 1764 he presented his *Lecture upon Heads*[1] at the Little Haymarket Theatre and his reputation was assured. Standing behind a long table covered with a green baize cloth and dozens of papier-mâché busts and wig blocks he began his two-hour long monologue satirizing one type after another: an Indian Chief, Alexander the Great, a London Blood, a Billingsgate Fishwife, a Horse Jockey, a Conjurer, a Frenchman, a Spaniard, a Dutchman, and finally a Methodist Parson. The floodgates were opened and a year later the small theatres, taverns, great rooms, and fairs of London were filled with his imitators. There were no copyright laws to protect him and he complained bitterly, but in vain. Before the vogue had run out in the early decades of the nineteenth century the *Lecture* had gone through some forty published editions and had received wholly, or in part, an uncounted number of performances which must have totaled close to a thousand. There were numerous spinoffs: *The Lecture on Hearts, The Lecture on No-Heads, The Lecture on Tails, Krainiographon* and others. As the years passed the original *Lecture* underwent numerous changes as characters were substituted and others were created to capitalize on their current topicality. Bits and pieces of the *Lecture* were often used as curtain raisers, entr'actes, and epilogues for evenings of varied entertainment. The molded busts were not always necessary; painted portraits were

1

Plate 1: The *Lecture* presented in a small room. (Harvard Theatre Collection.)

often substituted and it then became possible to pack all the accoutre-
ments of the performance into a single trunk allowing the performer
to give the *Lecture* wherever he could find an audience. The *Lecture*
became a staple of the one-man (or -woman) entertainer and brought
many back from the brink of penury. A typical example is given by
Cecil Price,[2] who recounting the trials of a small touring company in
Wales in 1779 tells of the Hillyard family, performers with the Portsmouth Company of Comedians who decided to withdraw because of a
financial dispute. Price writes, "Hillyard would not starve. When he left
... he had every intention of making his way to Monmouth and earning
a living by the performance of 'A Lecture upon Heads (Tails) and
Hearts.' He hoped for the patronage of the gentry."

The *Lecture* was given throughout the English-speaking world: England, Ireland, Scotland, Wales, India, Canada, Jamaica, and the eastern American seaboard. It had reached the American shores a year
after its London premiere and was performed by the major actors of
the time: Lewis Hallam, John Henry, Thomas Wignell, James Godwin,
and others. Henry, when he was manager of the American Company,
would often give abbreviated performances while he served as an
advance agent for his group seeking official approval for forthcoming
engagements.

Since the *Lecture* was not classified as a stage play, it was a boon to
many actors who were bedeviled by the Licensing Act or confronted by
the puritanical attitudes of several of the American colonies. It is little
wonder that it held the stage and print as long as it did.

Notes

1. George Alexander Stevens consistently called his work the *Lecture upon Heads* rather
   than the *Lecture on Heads*. Subsequent performers and editors used the latter title
   which has now become commonplace.
2. Cecil Price, *The English Theatre in Wales* (Cardiff, 1948), p. 30.

I

George Alexander Stevens:
His Life and Works

ALTHOUGH GEORGE ALEXANDER STEVENS was a well-known and generally admired figure during the latter half of the eighteenth century, there is no consistent or detailed account of his life. Unlike many of his contemporaries, prominent and otherwise, he did not write his memoirs, and his biography is limited to the sketchy and often contradictory entries in the standard dictionaries of the period. A few references are made to the "papers of Stevens," but if they exist they have not surfaced. Three of Stevens's prose works—*The History of Tom Fool* (1760); *The Dramatic History of Master Edward . . .* (1763), and *Adventures of Speculist* (published posthumously in 1788)—are in part pseudo-autobiographical, picaresque novels in the tradition of Smollett, Fielding, and Sterne. They yield several clues but it is impossible to separate fact from fiction and in the reconstruction of Stevens's life it is always best to align oneself on the side of discretion rather than optimistic conjecture. The difficulties are further compounded by the fact that the name Stevens abounds in the literary and theatrical world of the half century. Our subject has frequently been confused with the famous Shakespearean editor George Stevens. The two men could not be further apart, either in personality or talent. There are suggestive but confusing references to individuals who eventually turn out to be Castevens, William Stevens, Samuel Stephens, J. Stevens, Captain Stevens, and Young Stevens; and George Alexander himself often had his surname spelled Steevens and Stephens in the playbills and notices.

The biographical sources,[1] which provide us with some raw data, have limited use. They tend, as do so many works of this kind, to repeat the same information from work to work or edition to edition, occasionally compounding errors of fact or adding details that do not hold up under scrutiny or contrary, inconvertible fact. All seem to agree, however, that Stevens was born in London in 1710 in the parish of St. Andrew's, Holborn. This is a short distance from the patent theatres and Stevens may have frequented the playhouses at an early age. His "father was a London tradesman, who apprenticed him to a trade,"[2] "but the obscurity of his birth has cast a veil over the early part of his life."[3] The roster of those who made their way in the theatrical world is filled with the names of many who chose not to follow the course set out for them by their parents and Stevens is no exception to this company. Since we will not encounter a verifiable record until 1741, the first three decades of his life remain in darkness. There are a few hints. In the preface to the *Adventures of a Speculist* the editor writes "STEVENS has been often heard to say, that in the war of (we think) 1739 or 1740, he went aboard a man-of-war, and used frequently to relate the following story: 'During an engagement one of his brother sailors was wounded; another sailor took him in his arms in order to carry him to the cockpit, but before he had brought him off the deck, a chain-ball carried away his head, unperceived by the sailor who was bearing him. When the surgeon saw the trunk, he cursed the sailor for bringing him a man without a head. "Damn me (says the fellow) but he had his head on when I took him up."'"[4]

Throughout his literary career Stevens made constant use of classical references. He drew on Greek and Latin writings, personalities, and allusions and satirized them mercilessly. These classical references formed a large part of his appeal and endeared him, in part, to a select and discriminating audience. Charles Dibdin, writing of the English stage after Stevens's death, was one of his few detractors. He remarked that Stevens was "a *bon vivant* and a ready writer, who at pleasure could lug in the whole heathen mylothogy [*sic*] to electrify men into an admiration of poetry they were too far gone critically to examine . . ." and that he "had been so pampered by false praise that he fancied himself to the last moment a greater writer than Homer."[5] Stevens was demonstrably well read and his knowledge may have come from formal or self-education; his fertile brain was constantly alert to commercial opportunities. Isaac Sparks, a fellow actor and one of his drinking companions, "often said, that STEVENS was the best Greek scholar in England, and he seemed to think he had a college education."[6] One must consider the source, but the suggestion is intriguing.

Although Stevens will best be remembered for the *Lecture* and the many songs he wrote, he nevertheless spent a good part of his career in the theatre, legitimate and otherwise. His plays, most of which were produced, were minor efforts but received attention. Critical reaction tended to be derogatory or at best neutral, but some of his plays held the boards for respectable runs and were revived in and out of London. As an actor he performed a large variety of roles throughout his lifetime but met with little success. Mrs. Susanna Cibber said of him that "after having served two apprenticeships to the stage, he found himself as deficient in point of acting as at the first setting out."[7] Robert Hitchcock claimed he was "not possessed of much merit as an actor."[8] John Bernard in writing of one Charles Parker compared him with Stevens and others saying that they "considered acting their 'profession,' (and all other employments as mere modes of getting their bread,) [and had] the curious peculiarity of being clever at anything but acting."[9] All of these remarks are further reinforced by such biographical extracts as "his performances as an actor were contemptible";[10] "he acquired little fame in the profession";[11] "he showed little talent";[12] "as an actor, his merit was below mediocrity";[13] and a reference to his London engagement in 1753 "where he performed without any applause, to which indeed, his performances on the stage were in no respect entitled."[14] Stevens persevered, cajoled, and promoted himself at every opportunity, and at the end of a long career of major and minor successes, profligacy, dissipation, debt, illness, scorn, and adulation, he had compiled an impressive although critically undistinguished dossier.

The earliest discovered record of Stevens identifies him as an actor with an itinerant company operating out of Norwich in East Anglia in 1741. The group known as the Norwich Company of Comedians sponsored by the Duke of Grafton, Lord Chamberlain of His Majesty's Household, had established itself at the White Swan Playhouse and performed in that city generally from January through May. The remaining months they toured a local circuit which included such smaller towns as Ipswich, Woodbridge, Fakenham, Sudbury, and Hingham as well as the seasonal fairs. Since most of these towns did not have newspapers, the performance records outside Norwich are extremely scanty, but it is safe to assume that a good part of the Norwich repertory was also being done on the road. Sibyl Rosenfeld suggests that Stevens joined the company in 1741[15] (records are incomplete until January 1744), and the extensive list of his roles indicates that he was an important member of the troupe for the next four years. In addition to the plays documented below, the advertisements in the *Norwich Gazette* for these dates specify a large number of farces and pantomimes but the casts are very seldom listed. Stevens was almost certainly active in these entertainments as well. These were very important formative years for Stevens. He was now thirty-one and, although we may conjecture that he was involved in some form of theatrical activity during his twenties, his Norwich affiliation brought him into close contact with figures who were to become associates in his later life. Mr.

Herbert, the manager of the Lincoln Company, had been touring the area on and off between 1743 and 1746. Stevens probably met Herbert at this time and established the contact that was to bring him to Lincoln some years later.

Stevens's Roles at Norwich[16]

January 16, 1744. *The Provok'd Wife*. Sir John Brute.
January 23, 1744. *The Royal Convert*. Hengist.
January 31, 1744. *Don Quixote in England*. Don Quixote. *The Albion Queens*. Bridegroom.
February 6, 1744. *Sauny the Scot; or, The Taming of the Shrew*. Petrucio, the Tamer.
February 13, 1744. *The Bride-groom Bilked*. Bridegroom.
February 20, 27, 1744. *Macbeth*. Macbeth.
March 5, 1744. *The Provok'd Wife*. Sir John Brute.
March 12, 1744. *Love for Love*. Scandal.
March 19, 1744. *Jane Shore*. Duke of Glocester. *Birth and Adventures of Harlequin*. Squire Gawkey.
March 26, 1744. *Love's Last Shift*. Loveless.
April 2, 1744. *The Relapse*. Worthy.
April 9, 1744. *The Universal Passion*. (adapt. of *Much Ado about Nothing*). Gratiano.
April 16, 1744. *The Inconstant*. Mirabell (benefit for Stevens and Mrs. Bowman).
April 23, 1744. *The London Merchant*. Uncle.

End of Season

December 31, 1744. *The Beaux' Stratagem*. Dr. Foigard.
January 14, 1745. *Macbeth*. Macbeth.
January 21, 1745. *The Wife's Relief; or, The Husband's Cure*. Riot.
February 4, 1745. *The Funeral; or, Grief a-la Mode*. Campley. *The School-Boy*. Young Rakish.
February 11, 1745. *Hamlet*. The King.
February 18, 1745. *The Fatal Marriage* (competed this date with a company doing a one-night stand of *The London Merchant* at the Red Lion). Carlos.
February 25, 1745. *Richard the Third*. Richard, Duke of Glocester.
March 4, 1745. *The Roman Maid*. Dioclesian.

March 11, 1745. *King Lear, and his Three Daughters*. Edgar.
March 18, 25, 1745. *Sophonisba; or, Hannibal's Overthrow*. Hannibal.
April 1, 1745. *The Pilgrim; or, the Humours of Bedlam*. Mad Scholar.
April 2, 1745. *The Non-Juror* ("With a New Epilogue on Liberty by Mr. Stevens"). Colonel.
April 8, 1745. *The Tender Husband*. Pounce.
April 15, 1745. *The Universal Passion*. Protheus. *The Walking Statue*. Corporal Cuttum.
April 22, 1745. *The Constant Couple*. Colonel Standard.
April 29, 1745. *Theodosius*. Varames. *Varunea*
May 6, 1745. *Love's Last Shift*. Loveless.

Somehow Stevens was able to parlay his provincial experience into a minor engagement at Drury Lane for the 1745–46 season. It was the same season that Garrick had had his quarrel with Lacy at the patent house and had gone to Dublin. He missed Stevens's debut as Hamlet in the capital. The bills list the role as "attempted by a young actor" despite Stevens's advanced age. The opening night cast was a distinguished one: Charles Macklin played the gravedigger and Peg Woffington was Ophelia. In the November 29 revival Ophelia was performed by Kitty Clive. The play was revived on May 7, 1746 but the title role was played by Henry Giffard and Stevens was probably not with the company. Apparently Stevens had earlier played Hamlet in the provinces and, if the following anecdote is accurate, was to be disappointed by the more sophisticated audience's reception of his portrayal of the Prince.

From the applause he met with in his peregrinations, he became ambitious to try his fortune in London, where he made his first attempt in the character of Hamlet. There was something in the manner of his acting, so unusual and strange to a London audience, that, during the first act, they suspended their judgement; but in the second, they began to hiss violently; on which he came forward, and addressing himself to the audience, "What," said he, "you don't like it I find!—well, come—I'll give it you in a new taste." He then began to burlesque the character in such a manner as drew from the audience repeated bursts of laughter and applause.

But this species of performance was not calculated to afford permanent satisfaction, however it might entertain by its novelty; accordingly we find that, though a man of wit and learning, he never shone as a player, and was indeed rather below mediocrity."[17]

Stevens's Roles at Drury Lane

October 12, 1745. *Hamlet* "attempted by a young actor." Hamlet.
October 19, 1745. *The Orphan.* Polydor.
November 4, 5, 1745. *Tamerlane.* Axalla.
November 22, 1745. *Henry VIII.* Cromwell.
November 29, 1745. *Hamlet.* Hamlet.
December 17, 19, 1745. *Comus.* Younger Brother.
January 1, 1746. *Henry VIII.* Cromwell.
January 15, 1746. *Comus.* Younger Brother.
January 18, 20, 21, 1746. *Henry VI; or, The Popish Imposter.* King of Scotland.
February 17, 1746. *Comus.* Younger Brother.

There is evidence which suggests that Stevens may have been in London in 1748. An actor of that name is listed as Barnwell (his first performance on any stage) in *The London Merchant* on August 14 at the James Street Theatre. The performance was a benefit for James Stevens, a former bookseller who had taken to the stage and who may have been playing on his own behalf. During this season and the following, a Stevens is listed for the minor theatres. George Alexander may have played these and the booths at this time although the casts were generally not listed for James Street or the booths. One must constantly inquire into the possibility that Stevens was involved in the scripting, manufacture, and manipulation of the very popular puppet shows being performed at the booths and the fairs. We shall encounter very firm evidence of his activities in this sphere and later see its great significance as it relates to the *Lecture on Heads.* The Stevens who played Nicanor in *Busiris, King of Egypt* at the Haymarket on September 5, 1748, was the bookseller. On December 26 *Jane Shore* was given at James Street and a "*Dialogue,* written by Stevens" was offered, probably between the acts.

Stevens apparently had little success in London and returned to the provinces sometime near the end of the decade. In 1750 he was playing at Lincoln with Herbert's company.[18] It was probably here that he married Herbert's only daughter. She was also an actress and performed with him several years later.[19] Early in 1751 Stevens had undergone a severe illness and published some gloomy verses entitled "Religion; or, The Libertine Repentant," which delineated his earlier "dissipation, prodigality, want, idleness, [and] profligacy."[20] He wrote:

The following lines were lately wrote in a fit of illness, without any intention of ever troubling the public with them; but some very incorrect copies having been dispers'd, unknown to the author, occasion'd this edition.

The writer has look'd on life too long, and suffer'd too much in it, to be anxious for the event of these rhymes: they were wrote neither for profit, nor reputation; if he gets either of them, its more than he expected; or if he offends, its what he never design'd.

Bath, February 22, 1751.[21]

A typical passage is offered:

> By chance condemn'd to wander from my birth
> An erring exile o'er the face of earth;
> Wild thro' the world of vice,—licentious race:
> I've started folly, and enjoy'd the chace;
> Pleas'd with each passion, I pursu'd their aim,
> Cheer'd the gay pack, and grasp'd the guilty game;
> Revel'd regardless, leap'd reflection o'er,
> Till youth, till health, fame, fortune are no more.
> Too late I feel the heart-corroding pain
> Of sharp remembrance and severe disdain:
> Each painted pleasure its avenger breeds,
> Sorrow's sad train to riot's troop succeeds;
> Slow-wasting sickness steals on swift debauch;
> Contempt on pride, pale want on waste, approach.[22]

There is more than a touch of sadness reflected in these verses; and here in his earliest recorded publication is an unconscious forecast of the tribulations that were to beset his future career, particularly his frustration over the pirated and unauthorized editions and performances of his work in an age that lacked satisfactory copyright laws to protect the author.

Stevens went to Dublin in the fall of 1751 and spent a year and a half there as a member of the Smock Alley Company. Esther Sheldon claims that the 1751–52 season was its most brilliant.[23] Under the management of Thomas Sheridan, the company boasted the talents of Peg Woffington, Theophilus Cibber, West Digges, Isaac Sparks, and Sheridan himself. Stevens was for the most part relegated to small and supporting roles, but he remained active writing for the company and publishing several minor pieces. In August 1752 the *Covent-Garden*

Journal (Dublin) announced the publication of "A Week's Adventures; or, An Epistle from *England*, by George Alexander Stevens" and two months later advertised a second edition of the work under the revised title "A Week's Adventures in *England*: An Epistle from *George Alexander Stevens* to his Friend in *Dublin*." In the same year Stevens had published, in Dublin and then in London, his two-act farcical burlesque *Distress upon Distress; or, Tragedy in True Taste*. "This piece was never performed nor intended for the stage, but is only a banter on the bombast language and inextricable distress aimed at by some of our modern tragedy-writers."[24] We also learn that Stevens wrote the words for a new ballad, "In Honour of the True Blues," for a benefit for Mr. Kelly given at the Marlborough Green on June 4, 1752.[25]

The following anecdote, published after Stevens's death, vividly describes Stevens's return to the convivial life:

> He [Stevens] established in Dublin "The Nassau Court," over which Sparks, as LORD CHIEF JOKER presided. This court was held in a tavern in Nassau Street. Here subjects of humour were discussed, and all ranks of people were indiscriminately admitted into it to debate on them; but the greatest order and regularity were observed, fines being always inflicted and exacted for every offence, however trivial, against the established rules. A certain nobleman, now on the Continent, remarkable for folly and extravagance, having appeared in this court with his hat on, he was tried for the same. Just as sentence was going to be passed on him, Stevens, as his Lordship's advocate, started up and said, "that his client could not be punished for wearing a hat, because it was well known he had no *head*."[26]

Stevens's Roles at Smock Alley[27]

September 27, 1751. *The Twin Rivals*. Richmore.
November 16, 1751. *The Committee; or, the Faithful Irishman*. Obadiah.
December 7, 1751. *Zara*. Orasmin.
December 19, 1751. *The Man of Mode*. Shoemaker.
December 26, 1751. *The Necromancer; or, Harlequin Dr. Faustus*. Harlequin.
December 30, 1751. *The Tempest*. Trincolo.
January 2, 1752. *Sir Courtly Nice*. Hothead.
January 8, 1752. *The Relapse*. Lory.
January 20, 1752. *The Vintner Tricked*. Vizard.
January 22, 1752. *The Old Batchelor*. Setter.
January 28, 1752. *The Provoked Wife*. Razor.
January 29, 1752. *The Provoked Husband*. Squire Richard.

February 5, 1752. *The Way of the World.* Waitwell.

February 11, 1752. *Love for Love.* Ben.

February 29, 1752. *Coriolanus* (T. Sheridan adaptation). Volusius.

March 6, 1752. *The Alchemist.* Face.

April 2, 1752. *The Necromancer; or, Harlequin Dr. Faustus.* Harlequin.

April 9, 1752. *The Constant Captives.* Harlequin.

April 10, 1752. *The Provoked Wife.* Col. Bully.

April 27, 1752. *The [Beaux'] Stratagem.* Gibbet.

May 2, 1752. *The Roman Father.* Tullus Hostilius.

May 8, 1752. *The Rover.* Don Pedro.

May 13, 1752. *King Henry VIII.* King Henry.

May 15, 1752. *Harlequin Ranger.* Sharper.

May 30, 1752. *The Fatal Marriage.* Jaqueline.

End of Season

October 16, 1752. *The Beggar's Opera.* Opening night of season with Mrs. Stevens as Mrs. Vixen. Ben Budge.

November 29, 1752. *The Constant Couple.* Vizard.

January 31, 1753. *Love for Love.* Ben.

February 23, 1753. *The Constant Captives.* Bashaw.
The Merry Wives of Windsor. Host.

March 2, 1753. *The Way of the World.* Waitwell.

March 9, 1753. *The Lovers Revels.* Squire Gawky.

March 15, 1753. *The Pilgrim.*

April 11, 1753. For *The Provoked Husband* "A new Comic Epilogue to be spoken by Sparks and Stevens, in the characters of High Tragedy and Low Comedy . . ." Sparks benefit. Roderigo.

April 13, 1753. *Rule a Wife and Have a Wife.* Duke.

April 25, 1753. *The Humorous Trial of Ananias Overdone Swadler, before the Lord Chief Joker Sparks, according to the Rules and Manner of the Court of Nassau* (by particular Desire). Ananias.

May 5, 1753. (Same as above with slightly different title. For Stevens and Mrs. Crump benefit). Ananias.

What may appear to be the least significant among the three dozen roles listed above is, in the long view, probably the most important for our understanding of how Stevens was eventually to shape his career and establish his lasting identity. On April 25, 1753, and again on May 5, he presented his own *The Humorous Trial*; it was given again on August 25 after the regular season had ended. The following announcement is the earliest example I have found of Stevens and the satirical lecture. Other lectures followed before they reached a definitive form in his masterpiece, *The Lecture on Heads*.

AT THE MARLBOROUGH-GREEN On TUESDAY next the 25th Instant AUGUST 1752, will be perform'd a GRAND CONCERT OF VOCAL and INSTRUMENTAL MUSICK, consisting of TWO ACTS: Between which will be exhibited A SWADLER'S ORATION, By GEORGE ALEXANDER STEVENS In the Character of ANANIAS OVERDONE. Containing Observations on the *Light Within, Without* and *About*, LADIES of PLEASURE: Their *Light* Exemplified. A Dissertation upon the unclean Beast, call'd MAN. Ananias Description of his Cookmaid. The Event of his Amour. A Hint of the Bottle Conjurer. The great Sins of doing *Nothing* and of having *Nothing* to do. The Catechism of *Nothing*. Reflections upon MAMMON. The *Harangue* to conclude with a new Song, on the Benefit of Being MUM To conclude with GRAND FIRE-WORKS . . . Price 1s. 1d. The Concert to begin precisely at Six o'Clock DUBLIN: Printed by James Hoey, in *Skinner-Row*.[28]

A few months later Stevens was back in London, this time for an undistinguished two-season engagement at Covent Garden.

Stevens's Roles at Covent Garden

(1753–54 season)

November 12, 1753. *Volpone*. Corvino.
December 15, 1753. *Volpone*. Corvino.
February 12, 1754. *The Relapse*. Lory.
February 23, 25, 26, 28, 1754. *Constantine*. Marcellus.
March 9, 12, 16, 1754. *Julius Caesar*. Metellus.
March 25, 1754. *Florizel and Perdita* (Smock All. vers.). Clown.
April 20, 1754. *The Honest Yorkshireman*. Slango.
April 24, 1754. *Florizel and Perdita*. Clown.
May 21, 1754. *As You Like It*. Charles (role dropped for the Sept. 25 perf.).

(1754–55 season)

October 17, 1754. *Volpone*. Corvino.
November 4, 1754. *Tamerlane*. Stratocles.
November 6, 1754. *The Relapse*. Lory (replaced in the Nov. 29 perf.; role dropped for April 26, 1755, perf.).
November 27, 1754. *Cato*. Decius.

December 6, 1754. *Cato*. Decius.
December 10, 11, 12, 14, 18, 21, 1754. *Coriolanus* (Sheridan-Smock All. vers.). Brutus.
January 27, 1755. *Coriolanus*. Brutus.
January 28, 1755. *Julius Caesar*. Metellus.
February 7, 1755. *Cato*. Decius.
February 20, 1755. *The Mourning Bride*. Alonzo.
March 1, 1755. *The Mourning Bride*. Alonzo (replaced in the April 28 perf.).
March 6, 8, 10, 13, 15, 1755. *Appius*. Numitorius.
March 31, 1755. *Coriolanus*. Brutus.
May 12, 1755. *The Old Batchelor*. Bluff (this perf. a benefit for Costello, Bennet, and Stevens).

Stevens was again playing supporting roles and supplementing his tenuous career with various publications and further lectures as well as providing the well-known comedian Edward Shuter with songs, drolls, and benefit speeches. Shuter is claimed by some to bear a significant relationship to the genesis of the *Lecture on Heads*, but the two had a falling out toward the end of the decade. Shuter scorned Stevens and the latter expressed his bitterness in a mock dialogue that he inserted in his novel *The Dramatic History of Master Edward, Miss Ann . . .*, which was not published until 1763. In it Stevens has Miss Ann (Nancy Dawson, the popular singer, dancer, and mistress of Shuter) admonish Shuter for his ingratitude:

> I will say that for you Ned, that your gratitude and my virtue are two very fine things, if any body could but tell where to find them. There was *what's his name*, [Stevens] who wrote the Droll for you, and made you your *Dish of All Sorts*, and *The Day of Taste*, and several comic songs, which have been of much service to you in your benefits, both in town and in the country, how did you serve him? Didn't you expose him falsely and scandalously; and strove, by what you said of him publicly, in some of the most infamous bawdy-houses that you frequent, to render him contemptible? and he had never done anything, to my knowledge, to merit such treatment.—I wish he would write something about you; I wish he would; nothing he could print against you could be half so bad as the abuse you have loaded him with Neddy; but he don't value you nor I neither.[29]

Stevens seems to have been on better terms with Nancy Dawson than with Shuter. She had become very popular by 1760 and had danced the Hornpipe in the third act of the Covent Garden revival of *The Beggar's Opera*. The piece was danced to the tune of "Here we go round the

mulberry bush" and the words were attributed to Stevens. It came to be
known as "The Ballad of Nancy Dawson" and is mentioned in the
epilogue to *She Stoops to Conquer*. Stevens said of Nancy: "As she was
extremely agreeable in her figure, and the novelty of her dancing
added to it, with her excellence in execution, she soon grew a favourite
with the town, and became vastly celebrated, admired, imitated, and
followed."[30]

From the "Nassau Court" of Dublin, Stevens had now become a
contributing and imbibing member of several equivalent London
clubs. He became associated with "High Borlace," "Comus' Court,"
"The Choice Spirits," and perhaps others. In 1754 he published *The
Choice Spirits Feast: A Comic Ode*, which was "concerned with celebrating
a meeting of . . . his club, where the members enjoy good drink and pass
a pleasant time."[31] (See plate 2.) In *The Adventures of a Speculist* (written
ca. 1762, published 1788) Stevens describes the members of "Comus'
Court" and does his self-sketch: "That fresh-colored fellow [Stevens]
who follows him is an unaccountable being. He has wrote some tolerably droll songs, but spoils them by his attempting to sing them. He has
belonged to both Theatres, and never could make himself of any
consequence in either: he has too much sense for a fool, and too little to
be prudent. He might be either better or worse than he is, if he would
take any pains to bring it about. GEORGE, however, is either unable or
unwilling to think as he should do, but lets things come or go, just as it
may happen; too careless to consider of any moment but the present,
and, grasshopperlike, merry one half the year, the other half
miserable.[32]

In *The Dramatic History* he invents a ludicrous story which further
describes his talents and reflects his typical humor. He tells of a Corporal Knott, who has fallen in love with the married Madame Llwhyddwhuydd. In the wooing process Knott decides to have a song written
for her. He goes to the "Choice Spirits" meeting where

> he was inducted to the president, whom you see in the print, one George
> Alexander Stevens, and who was recommended to the Corporal as a
> songwriter.
>
> Stevens received six-pence from him as earnest, for it was a rule, which the
> poets of that club had made, to always have half the money down; and the
> president declared he would write the song, as soon as ever the disputa-
> tion was over, which the gentleman's entrance had put a stop to . . .
>
> All gentleman performers in the pen and ink way of song-making, must
> acknowledge it is extremely unlucky, when the lady's name, whose person
> they are to celebrate, won't make a proper rhime [*sic*].

Plate 2: *The Choice Spirits Assembly*. Probably a caricature of Stevens at center. From *Songs, Comic and Satyrical* (Oxford, 1772). (British Library.)

The number of pretty ballads which are sung every summer season, at all
public places of entertainment, would lose one part of their merit, were it
not for the name jingle, which so aptly terminates every stanza, such as

Kitty Downs	Polly Savage
And Zouns	And Cabbage
Miss Apple	Love Miss Harriot
And Couple	And Judas Iscariot

What then could a song maker do with Llwhyddwhuydd? had he not
cunningly supplied that defect, by verifying her Aeolian name Chloe; and
fitted up so tasty a love-song for the Corporal, that Mr. Knott, taking the
bard by the hand, swore, had he any more money about him to signify, he
would have made George a handsome present.[33]

The year 1754 also saw the publication of Stevens's "heroi-comical"
poem "The Birth-Day of Folly" written in imitation of Alexander
Pope's *Dunciad*. It is a slight work satirizing folly and various contemporary figures. One of the attacks is directed at Charles Macklin, the
great actor whose life was to span nearly the entire century. Macklin
"retired" from the stage in 1753 and set out on a new career as caterer
and host. At great expense he had a large room fitted out on Hart
Street in the Covent Garden Piazza and in March 1754 opened his
elegant dinner-coffee house. He turned out to be a poor businessman;
he extended credit unwisely, was fleeced by his servants, and eventually
was eaten out of house and home. In part to ameliorate these losses and
in part to satisfy his own aspirations as a lecturer and orator, Macklin
turned to another scheme. He refurbished his property and on
November 22, 1754, announced his opening of "The British Inquisition." This venture was designed to present his auditors with a series of
public lectures on a wide variety of topics. The first lecture was on
Hamlet, and a few weeks later his topics gradually extended to the
debating of such questions as "Whether a better Method may not be
found out of Manning the British Fleet, than is practised at present?"
and "Whether Women of Reputation are as justifiable as Women of
Pleasure, in the Use of Paint for their Complexion?" In the beginning
the project was reasonably successful, but it soon became a subject of
scorn and mockery. Not to be outdone, Samuel Foote, that "son of
Fun," began his own series of burlesque oratories at the Haymarket
and also tried to humiliate Macklin by attending the "Inquisition" and
harassing him in public. Stevens was late to join the fray. On December
24 it was announced: "AT the LECTURE ROOM, formerly the Theatre in
James-street, near the Tennis-Court, Haymarket, This Evening will be
read, A Comic Lecture on the Pilgrim's Progress, A Disquisition on the
Inquisition, and Orators Oratorised By GEORGE ALEX. STEVENS. The

Question, in which Specimens of true and false Eloquence will be given by the ROSTRATOR, is How far the Parabola of a Comet affects the Vegetation of a Cucumber. Ladies will be admitted—not to speak. Price Two Shillings and One Shilling."[34]

After the beginning of the new year Stevens modified the lecture and moved it to the Little Haymarket after Foote had yielded the premises. The announcement for the January 8 performances was thus described: "A Course of Comic Lectures will be opened by George Alexander Stevens. (Comment) At the New Theatre in the Haymarket (Where Mr Foote lately appeared), an Orator's head will be dissected *secundum artem*. The Orators will be shewn lying in state with Heiroglyphicks and Monumental Inscriptions. The question will be whether they will be allow'd Christian burial? If 't'is granted, a funeral Oration will be pronounced by *Martinus Scriblerus*. Places for the Boxes to be taken at the theatre. 'Thus orator to orator succeeds / Another and another after him / and the last.'"[35]

The lecture was repeated five days later on January 13 with an enticing new description of the contents. Despite the disclaimer, Stevens was certainly the author of the entire work.

AT GEORGE ALEXANDER STEVENS DISQUISITION (held at the New Theatre in the Haymarket) This Day the Comic Lectures will be continued. The proemium will be on the Use of Allegory in Speech, and a Specimen of true Allegory in which will be introduced the History of Humbugging. In the Genealogy of Riches and the Adventures of Flattery, the Monuments and Hieroplyphics [*sic*] of the Orators will be explained and commented upon. A Specimen of Triumvirate Oratory. A Dissertation on the Contention of modern Disputants, with the Quadrupede Syllogism. A Proposal for a Coalition of Orators. An Orator's Head dissected. To conclude with a new Peroration in Verse, not written by Geo. Alex. Stevens. * * * As there is nothing in this Undertaking contradictory to the rules of Good Manners, the Ladies need not be alarmed, nor fear that Decency should meet with the same Usage there she has suffered at other Oratories.[36] [See plate 3.]

Stevens was once again in financial difficulty. Neither the satirical lectures nor his engagement at Covent Garden was sufficient to sustain him, and he was forced to print the following public notice on January 18: "All persons who have Bonds, Notes, or any other legal Demands, on George Alexander Stevens, of Covent-Garden Theatre, are desired to send in an Account what their several claims are. Direct to A.M. at the Dog Tavern in St. James's Market, or for the same at Jack Speed's, White-Horse, Fetter-Lane.[37]

GEORGE ALEXANDER STEVENS,

In the Character of a POET. _ EPILOGUE to the DISQUISITION.

"*Propitious hear thy Votary in distreſs,*
"*O make his troubles or sensations leſs!*

Lod. del.   Publiſh'd by Fielding & Walker Janʸ 1.1780.   Cook Sc.

Plate 3: Stevens in *The Disquisition*, January 1755. (Folger
Shakespeare Library.)

He struggled on for the next three weeks in an attempt to supplement his income. A curious set of events followed, beginning with this announcement:

At the particular Desire of several Persons of Quality. At the New Theatre in the Hay-Market, on Tuesday Jan. 28 will be open'd The FEMALE INQUISITION. By a LADY. The first Dissertation will be on the superiority of the lovelier and better Sex over their pretended Lords and Masters. After the Dissertation will be a Debate, by a Disquisitor and the Lady of the Inquisition. And, after the Debate, the Preference contended for will be demonstrated by the astonishing Performance of Miss ISABELLA WILKINSON on the WIRE. With a proemium and Peroration, to be spoke by GEORGE ALEXANDER STEVENS. To begin exactly at Seven o'Clock. Places for the Boxes to be had at the Theatre. And those Ladies who have already taken Places, are earnestly requested to send their Servants early.[38]

Other than the fact that Stevens was again scraping by with bits and pieces there might be little to comment on here. It is curious, however, that he was also listed in the bills as playing Metellus in *Julius Caesar* at Covent Garden that same evening. If both notices are accurate, we are forced to visualize our actor/lecturer dashing across the street frantically changing his costume in time for his performance since his role in Shakespeare's play required him to be on stage at the beginning of the second act and to participate in the assassination. This must have been the case unless one of the bills is incorrect, or unless the part was cut that evening, or unless Stevens had made arrangements for a substitute. *The Female Inquisition* continued for two additional performances, the next on January 31 and the last on February 4. On these occasions they were described as "a short Comic ORATORIO." Miss Wilkinson continued on the high wire but Stevens now presented only the proemium. The ticket prices were listed as Boxes 5s., Pit 3s., and the Gallery at 2s.[39]

Stevens's activities are difficult to trace for the next six years. In 1759 Stevens published his *Collection of New Comic Songs*, which included the "Swadler's Harangue" he had performed earlier in Dublin. Also in 1759 he composed a droll entitled *The French Flogged; or, The English Sailors in America* for Edward Shuter, who offered it at his booth at Bartholomew Fair (September 3–6) and at his Southwark Fair booth (September 18–21). On March 20, 1760, it was performed for Shuter's benefit at Covent Garden when Stevens definitely played the role of Ben. On March 30, 1761, it was given at Covent Garden under the title *The English Tars in America*; on October 9, 1777, it was revived at the Haymarket as *The True-Born Irishman; or, The English Soldiers and Sailors in America*; and finally it was updated by Frederick Pilon for its premiere in Cork on October 24, 1780, and offered as the last play of the season. John Genest printed the following synopsis:

> An English Captain had been sent to America with 200 men under his command—he was forced by a storm to land on an island—He rescues a White Lady from 3 Frenchmen—her mother was an English woman who had married the Indian King—the King had adopted her as his daughter—the King gives the Captain the command of his troops and promises him the Princess if he should succeed in defeating the French.—Macfinen marries the Black Lady—this is a poor piece—it is attributed to G. A. Stevens—it was printed in 1767 as French Flogged, or British Sailors in America—it seems to have been acted in that year as the names of Miss Dawson and Miss Smith stand to the female characters—Stevens acted one of the sailors, and Davies the English Captain.[40]

There are strong indications that Stevens had another stint with the strolling players at this period of his career. He appears to have been attached to the Lincoln Company which was under Herbert's management. The group opened a playhouse at Grantham about 1757 which served as its base while touring the local circuit. Herbert died shortly afterward, leaving the company to his wife, who in turn assigned it to Stevens, who eventually turned it over to Dyer, one of his principal performers.[41] Once again Stevens ran into financial distress. He was deserted by his company in March 1761 and jailed in Nottingham for a debt he had incurred earlier in London. He wrote to an acquaintance, Dr. Edward Miller, organist at the church in Doncaster, asking the musician to raise funds to settle his obligation. Apparently he was successful since Stevens was back in London at the end of the year acting at Drury Lane. The text of the letter dated March 27, 1761, from Nottingham Gaol follows:

> SIR,
> When I parted from you at Doncaster, I imagined, long before this, to have met with some oddities worth acquainting you with. It is grown a fashion of late to write Lives;—I have now and for a long time have had leisure enough to undertake mine, but want materials for the latter part of it; for my existence now cannot properly be called Living, but what the painters term *still-life*; having, ever since March 13, been confined in this town gaol, for a London debt.

> As a hunted deer is always shunned by the happier herd, so am I deserted by the Company*, my share taken off, and no support left me, save what my wife can spare me out of her's:—

"Deserted in my utmost need
"By those my former bounty fed,"

With an oeconomy which till now I was a stranger to, I have made shift to victual hither to my little garrison, but then it has been with the aid of my good friends and allies—my clothes.—This week's eating finished my last waistcoat; and next, I must atone for my errors upon bread and water.

Themistocles had many towns to furnish his table, and a whole city bore the charge of his meals. In some respects I am like him, for I am furnished by the labours of a multitude. A wig has fed me two days: the trimming of a waistcoat as long: a pair of velvet breeches paid my washerwoman, and a ruffled shirt has found me in shaving. My coat I swallowed by degrees. The sleeves I breakfasted upon for weeks: the body, skirts, &c. served me for dinner two months. My silk stockings have paid my lodgings; and two pair of new pumps enabled me to smoke several pipes. It is incredible how my appetite (barometer-like) rises in proportion as my necessities make their terrible advances. I here could say something droll about a good stomach, but it is ill jesting with edge tools, and I am sure that's the sharpest thing about me. You may think I have no sense of my condition, that, while I am thus wretched, I should offer at ridicule: but, sir, people constitutioned like me, with a disproportioned levity of spirits, are always most merry when they are most miserable; and quicken like the eyes of the consumptive, which are always brightest the nearer the patient approaches his dissolution. However, sir, to shew you I am not lost to all reflection, I think myself poor enough to want a favour, and humble enough to ask it here. Sir, I might make an ecomium on your good-nature, humanity, &c. but I shall not pay so bad a compliment to your understanding, as to endeavour, by a parade of phrases, to win it over to my interest. If you could any night at a concert make a small collection for me, it might be a means of my obtaining my liberty; and you well know, sir, the first people of rank abroad will perform the most friendly offices for the sick: Be not, therefore, offended at the request of a poor (tho' a deservedly punished) debtor.

GEO. ALEXANDER STEEVENS.[42]

Several anecdotes concerning Stevens in the provinces were published after his death. They shed additional light on his tribulations and sense of humor: "He began his career at Norwich, and afterwards joined several strolling companies. His itinerant situation frequently threw him and his troop into laughable situations. One night when they were performing in a barn, they were too attentive to business to observe several large apertures in the boards, which afforded much enjoyment to the outside auditors: one of whom took the first opportunity of tearing away the train of a pompous heroine. Her duty soon after requiring her attendance on the stage, she stalked on, and in the height of tragic rant, exclaimed, 'Why do I bear about this gaudy train?' (at the same time turning round to observe it) added, 'D——n the dirty scoundrels, they have cut it off.'"[43] And elsewhere:

> When . . . Geo. Alexander Stevens was a first actor in a strolling company of players in England, he performed the part of Horatio in the Fair Penitent.—The Calista was a Mrs. B. who had been long the celebrated heroine in tragedies, and the fine lady in comedies. Mrs. B. in her decline, sacrificed too often to the intoxicating god. In proportion as the action of the play advanced to a conclusion, by endeavouring to raise her spirits with a chearful glass, she became totally unfit to represent the character. In her last scene of Calista, it was so long before she died, that George, after giving her several gentle hints, cried out, "Why don't you die, you b(itch)?" She retorted, as loud as she could, "You robbed the Bristol mail, you dog!" This spirited dialogue so diverted the audience, that much and loud clapping ensued. The manager seeing no end of this merry business, dropt the curtain and put an end to the tumult.[44]

Stevens retained loyalty and respect for provincial actors and the acting career that nurtured him. In 1766, after his reputation had been established by the success of his *Lecture on Heads*, Stevens contributed a prologue for the opening of the theatre season at Sheffield. He probably did not speak the piece but wrote with strong conviction:

> Let not stale prejudice your minds affect,
> Saying frightful! how should country players act?
> Is there no acre of dramatic earth,
> But London soil, to give an actor birth?
> Yes, like field flowers they blossom wild 'tis granted,
> But not the thing, until to town transplanted.
> And yet in town—but scandal's not my theme.
> To assist the country stage my fav'rite scheme,
> To prove that rural troops have real merit,
> When manag'd as they ought with proper spirit.
> To night's the trial, I'll not meanly sue;
> You sit in judgment: give the judgment due;
> Give it impartial, I'll give thanks to you.[45]

Stevens's two-volume novel *The History of Tom Fool* was published in 1760. It is a long discursive work heavy on sentimentality, morality, and the follies and affectations of the age, but it yields little, if any, autobiographical material. It is, however, typical of the author's satirical approach and his preoccupation with London types, excessive behavior, and bizarre incidents.

When Stevens returned to London after his Nottingham misadventure, he began what seems to be the busiest and most productive period of his life. He was with the Drury Lane Company from October 1761 until February 1764. Again his roles were mostly small ones, but Garrick must have taken a liking to him for Stevens was kept on, his wife was employed, and he received a benefit and wrote an afterpiece, *Hearts of Oak*, for the repertory. Stevens played the Doctor to Garrick's Macbeth and associated with the leading performers of the stage. These were exciting times and significant events were taking place in the theatre. In 1761–62 Garrick made his first move to banish spectators from the stage and completely enforced this rule the following season, and the opening months of 1763 were marked by the half-price riots at both patent houses.

Stevens's Roles at Drury Lane

(1761–62 season)

October 31, 1761. *Macbeth* (w/Garrick). Doctor.
January 9, 1762. *Macbeth* (w/Garrick). Doctor.
January 15, 16, 18, 20, 22, 23, 27, 28, 29, 1762. *Hearts of Oak* (Stevens's afterpiece).
February 27, 1762. *Hearts of Oak*.
March 2, 9, 15, 18, 23, 27, 1762. *Hearts of Oak*.
April 3, 21, 1762. *Hearts of Oak*.
April 28, 1762. *Cymbeline* (Garrick as Posthumus). Cornelius.
May 7, 8, 17, 18, 19, 21, 24, 1762. *Hearts of Oak*.
May 17, 1762. *The Merry Wives of Windsor*. Falstaff (benefit for Stevens, Weston, and Courtney).

(1762–63 season)

September 25, 1762. *1 Henry IV* (also *Hearts of Oak*). Glendower.
October 4, 22, 1762. *Hearts of Oak*.
November 3, 5, 11, 15, 1762. *2 Henry IV*. Mowbray.
November 4, 10, 13, 16, 1762. *Hearts of Oak*.
December 3, 1762. *2 Henry IV*. Mowbray.
December 22, 28, 30, 1762. *Two Gentlemen of Verona*. Panthino.

January 4, 6, 25, 1763. *Two Gentlemen of Verona*. Panthino.
January 7, 17, 21, 1763. *The Old Maid*. Hartwell.
January 10, 18, 21, 1763. *2 Henry IV*. Mowbray.
January 15, 19, 1763. *The Male Coquette*. Spinner.
January 17, 1763. *Macbeth*. Doctor.
February 2, 1763. *Two Gentlemen of Verona*. Panthino.
February 10, 1763. *2 Henry IV*. Mowbray.
March 17, 1763. *Macbeth*. Doctor.
March 24, 1763. *The Old Maid*. Hartwell.
April 13, 1763. *Macbeth* (also—Mrs. Steevens [*sic*] "1st appearance this
    stage" played Melissa in *The Lying Valet*; Stevens also delivered tickets
    for this performance). Doctor.
May 2, 20, 1763. *Macbeth*. Doctor.
May 6, 1763. *Hearts of Oak*.

(1763–64 season)

November 9, 16, 1763. *1 Henry IV*. Sheriff.
November 29, 1763. *Macbeth*. Doctor.
February 28, 1764. *Macbeth*. Doctor.

An obscure but revealing sidelight yields an additional facet of
Stevens's life. An actor-playwright, George Downing, had been acting
with Herbert's company in early 1761. The two quarreled and Downing came to London hoping to join the Drury Lane Company. He was
penniless when he befriended Stevens at a tavern. Stevens lent him
some money and was instrumental in getting him an acting job at
Borough Fair in Islington, where he played a king in Stevens's
St. George for England, "a kind of Medley, a compound of Tragedy and
Comedy, intermixed with Songs and Dances."[46] The play has not been
published and this is the only reference I have seen to the work.

Stevens is credited with writing the brief *Hearts of Oak*, which was
extensively performed as an afterpiece in 1762 and 1763. It is a musical
interlude comprising a song and dance by sailors. The piece "being a
mere temporary affair on the declaration of war with Spain, met with
good success."[47]

In 1762 another of those ubiquitous stage satires reached the bookseller's stall. Obviously prompted by the great popularity of Charles
Churchill's *Rosciad* (1761), which is said to have sold 10,000 copies, this
one, entitled *The Battle of the Players*, directed its attack at the rivalry
between Garrick and Rich, who managed Drury Lane and Covent
Garden respectively. It is a bitter work, occasionally confused but

consistently vengeful. Poor Stevens comes in for an unwarranted share of spite, not as an actor but as a writer.

> Two *Richerian* Officers endeavour to stop the Fury of his Arms, and oppose his further Progress. The first was named *Stevinus:** A Man, who having been Link-boy to the Muses, thought himself beloved by them; and who, mistaking Scurrility for Satire, and the grossest Dulness for the purest Wit, had been permitted by *Cloacina*, with Permission to deposite the excrementitious Works of his hard-bound Brain, in her sacred Temple; and, elated with a real Confidence, and an imaginary Valour, was grown so military mad in the Cause of Obscenity, that he swore he would wage eternal War with Delicacy and Virtue. The Name of the other was Dickius Smitherus [Richard Smith]: A Person of good and gentle Disposition, much respected as a Man, but not brilliant as a Soldier. Both these at once attack *Daviesius* [Thomas Davies]. and throw with all their Force their Spears against him. That of *Stevinus*, excessively blunt, and sent by a feeble, 'though revengeful Hand, scarce reaches the well-tempered Shield, and falls harmless on the Ground. As these two Warriors, now standing in an oblique posture, attempt to draw their Swords, a strong Lance sent from the powerful Arm of their Antagonist, transfixes them Side to Side, and they pour out their Souls in a Torrent of gushing blood.

> *Author of a thousand bawdy Songs and obscene Treatises; a constant Attendant at the Bucks nocturnal Meetings, and a great Pretender to Wit and Humour.

> Our Author has been guilty here of a very palpable Mistake. The obscene Writer he introduces, is not at C——t G——n Theatre, but on that of D ——y L——e. I applaud him, however, for satirizing him, on Account of his indecent Writings; 'though I must own, I cannot at the same Time exculpate our Author, in this very Work, for his *Double Entendres*. The Editor.[48]

Between 1762 and 1764 Stevens was the editor of a periodical called *The Beauties of All the Magazines Selected*. It was a kind of eighteenth-century *Reader's Digest* comprising interesting extracts from current magazines but also including a good bit of original material by Stevens. It was a dismal failure which had less than five hundred readers, but it is of importance to us because Stevens's contributions are so closely linked to the *Lecture on Heads*, which was to appear in a few years. He deals with such subjects as women's headdresses, male wigs, and oratory. He also refers in the 1762 volume to "the *Peroration* which Mrs. Clive has lately sung at Drury Lane Theatre, wrote by G. A. Stevens, to the tune of *Which nobody can deny*. It is called Fanny's Phaenomenon" and deals with the incident of the Cock Lane Ghost which had recently captured the public's imagination.[49]

Stevens's *The Adventures of a Speculist; or, A Journey through London*[50] referred to earlier was not published until 1788 although originally written about the same time as *The Beauties*. . . . It is another long novel, even more discursive than *Tom Fool* and also devoted to the satirizing of current follies and character types. He treats such topics as stockjobbers, inmates of Fleet Prison and Bedlam, prostitutes, rakes, oratory, fashion, wigs, and Methodism, and he includes the text of the comic paraphrase of Shakespeare's *Seven Ages of Man* which Stevens wrote for Shuter, who presented it at his own benefit at Covent Garden on March 21, 1763. There can be little doubt that much of the material in *Speculist* found its way into the *Lecture on Heads* and we shall shortly examine this connection. It is uncertain why *Speculist* was never published during Stevens's lifetime,[51] but its link with *The Beauties* . . . is unmistakeable. In the preface to *Speculist* the editor writes:

> It is a common remark, that "Genius can never die," and true may it be in the *metaphorical* sense of the word dying; but that the *production*, at least, of Genius are liable literally to perish, and insensibly to be swallowed up in the guelph of oblivion, we have too striking a proof in the untimely fate which the following admirable little pieces had nearly experienced.
>
> For their preservation they are now solely indebted to the care and industry which have been employed in the compilation of these volumes.—Almost thirty years have elapsed since they originally made their appearance; and then under the most unfavourable auspices were they ushered forth, having been published in an unsuccessful periodical work; —a work, to which there were many contributors beside our author, and of which, at no period of its short existence, there were known to be even five hundred readers, supported as it was with all the wit, and with all the humour—aye, with all the MANLY SENSE too—that, in the brightest moments of his literary career, ever animated the prolific brain of the mirth-inspiring GEORGE ALEXANDER STEVENS.[52]

In 1763 Stevens published his third novel, *The Dramatic History of Master Edward, Miss Ann, and Others, the Extraordinaries of These Times*. It too provides important information as seen in the previously quoted extracts. As with the first two novels, it deals largely with satirical comments on the personalities and follies of the time.

When Stevens performed the Doctor in *Macbeth* at Drury Lane on February 28, 1764, it was to be his last appearance on those boards for a decade. He was on the verge of his crowning success. Two months later, at 12:30 P.M. on April 30, he opened his *Lecture on Heads* at the Little Haymarket Theatre. It was an instantaneous and resounding success, to be quoted, pirated, adapted, printed, revised, spun-off, satirized, and applauded for the next half century. The remainder of this study will deal with the various aspects of the *Lecture* in great detail. At present we shall concern ourselves only with the dates and locales of Stevens's own performances of the work as we trace him to the end of his career.

The initial Haymarket production lasted twelve performances, closing on April 26 when Stevens's contract with the theatre ran out and could not be renewed because of a prior commitment. He then took to the road giving the *Lecture* in Dublin[53] and Manchester in July, in Bath in November and December, and in Bristol at the end of the year. On March 4, 1765, he returned to the Haymarket and during that month repeated the *Lecture*, with additions, for twenty-seven performances, moved to the Old Theatre at Richmond in early August, and then played at the Plaisterer's Hall, Aldermanbury, for thirty-five performances between October 21 and December 7. As we shall see later, these two years were a source of great irritation and distress to Stevens. Not only had many unauthorized and abbreviated versions of the *Lecture* been printed, but it was also staged by others, without permission—in some cases on the very same days Stevens was performing. He resorted to protest letters to the editors, reiterated the authenticity of his own version in the playbills, threatened law suits, wrote puffs, and added new material. It was all to no avail. Heads-mania swept England but Stevens, although he apparently earned a good income, never had complete control of his material.

At this point it is necessary to confront one extremely vexing problem. Many of Stevens's biographers categorically state that after his successful tour he took the *Lecture* to America, where he also performed it with great success. A typical entry reads: "After exhibiting it with great success all through England, he visited America, and was well received in all the capital towns; at Boston his reception was far beyond what he expected; he was apprehensive that the gloom of bigoted presbytery would prevent the humour of his lecture from being relished, but crowded audiences for the space of six weeks convinced him of his error; at Philadelphia his reception was equally flattering and profitable. After an absence of two years he returned to England, and soon after paid a visit to Ireland."[54]

If one traces the activities of Stevens from April 1764 through August 1766 it becomes highly improbable, actually impossible, for him to have been in America at the time stated. There is no other mention of such a visit in any of the sources consulted, and surely had a person of Stevens's prominence been in Boston or Philadelphia his presence would have been noted. The *Lecture* was first performed in America in February 1766 in Philadelphia and was repeated up and down the eastern seaboard for the remainder of the century. The *Lecture* was probably performed more frequently in America in this period than it was in Europe. The excerpt from the biographical entry quoted in the previous paragraph was printed as part of Stevens's obituary and repeats similar statements made in earlier biographies, but the particular difficulty is in the concluding sentence: "The writer of the greater part of this account received his information on the subject from Mr. S."[55]

The best guess is that this inaccuracy was handed down over the years and was originally based on a misrepresentation of the facts— namely that the *Lecture* was popular in America in the sixties but was being done by persons other than Stevens. Other accounts tell us that Stevens made close to £10,000 with the *Lecture*, some affirming that it "melted from his hands before his death,"[56] others that "he secured himself in affluence during the rest of his life."[57]

In an attempt to gain some measure of control over his *Lecture*, Stevens prepared an altered version called *The Supplement*. He adver- tised it as "an entire new lecture upon heads, portraits, and whole lengths" and opened it at the Haymarket on February 25, 1766. In a lengthy and bitter prologue he decries the "poaching Curs [who] meanly stole my game" and satirizes his fruitless attempts at legal redress. *The Supplement* was not well received, and after six perform- ances he stated his intention of adding new scenes, meanwhile return- ing to four performances of the original *Lecture*. At this time he peti- tioned the Lord Chamberlain to allow his wife to act with him in the *Lecture*, but I have found no record to confirm that she did so.[58] On April 3 he resumed the revised *Supplement* for twelve additional per- formances, closing on April 24.

Stevens returned to Manchester in August but does not seem to have presented the *Lecture*. He was there when it was done by Collins and is said to have expressed great displeasure. Stevens was on tour during the latter part of the year. He played at Whitehaven and while there spoke with a Mr. Dunn, who wished to publish some of Stevens's songs. This collection eventually appeared in 1771 under the title *The Choice Spirits' Chaplet; or, A Poesy from Parnassus*. Stevens claimed the publica- tion was unauthorized and rectified the situation with the publication of his *Songs, Comic and Satyrical* in 1772. Here is his account of the matter:

A paltry collection of Songs having lately made its Appearance, in which the Publisher has, with uncommon Effrontery, prefixed my name as Editor, and upon my disclaiming the imposition, has even had the Assurance, in a public Advertisement, to assert that he had my Authority for so doing; although I have more Veneration for the Public, than either to trouble them, or load the Daily Papers with an Altercation between a little Country Shop-Keeper and a Ballad-Maker, yet I once for all beg Leave to state the real fact.

About four years ago I exhibited my LECTURE at *Whitehaven*, and having Occasion to use this Man's Shop, he took the opportunity of soliciting me to give him a few Comic Songs, "because he had a Mind to publish a Volume to please his Customers in the Part of the Country where he lived;" and at the same Time opening a Song Book, shewed me several under my Name, which he told me he purposed to print in his Collection:—My Reply was; *"Sir, There is not one of those printed as I wrote them; and some to which my Name is affixed are really not mine."*—"But, Sir, replied my Chapman, will you please to give yourself the Trouble to mark such of them as are yours."—*"Why, really, Sir, I am ashamed of them."*—"Lord, Sir, they'll do very well here; pray Sir, take the Book home, and be so obliging as to mark them for me.—And if it would not give Mr. *Stevens* too much trouble, I should be greatly obliged if he would just put a Mark upon any other Songs in the Book that he thinks worth printing."—This was done, and the Volume returned the next Day.

From hence I could not imagine he would no *more* than insert my *Name* to the Songs I had owned; and I solemnly declare he had no Authority from me to use it otherwise.—What I did was a mere Act of common Civility;—I had not then, nor have I since had any Connection with the Man; and upon this Ground alone he has had the *Modesty* to charge me with a Breach of Promise by my Disavowal.—This among other Reasons, has induced me to publish my own Songs, which I now claim as property, and have entered in the Hall Books of the Stationers Company. G.A. STEVENS.[59]

Stevens visited Stratford at the end of 1767, presumably to deliver his *Lecture* and became involved in the deliberations that were to culminate in the Shakespeare Jubilee in the summer of 1769. The story of the festival as well as Stevens's involvement are told by Christian Deelman in *The Great Shakespeare Jubilee*,[60] and the details that follow are largely drawn from this book. The idea had germinated earlier that year when the Stratford Town Council decided to rebuild its Town Hall. Francis Wheler, the Steward of the Court of Records of the Borough of Stratford, wrote to David Garrick asking the actor to contribute an "Ornamental Memorial" for the building. Wheler promised to pair this with a picture of Garrick himself, and he offered

Garrick a membership in the Corporation of Stratford which would be
delivered in a box made of the wood of the mulberry tree Shakespeare
was said to have planted. The vain Garrick, always susceptible to
flattery, accepted without hesitation. Stevens learned of these preliminary negotiations one evening at a party given for him by his friend
John Payton, landlord of the White Lion Tavern. He strongly en-
dorsed the plan and on his return to London visited with Garrick. On
December 28 he wrote to Payton:

> Friend
>
> On Saturday night as soon as I arrived went to Mr. Garricks, acquainted
> Him with what the Inhabitants of Stratford wishd for relative to
> Shakespear—
>
> He informed me your Recorder had been with Him & told him about
> Shakespear Picture to be *in* the Town Hall—
>
> *Out* S^r was my answer: Mr Recorder was out S^r, & the Corporation of
> Stratford want Shakespear to be out—out I mean, to Every bodys view:
> there is a Nich, on purpose for his Statue—or Bust was Mr Garricks Reply.
>
> Here we were Interrupted, & I was obliged to go soon after about my own
> Business.
>
> Now friend. I am Certain Mr Garrick; (at least as well as I can guess,) will
> present ye Town & Town Hall with either a Statue or Bust of
> Shakespear—but by all means address Him by Letter properly. Set forth
> his great merits, & that there is not a man in England (except himself) to
> whom you could apply with equal propriety for a Bust, or Statue. Say
> Shakespear the father of the English Stage, Garrick the Restorer of
> Shakespear—& some other such phrases for all great men Love to be
> prais'd. Without praise but with great Sincerity.
>
> I am Your wellwisher
G. Alex^r Stevens.[61]

Deelman goes on to explain that Stevens visited Garrick two days
later and on December 30 again wrote Payton that Garrick had agreed
to send the statue. Stevens, now completely caught up in the idea, even
offered his own talents: "I told him I wou'd write something to be cut
upon it [the statue]—very short in Latin and English or all in English . . .
describing the Donor as well as the Great originall for whom the Bust
or the Statue was design'd."[62]

Stevens continued his tour, and on January 10, 1768, he wrote to
Payton from Worcester, this time penning the first suggestion of a
Jubilee:

[I] intend (if God spares my Life) this Summer, to be at the opening of your Town Hall, if you can tell me nearly when it will [be] finish'd, & the Statue or Bust put up.

And I will have a sort of new Oration, Ready set proper for the occasion, by one of our best Composers. & I will exhibit it my self one Consort there for the Benefit of the Building.—if it shou'd be approved.

Do me the Justice to beleive [sic] That this my proposal can have no view but that of offering my mite in Honour of the prince of Poets. . . .[63]

Although Stevens's contributions to the venture remain enigmatic and inconclusive, there is, despite his disclaimer, more than a touch of self-promotion: "Stratford took notice of the idea, for Hunt [the Town Clerk of Stratford] mentions it in his reply to Stevens. He probably passed the suggestion on to Garrick when the opening of the Town Hall was discussed. It seems to have borne fruit; and may, indeed, have been the first seed of the whole festival."[64]

Stevens probably toured the remainder of 1768. He was lecturing at Worcester in January, and there are records of a ten-day stay at Bristol in December followed by a similar period in nearby Bath in January 1769. On March 28 he opened a two-month stand in London at the Haymarket Theatre during which he presented the *Lecture* sixteen times. Samuel Foote, manager of the theatre, then closed the Haymarket in early May for alterations in anticipation of the summer season.

Stevens was back in the provinces during 1769. His old friend and fellow actor Thomas Death and his wife Margaret were members of Herbert's Norwich Company. Margaret Death died on April 10, 1769.

Some time after this mournful intrusion on the domestic happiness of Mr. Death, G. A. Stevens came to deliver his lecture at Norwich, and wrote some lines for a tablet which had been erected to the memory of the departed, which we insert, more for the satisfaction of the reader, as coming from the pen of such a man, than for any merit in their composition or novelty in the thought.

Her form once lovely now can please no more,
And all her melody on earth is o'er;
A wife and mother, tender and sincere,
These she hath been, now alas, she's here.[65]

We have further evidence of Stevens during this year. Another fellow actor and friend refers to him at some length in his memoirs. Thomas Snagg, who played under the stage name of Thomas Wilks, was with the Lincoln Company in 1769 and wrote:

I can't forbear remembering the pleasure of this my first intimate acquaintance with Mr George Alexander Stevens who was at this time in his full health, spirits and comicality. He was just returned from the farce of Mr Garrick's, at the Stratford Jubilee [September, 1769]. . . .

When we returned to Lincoln, which was our next march, Mr Stevens united in the Management. Then we removed to Newark-upon-Trent, and from thence to Grantham (for some reason we lost Sheffield this year) and arrived at Lynn by the time of the mart as usual."[66]

Stevens's major activity in 1770 was the composition and publication of his comic opera *The Court of Alexander*, which opened as an afterpiece to *The Orphan* at Covent Garden on Friday, January 5, and (with the exception of Sunday) played for seven consecutive evenings. The music was composed by J. A. Fisher, "a young genius, who has hitherto been but little known in the musical world,"[67] and the title role was played by Edward Shuter. The *London Stage* describes the opening scene: "The Court awakes with total hangover. Alexander orders a pot of coffee to clear his head. Thais begs him to leave the 'gout giving juice—Retire with me / In my Chinese pavilion, drink some Tea.'"[68] Another critic writes:

In this piece Mr. G. A. Stevens . . . directs his humour, of which he is allowed to possess a great share, against the absurd taste which still prevails for serious Italian operas. For this purpose, he introduces great personages speaking low and absurd dialogue, to fine music.

As a specimen of the author's talents for this droll manner of writing, we shall select his description of Orpheus.

Orpheus was music-maker to the woods,
Gave groves a gamut, put in tune the floods;
He made tall trees a minuet-step advance in,
Taught hedges hornpipes, shrubberies country-dancing;
For every reptile he had songs and jigs,
And symphonies compos'd for guinea pigs.
   For weazles and rats,
   He had both sharps and flats,
     For dogs barking *largo* and *affetto*;
   From the grinding of knives,
   And the scolding of wives,
     He compos'd a dismallo duetto. . . .[69]

An interesting sidelight occurred the following year. Nathaniel Halhed, a friend and former fellow student of Richard Brinsley Sheridan at Harrow, had written a farce called *Ixion* and asked Sheridan to help doctor it. Halhed had written a song for Ixion, who was trying to ingratiate himself with Juno, and "Sheridan was told by his friend that this 'was intended to ridicule a part of the farce called *The Court of Alexander*, which was brought on the stage at Covent Garden last year by George Alexander Stephens.'"[70]

Two additional works of Stevens's were published in 1770. The first was *The Humours of London: A Choice Collection of Songs*, an anthology which included a "Choice Variety by Geo. Alex. Stevens" (and others), and the second was "The Storm," one of his best-remembered songs and one frequently sung by Mr. Incledon. He performed it at Birmingham in 1796, and, more memorably, on May 17, 1820, Mr. Elliston asked him to sing "The Storm," and Incledon "replied he could not till he got some new teeth."[71]

Somehow Stevens managed to ingratiate himself in the management of Covent Garden for on April 5, 1771, he performed Touchstone in *As You Like It* at that theatre "by Particular desire, and for that night only."

A quite detailed and revealing account of Stevens's activities in 1771 is provided by Thomas Snagg in his *Recollections*. After his association with Stevens at Lincoln in 1769, Snagg was enticed to Norwich and was with that company in 1771. He resumes his narrative as he describes his activities in the fall of that year when he went to London to manage some private affairs.

This might be ranked as one of the most unfortunate of my travels, for here I had formed a kind of wild goose scheme with Mr G. A. Stevens to establish a Burletta Company, which was to be our joint property and to be conducted under my direction on a small scale with few performers and at little expense.

It was to comprise musical and comic dramas in which Mr Stevens was to assist, with writing new and whimsical pieces. To accomplish this, cash was necessary for our apparatus, as scenes, clothes, music and the numberless etceteras that would be properly wanting to embark in this mad business. [Snagg describes some of his attempts to raise money for the project including the foolish lease of piece of his rental property.] . . .

Thus I spent my time with Mr Stevens planning these our "castles high in the air" and returned in the stage coach to Ipswich and my dramatic pursuits where every matter kept its accustomary track and then the Company decamped for Yarmouth where I was to receive my yearly Benefit. . . .

I passed my leisure moments (when the Theatre did not demand my attendance) in contemplation and preparation for mine and Mr Stevens' new undertaking in which we had high dreams of expectation.

The scenes were painting, the dresses making, the performers engaging and myself labouring and calculating without ceasing, to hatch this egg of improbability. Mr Stevens was likewise not idle, for his ideas on success were as blooming as my own. We purposed to take the field not very distant from the Capital of Norfolk, because of the expense and as our few performers were nearly all upon the spot.

Yarmouth, being a populous Sea Port and the residents a play-admiring audience, was conceived a proper spot to pitch our tent, but we being unfortunately considered by the Mayor as a kind of revolutionary band, he would not consent to our renting the theatre, tho' as he would not prevent any amusement or advantage to the town there would be no objection to our performing.

The obstruction of the use of the Playhouse was soon removed, for money will move mountains, and that was a necessary auxiliary we were at present in possession of. A spot of ground was hired and carpenters or a sort of builders agreed with for the erecting of a temporary building.

Thus everything went before the wind and we invested the town in form, pasted up a large posting bill and announced for our first representation the Burletta of *The Mad Captain*. (To be sure the title might have been construed into some little affinity to our undertaking.) This was an altered piece from an old and obsolete farce with songs and local jokes written and appropriated by Mr G. A. Stevens and music compiled and set by Mr Wat Clagget and an introductory prelude which I, the Manager, delivered and sang as follows:—

PRELUDE TO THE BURLETTAS

In London oft at shop doors men appear
Armed with strong lungs and bawling, "walk in here."
Ladies and Genmen, please to walk in,
Don't lose time, we're just going to begin.

Snagg quotes an additional fifty-six lines including, most significantly, the same description of Orpheus that Stevens had written for *The Court of Alexander*. One gets the distinct impression that Stevens did not bring very much original creative effort to this venture but was content to write pastiches comprising songs and ditties he had composed for earlier works. Snagg continues:

Tho' there might be some merit in the lines, as few things are devoid of that which come from the pen of Mr G. A. Stevens, and our performance was received by the few that honoured our first representation with much applause, it had not the fascinating power to draw a second house, really not. Then we clapped musical farces to our pieces as *The Chaplet* etc. In short, the sun and fine weather were playing such captivating beams against our flimsy productions that the folks thought it pleasanter and more healthful to walk and enjoy the sea breezes than to pay and be shut up to hear our contemptible warbling, for we had neither name, merit nor interest to support us.

After performing till the middle of July from the same time of the preceding month we were obliged to conform to the taste of the people by returning to theatrical plain comedy and farce and tho' Mr Stevens came down and did part of his Lecture on Heads, then in high estimation, we were under the necessity to sit down with a great loss of time and cash, labour and reputation. In short, we decamped like a dog who had burnt his tail, tho' with an invitation to perform plays at a small town near Harleston, which to make good our retreat we accepted, received permission from the Justice of the District, or at least his word to overlook us as vagabonds, formed a respectable strolling Company and played to overflowing houses. The nights were bespoke one over another by the neighboring gentry and from our small receipts were distributed a profitable sharing livelihood and we were "accounted great performers."

We then weighed seriously our situation and the improbability of profit or reputation ensuing and resolved to disband our troop and lay down our Managerial dignities.[72]

If Snagg's poor opinion of his company is valid, it is small wonder that it met with so little success. Stevens moved on, and by March 1772 he was again at the Haymarket, where he delivered the *Lecture* sixteen times between March 26 and May 11. The performance began at seven and ended at nine-thirty in the evening. He was now sixty-two years old and seemingly his energies were on the decline. He noted in the newspapers that "the great Exertion requisite to support this Lecture by a single Person in so extensive a Place as a Theatre Royal, deters the Exhibitor from attempting it oftener than twice a week."[73] Filling the vast confines of the Haymarket was challenge enough even in a demanding role; consider the staying power necessary for the solo performer who was on stage continuously for two and a half hours! Some time during the year Stevens saw the publication of his *Songs, Comic and Satirical*, which contained the texts of 134 of his songs. In September he was at Cambridge for the fair, where he managed, and probably performed at, one of the three theatrical booths "in the Cheese Fair where he presented *The Clandestine Marriage, Midas, Douglas, The Mayor of Garratt* and, by desire of Sir Thomas Halton, *The West*

Indian followed by the popular *Padlock*. His charges were in line with the usual ones at country theatres, boxes 3s., pit 2s., gallery 1s., and tickets were to be had at Sharp's near Sidney Sussex College and at the Printing Office. . . . The only member of the company mentioned, besides Stevens, is Master Blanchard, who sang."[74]

At the beginning of 1773 Stevens formed a brief association with Samuel Foote as a puppet-maker. On February 15 Foote presented his "Primitive Puppet Show" entitled *Piety in Pattens*, a one-act satire on the sentimental comedies so popular at the time.[75] The play utilized life-sized marionettes until its August revision when it was adapted for live actors. While Stevens's total involvement with the production is uncertain, there is little doubt that he was closely connected with the construction and perhaps even the manipulation of the figures. The first public announcement, or puff, which appeared more than a month before the opening night, noted that "Mr. Foote and Mr. George Alexander Stevens are going to amuse the town with a new species of entertainment, or rather an old one revived, called 'A Puppet-shew, where will be laughing Tragedies, weeping Comedies, and squeaking Operas, by Figures as large as some living Theatrical heroes.'"[76] Still another early article prepared the public for Foote's play and reinforced Stevens's contributions. We are told that "G. A. Stevens entered into partnership with the Son of Fun [Foote], and began to compose a new species of creatures, with features so similar to the originals, that you will not know the man of paste-board from the man of nature. . . . Such are the imitative perfections of Stevens, who surpasses all statuaries we have seen!"[77] Further evidence of Stevens's talent and reputation appeared in two reviews published shortly after the opening of the play. The first made specific reference to the marionettes: "The figures are nearly as large as the life, constructed with admirable skill, were all exceedingly well dressed, their action managed with great adroitness, and their features made striking and expressive."[78] The other reported that "Mr. Foote is said to be busy in lengthening and adding to his Primitive Entertainment. We hear that a Punch is made by that humourous human Carpenter, George Alexander Stevens, and that the celebrated Mimic who directs the Theatre Royal at York is sent for to speak for the hump-backed Hero.[79]

Stevens stayed busy during the year. Oliver Goldsmith's *She Stoops to Conquer* opened in mid-March. Several days after the premiere the playwright received the following letter: "G. Alexander Stevens presents his respects to Dr. Goldsmith and will esteem it a great favor If He will condescend to grant to get Stevens two neices an order to see the new Comedy to night. Russell Street, Covent Garden—Thursday."[80]

On May 12 Stevens did a guest performance as Stephano in *The Tempest* at Drury Lane "for that night only."

Three months later, on August 11, the Haymarket opened Stevens's afterpiece *The Trip to Portsmouth*. The work was a comic opera sketch consisting of four detached scenes, with songs, based on a recent naval review for George III at Portsmouth. It was "begun and finished in five days. He performed in this piece for the last time himself."[81] This latter statement is inaccurate. Stevens's name is not mentioned in any of the bills; the source of the confusion may be a Mr. Castevens who is listed in the cast for two performances in 1775. The sketch received thirteen performances after its opening and was revived at the Haymarket three times in 1774 and twice in 1775. On December 3, 1773, it began a short but successful engagement in Belfast: "loud applause greeted G. A. Stevens's operatic farce, *A Trip to Portsmouth.* . . . Similar to the harlequinades in scenic and musical emphasis, but catering more directly to the growing patriotic fervour, it culminated in 'a grand view of the British fleet.' The loyal sentiments of an aroused Belfast public demanded seven performances within six weeks."[82] In addition, it was staged at Smock Alley and Newcastle-upon-Tyne in 1774. The text of the opera and the songs were published separately in 1773.

In the fall of 1773 Stevens was lecturing again. It is pleasing to note that after twenty years of professional and personal contact with the mecurial and often irascible David Garrick, the great actor still retained an enduring respect and affection for him. In anticipation of the tour, Garrick wrote his brother Peter in Lichfield and informed him that Stevens would be doing the *Lecture* in their hometown. He referred to him as "my old Friend," "deservedly applauded," and "a very honest, liberal-minded Man," and asked Peter to drum up as much business as he could. Garrick even offered a money-back guarantee to those who were not satisfied with the *Lecture*.[83]

At Christmas, Stevens lectured in Manchester and sometime during 1774 was in Dublin with the *Lecture* at the Music Hall in Fishamble Street. At the end of that year he gave seven performances between November 24 and December 9 in Bristol advertising it as "positively the last Time the Lecture ever will be exhibited in this Town." In August 1775 Stevens delivered the *Lecture* several times in Belfast and in 1777 was again at the Haymarket Theatre for the two-month run. The *Lecture* was performed eighteen times between March 11 and May 5 but never on any two consecutive days. It was advertised as "the last season of its ever being done in London." And so it was, at least by Stevens.

Many sources assert that Stevens, his facilities and senses impaired by old age, "disposed of his original 'Lecture' [in 1774] for a moderate sum to the actor, Charles Lee Lewes . . . who 'improved' it from time to time, but failed to reproduce the full success of the inventor."[84] This early date is probably inaccurate since Stevens was lecturing for several more years. It is also unclear whether Stevens sold the rights to performance or the production paraphernalia, or both.

In any event, Stevens again gave the *Lecture*—three times in Manchester in the summer of 1779, twice at the Theatre Royal in Chester in November and December, and his final recorded performances on December 8 and 10 at the Town Hall in Wrexham, Wales.

By 1780 Stevens, now seventy years old, was in rapid decline. According to most of his biographers, his intellect had started to decay and he had retired to Hampstead. His encroaching senility, however, did not deter him from one final effort. On October 30, 1780, *The Cabinet of Fancy; or, Evening Exhibition* opened at the Theatre Royal, Haymarket. It was described as: "Consisting of variety of Paintings, serious and comic; Satirical, Portrait and Caricature Designs; Emblematical, Pantomimical, Farcical and Puppet-showical Representations, mostly Transparency. Instead of delivering a Catalogue, the Designs will be explained by at present an unknown Artist [Wilks]. . . . As the Time of viewing the Exhibition is limited, and as it is the wish to render it as amusing as possible, an excellent band of Music will be provided for the entertainment of the Spectators. In the course of the explanation of the Pictures several Songs will be introduced. . . . The Songs, written by G. A. Stevens, are to be had at the Theatre.[85] The piece, which was also performed five additional times in November, was a minor effort. The songs were published separately that same year. Stevens's very popular song "The Vicar and Moses" (suggested by "The Vicar of Wakefield") was also published in 1780.

George Alexander Stevens died on September 6, 1784. Even the last day of his life has an element of uncertainty about it. Most of the notices claim he died in Biggleswade, Bedfordshire, but several indicate that it was at Baldock, eight miles to the southeast. A curious note recalls that "the papers say that on the 24 last he ment[d] to his wife and others that he sho'd die within a fortnight and desired them to take notice of the day and a few days after reminded them he sho'd keep his time. He was then as well as he had usually been."[86]

Several epitaphs were subsequently printed.

> A second *Alexander* here lies dead;
> And not less fam'd—*at taking off a Head.*[87]

and

Poor Stevens, alas! thy *Head* is laid low,
   Who all *Heads* has lectur'd upon;
The tribute though just, is small to bestow,
   To say an *Original's* gone.[88]

Notes

 1. Some of these consulted include: *Biographia Dramatica*, 2 vols., ed. I. Reed (London,
    1782); *Biographia Dramatica*, 3 vols., ed. I. Reed and S. Jones (London, 1812),
    hereafter *B.D.*; *Dictionary of National Biography*, ed. L. Stephen and S. Lee, vol. 18
    (Oxford 1897–98), hereafter *D.N.B.; A New General Biographical Dictionary*, ed. H. J.
    Rose, vol. 12 (London, 1857); *The Thespian Dictionary; or, Dramatic Biography* . . .
    (London, 1805); *An Universal Biographical and Historical Dictionary*, ed. J. Watkins
    (London, 1800); *Gentleman's Magazine*, vol. 54 (London, 1784); *The European Maga-
    zine and London Review*, vol. 6 (London, 1784); *Scots Magazine*, vol. 46 (1784).
 2. *D.N.B.*, p. 1116.
 3. *Gentleman's Magazine*, p. 795.
 4. G. A. Stevens, *Adventures of a Speculist* (London, 1788), vol. 1, pp. xvii–xviii.
 5. Charles Dibdin, *A Complete History of the Stage* (London, 1800), vol. 5, p. 189.
 6. *Speculist*, p. xix.
 7. Mrs. Cibber, *Dialogue in the Shades* (1766). Quoted in John Genest, *Some Account of the
    English Stage from the Restoration in 1660 to 1830* (Bath, 1832), vol. 10, p. 177.
 8. Robert Hitchcock, *An Historical View of the Irish Stage* (Dublin, 1794), vol. 2, p. 153.
 9. John Bernard, *Retrospections of the Stage* (Boston, 1832), vol. 1, p. 39.
10. *An Universal Biographical and Historical Dictionary*, unpaginated.
11. *Thespian Dictionary*, unpaginated.
12. *D.N.B.*, p. 116.
13. *Gentleman's Magazine*, p. 717.
14. Ibid., p. 795 and *B.D.* (1812), p. 688.
15. Sibyl Rosenfeld, *Strolling Players and Drama in the Provinces, 1660–1765* (New York,
    1970), p. 60.
16. Data from the *Norwich Gazette*.
17. From "A Short Account of the Life of Geo. Alex. Stevens," in *A Lecture on Heads*,
    (Belfast, 1807 edition), pp. 117–18.
18. *D.N.B.*, p. 1116.
19. She outlived Stevens by thirty years, dying September 2, 1813. "Suddenly at the
    house of C. P. Herbert, Esq. of Setch, in Norfolk, in her 84th year . . ." (obituary in
    European Magazine, September, 1813, p. 274).
20. *Gentleman's Magazine*, p. 795.
21. "To the Reader"—from "Religion; or, The Libertine Repentant. A Rhapsody"
    (London, 1751).
22. *Gentleman's Magazine*, p. 795.
23. Esther Sheldon, *Thomas Sheridan of Smock-Alley* (Princeton, 1967), p. 170.
24. *B.D.* (1782), vol. 2, p. 88. Churchill borrowed the line "And common sense stood
    trembling at the door!" and inserted it in his "Rosciad."
25. *Dublin Journal*, May 26–30, 1752.
26. *Pennsylvania Packet*, April 20, 1785.
27. Data taken primarily from Sheldon.

28. Broadside in British Museum, no. 1890. e. 5. (80).

29. *The Dramatic History of Master Edward* . . . (London, 1763), p. 145.

30. *Catalog Raisonnée of Mr. Mathews's Gallery of Theatrical Portraits* . . . (London, 1833), p. 51.

31. Robert B. Thomas, *The Life and Work of George Alexander Stevens* (Ph.D. diss., Louisiana State University, 1961), p. 41.

32. *Speculist*, vol. 2, pp. 20–21.

33. *Dramatic History*, p. 41ff.

34. *Public Advertiser*, December 24, 1754.

35. *The London Stage*, pt. 4, vol. 1, p. 462.

36. *Public Advertiser*, January 13, 1755.

37. *Daily Advertiser*, January 18, 1755.

38. Ibid., January 20, 1755.

39. Ibid., January 31, February 1, 3, 4, 1755.

40. The Larpent manuscript of the farce (no. 6. L.) is dated February 28, 1760. Dibdin, vitriolic as ever, said the piece was "damned in the theatre" (vol. 5, p. 188). The 1777 production is not to be confused with Charles Macklin's play *The True-Born Irishman*, which was published in 1795. Frederick Pilon was familiar with Stevens's work. It was he who provided a prologue and textual additions to Lee Lewes's edition of the *Lecture* after the latter had purchased the property from Stevens. Genest (vol. 4, pp. 627–28) is confused about a 1767 performance. Although the play was published in that year the printed dramatis personae refers to an earlier production.

41. Thomas Gilleland, *The Dramatic Mirror* 2 vols. (London, 1808), vol. 1, p. 211; Frederick T. Wood, "Notes on English Provincial Playhouses in the Eighteenth Century," in *Notes and Queries*, vol. 160 (1931), p. 166.

42. *European Magazine*, October 1786, pp. 274–75. Other published copies of the letter vary in some details, most conspicuously the *B.D.* (1812) version, p. 690, which gives Stevens's incarceration date as *February 13* in *Yarmouth* Gaol. Curiously, the version quoted here footnotes the company which deserted Stevens as the Norwich rather than the Lincoln Company. It also spells his name Steevens.

43. From "A Short Account of the Life of . . . ," p. 116.

44. *Pennsylvania Packet*, April 12, 1785. The anecdote had been printed earlier (*European Magazine*, December 1784, p. 459) and Winston cites it in part 1 of his manuscript cataloged as "Theatric Tourist" (Folger) stating he got it from *The Weekly Entertainer*, (vol. 5, March 28, 1875, p. 306). Winston has Mrs. B. exclaiming "*Who* robbed the Bristol mail" which certainly weakens the joke.

45. *London Chronicle*, November 1–4, 1766.

46. P. Highfill, Jr., K. Burnim, and E. Langhans, A *Biographical Dictionary of Actors, Actresses, Musicians* . . . *in London, 1660–1800* (Carbondale and Edwardsville, 1973–78), vol. 4, p. 464. At the present writing this invaluable dictionary is in its sixth volume through the letter *G*.

47. *B.D.* (1782), vol. 2, p. 146. The work is unpublished but exists in the Larpent manucript (7. L.) dated January 13, 1762. The *D.N.B.* questions Stevens's authorship: "The well-known sea song 'Hearts of Oak' (originally 'Heart of Oak') was first given in 'Harlequin's Invasion,' a Christmas pantomime of 1759, and has generally been attributed to David Garrick. It is quite certain that Stevens would have included it among his 'Songs' if he had any claim to it" (p. 1116). It is by no means certain, however, that the interlude and the song are one and the same.

48. Anonymous, *The Battle of the Players* (London, 1762), pp. 31–32. This work is not to be confused with one of the same main title printed in the same year in Dublin, which

deals with the Irish stage. The author, of course, has placed Stevens in the wrong theatre. His partner in crime, Richard Smith, had been with Rich at Covent Garden for a number of years. Rich, incidentally, had died in November 1761. The adversary, Thomas Davies, was one of Stevens's old colleagues. The two were at Smock Alley in 1752 and appeared together in *The Way of the World, Coriolanus, The Alchemist,* and possibly other plays. He was Garrick's first biographer and also was responsible for introducing Boswell to Samuel Johnson.

49. *The Beauties of All the Magazines Selected* (London, 1762–64), 1762, p. 12.

50. *Speculist.* See *supra.*

51. Thomas suggests that "Stevens had insufficient confidence in the work to attempt to publish it during his own lifetime, so perhaps he recognized the deficiencies" (p. 109). It may also be that the potential printers saw little chance of its repaying their investment.

52. *Speculist,* pp. iii–v.

53. Hitchcock, pp. 152–53.

54. *Gentleman's Magazine,* p. 717.

55. Ibid.

56. Ibid.

57. *B.D.* (1812), p. 689. The 1782 edition, however, published while Stevens was still alive, makes no mention of an American tour.

58. "If it should not be looked upon as an impertinent Request May I beg his Grace's Permission for Mrs. Stevens to repeat part of my Lecture with me. I hope this Intrusion may not offend. I am &c. With great respect Your most Humble Servant G: Alexander Stevens." P.R.O. L.C. 7.3. 10 March 1766.

59. "Address to the Public" from *Songs, Comic and Satyrical by George Alexander Stevens* (London, 1772).

60. Christian Deelman, *The Great Shakespeare Jubilee* (New York, 1964) p. 56ff. and passim. Some biographers of Garrick have incorrectly linked this development with George Steevens, the Shakespearean editor.

61. Cited in Deelman, p. 65.

62. Ibid.

63. Ibid., p. 66.

64. Ibid.

65. *General Magazine,* November 1788, p. 566. Also *Biographical Dictionary,* vol. 4, p. 250. I am very grateful to Professor Highfill for calling my attention to this information. Death's entry in the *Biographical Dictionary* also describes him as a lecturer. Although I have not been able to confirm it, there is a strong possibility that he presented Stevens's *Lecture* sometime during his career.

66. Thomas Snagg, *Recollections of Occurrences* (London, 1951), pp. 74–75.

67. *Freeholder's Magazine,* January 1770. Cf. Dibdin ". . . wretchedly composed by the curiously celebrated Dr. FISHER . . . ," p. 188.

68. *The London Stage,* pt. 4, vol. 3, p. 1446.

69. "A Criticism on the Court of Alexander. From the *Critical Review*" (bound in with the third edition of the play).

70. W. Fraser Rae, *Sheridan: A Biography* (London, 1896), vol. 1, p. 103.

71. A. L. Nelson and G. B. Cross, eds., *Drury Lane Journal: Selections from James Winston's Diaries, 1819–1827* (London, 1974), p. 10.

72. Snagg, pp. 75–80. The original of the altered piece, *The Mad Captain,* to which Snagg alludes is almost certainly an opera of the same name by Robert Drury acted at Goodman's Fields in 1733 and published in octavo. See *B.D.* (1782), vol. 2, p. 212 and

Allardyce Nicoll, *A History of English Drama 1660–1900* (Cambridge, 1969), vol. 3, pp. 334, 396, who attributes the work to Stevens. Nicoll, in the same book (p. 326), credits Stevens with the comic opera *The Fair Orphan* "perf. Lynn, 1771 by G. A. Stevens' company." It was published in octavo in 1771 This was probably done with Snagg and the Burletta Company.

73. *Public Advertiser*, March 26, 1772.

74. Sibyl Rosenfeld, "The Players in Cambridge, 1662–1800," in *Studies in English Theatre History* (London, 1952), p. 31.

75. For an excellent detailed account of the play and its production history, see Samuel N. Bogorad and Robert G. Noyes, "Samuel Foote's Primitive Puppet-Shew," in *Theatre Survey*, vol. 14, no. 1a. (1973). Please note that I have used "puppet" and "marionette" in the same sense, i.e., as string-manipulated figures.

76. *London Chronicle*, January 12, 1773. (N.B. This is Bogorad's citation. I haven't found it.)

77. *Westminister Magazine: or, The Pantheon of Taste*, January 1773, p. 69.

78. *Morning Chronicle and London Advertiser*, February 16, 1773.

79. *Lloyd's Evening Post and British Chronicle*, February 24–26, 1773. "The director of the Theatre Royal at York at this time was Foote's old associate, Tate Wilkinson; there is no reason to believe the suggestion made here is serious" (Bogorad and Noyes, n. 77, p. 109).

80. Manuscript letter in the British Museum dated March 18, 1773. BM42515 f. 117. Edward Shuter and Lee Lewes were both in the original production. Goldsmith was a paper saver. He used the verso of the letter for a receipt. "Recd of Dr. Goldsmith the Sum of Nine Pounds One Shilling in full of all demands. J(?). W. Hawes," dated March 26, 1773.

81. *Gentleman's Magazine*, p. 796.

82. W. S. Clark, *The Irish Stage in the County Towns, 1720–1800* (Oxford, 1965), p. 234.

83. D. M. Little and G. M. Kahrl, eds., *The Letters of David Garrick* (Cambridge, Mass., 1963), vol. 2, pp. 899–900.

84. *D.N.B.*, p. 1117.

85. *The London Stage*, pt. 5, vol. 1, p. 382.

86. This has been drawn from a note in the *Biographical Dictionary* files at the Folger. The original is in Joseph Reed's "Noticia Dramatica," vol. 2, fol. 188, p. 328ff, at the British Museum. I have not found this in the papers of the day.

87. "Epitaph, Extempore . . . by Capt. Thompson" *Morning Herald* (London), October 7, 1784.

88. *Public Advertiser*, September 15, 1784. This was published elsewhere with some frequency. The most interesting appeared in the *Pennsylvania Packet* on January 14, 1785, on the same page as a notice for a performance of the *Lecture* to be done, probably by Hallam.

II

Background for the *Lecture*

TRACING THE GENESIS of the *Lecture on Heads* is an exercise in the fusion of numerous variables. When Stevens first appeared on the stage of the Little Haymarket Theatre that April day in 1764 he stood ready with a work perfectly suited to its time and place. Social attitudes, theatrical tastes, and Stevens's own very special talents and experience had melded, making possible a unique piece of entertainment. None of Stevens's biographers or critics understood completely how it had come about; each saw it from a limited, and sometimes distorted, perspective because he did not have access to all the facts. The *Biographia Dramatica* tells us the *Lecture* "is said to have owed its origin to his meeting, in one of his strolling excursions, with a country mechanic who described the members of the corporation with great force of humour."[1] There must be a grain of truth in this somewhere, but as it stands it is little more than an unverified oversimplification. The chief value of this kind of statement is in the implicit reminder that we must tread very cautiously among the apocrypha, puffs, generalizations, errors of fact, bad memory, acrimony, and adulation that abound in the documents.

The single most important observation is that the middle of the eighteenth century in England was a marvelously fertile period for satire.[2] Henry Fielding, Tobias Smollett, and Laurence Sterne had extended the style and range of the novel and certainly influenced the several works Stevens wrote in the genre. The satirical print, plain and colored, was sold by the thousands and adorned the homes of the rich and poor alike. William Hogarth and Matthew Darly, both contemporary with Stevens, and James Gillray, George and Isaac Cruickshank, G. M. Woodward, and Thomas Rowlandson, who worked later, all, at one time or another, did satirical theatre pieces. The latter two even illustrated late editions of the *Lecture*. Hogarth did some of his best work in this category and will continue to be admired for such prints as "Masquerades and Operas," "Strolling Actresses Dressing in a Barn," "Rich's Glory," "The Laughing Audience," and "The Crying Audience." Stevens was well aware of Hogarth's work and was significantly impressed by his satirical print "The Five Orders of Perriwigs." All these artists directed their barbs at many topics: the professions, foreigners, excesses of manners and fashion, public taste, city types, the government—their targets were endless. Stevens was their histrionic counterpart as he lashed out against the follies of his age; more genial perhaps, but no less incisive. The theatre itself was another satirical battleground with the tradition extending as far back as John Skelton and the early interludes through Jonson and the Restoration. Indeed, theatrical satire was a major factor in the establishment of the Licensing Act from John Gay's *The Beggar's Opera*, which so enriched the London stage, to the culminating event, Henry Fielding's attack on Walpole in *The Historical Register for the Year 1736*, which eventually led to the author's retirement from the theatre. And, ironically, one of the consequences of the act was to create and encourage the vogue for the spate of nonlegitimate theatricals of which the *Lecture*, and other solo entertainments, was such a popular example. Not only did the stage lampoon society but it even became its own victim. When Alexander Pope published his *Dunciad* in 1728 he set the tone for the countless mock epistles to follow. Charles Churchill's *Rosciad* was the diadem in the crown and spawned the likes of the *Churchiliad*, the *Fribbleriad*, the *Kellyad*, the *Strolliad*, the *Garriciad*, the *Druriad*, the *Thespiad*, and many others. With time agreeing, Stevens was ready for his world.

The castigation of social behavior and appearance had long been a theme of Stevens's, and it found its way into many of his works prior to the *Lecture*. As early as 1754 Stevens was directing his attacks against Macklin, Foote, Quin, quack doctors, and orators in *The Birth-Day of Folly*; and in his *Disquisition* of 1754–55 Macklin and oratory share the critical spotlight with humbugging and flattery. *Tom Fool*, in 1760, paints English life on a large canvas and aims at indolence, gossiping, Methodism, and card playing in a world peopled by such Jonsonian types as Squire Tasty, Ephraim Invoice, Mrs. Flimm, and the Misses Demirep and Ninny. *Adventures of a Speculist*, purportedly written (ca. 1763–64) to preserve some of the better pieces from the ill-fated *Beauties of All the Magazines Selected*, comes even closer to the mark. It abounds with satires on stockjobbers, gamblers, women orators, and male and female fashions. Stevens calls attention to Hogarth's "The Five Orders of Perriwig" (see plate 4), proceeds to satirize them—the Episcopal, the Aldermanic, the Lexonical—and even suggests that the reader buy a copy of the print.[3] His section on female fashions touches on the French Night Cap, the Ranelagh Hood, the Mary Queen of Scots Cap, the Fly Cap, and many others which are to appear in the

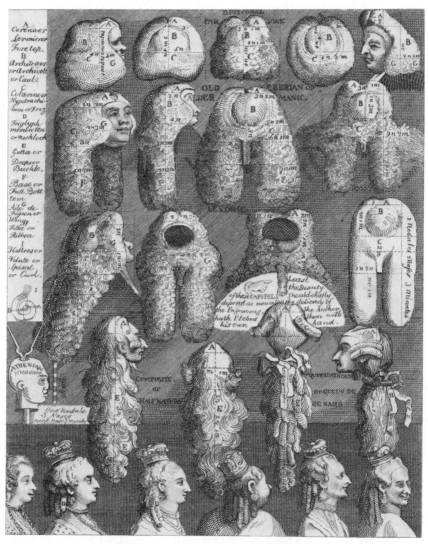

Plate 4: Hogarth's *The Five Orders of Perriwigs*. (Author's copy.)

Lecture. As the editor observed: "Little, at this period of his gloomy gaiety, (and who, without, perhaps a shilling in his pocket, can in his heart be otherwise than gloomy gay?) did George think, that with the assistance of Hats, as well as Wigs, cocked, and dressed according to his own original fashion, to decorate the heads of Fools, he should have the happiness to finish his days with all the *otium cum dignitate* that can flow from the possession, blessing while it is always blessed, of an independent fortune."[4] Before the year was out Stevens was enacting these foibles and follies instead of writing about them.

When a reader examines the newspapers and various periodical publications of the mid eighteenth century in London and some of the larger cities in England, he is immediately struck by the broad dissemination of information and by the avid curiosity about natural history, the sciences, politics, religion, economics, literature, the theatre, travel, and prominent personalities. The literati and reasonably affluent population had access to a wide variety of reading matter including cheap editions of books, plays, and pamphlets constantly being advertised by the booksellers. Ideas were exchanged in other ways as well. Debating societies were popular, including women orators, who often came in for a large share of ridicule. And there were the lectures, which were often given in private rooms by specialists, learned and otherwise. The curious could attend lectures on the principles of "mechanick" science, the nature of vision in the eyes of insects, the principles and rationale of navigation, experimental philosophy, the elements of geography, the theory and practice of midwifery, and so forth. The format was ready-made for Stevens and others. Here was the solo performer relying on his own intelligence and skill, holding the attention of an audience for several hours, left to his own devices unencumbered by the pressures of salary negotiations, benefits, wardrobes, learning new roles, reliance on elaborate staging, or fellow actors who missed lines or performances. It was an obvious and practical way of circumventing the Licensing Act and became one of the entertainment staples outside the patent houses.

Samuel Foote was largely responsible for popularizing the lecture genre and evading the law with such subterfuges as *Diversions of the Morning, Cup of Tea, Dish of Chocolate, Auction of Pictures*, and *Orations*. He started his performances at noon[5] in order not to compete with the royal playhouses for the limited audiences. Various other actors and entertainers added solo pieces to their repertories. Most notable was Ned Shuter, one of the most popular comedians of the day, who relied heavily on Stevens to supply him with material. The *Biographia Dramatica* says that "for Shuter he composed the first sketch of his *Lecture on*

Heads. . . . Whether the humour of the piece was not congenial with that of Shuter, or whether he was inadequate to the task, it is certain it was at first scarcely noticed. Luckily for the author, he was prompted to enlarge his plan; and, having furnished himself with a complete apparatus, he went into the country, and repeated his Lecture."[6] My instincts tell me that Stevens probably did prepare the piece for Shuter, but it is certainly incorrect to state that "the humour of the piece was not congenial" or that he "was inadequate to the task" since Shuter performed the *Lecture* many times during his career; in fact, on one occasion he was even doing it simultaneously with Stevens at a different location.

Finally, we must take special note of Stevens's use of the modeled papier-mâché heads in the *Lecture* and how it reflects his interest in and experience with puppets. For a writer like Stevens, whose corpus was almost entirely satirical in nature, the world of the puppet theatre was an inevitable magnet: "The marionette theatres were, in fact, miniature theatres, and the eighteenth century was their heyday as a form of entertainment."[7] The existence of puppets in England can be traced to the fourteenth century. Chaucer refers to them, and it soon becomes apparent that "both glove puppets and marionettes, used in a fully dramatic manner, were familiar forms of popular entertainment by the fifteenth century, and that a tradition of both secular and religious puppet shows had been established here long before the Elizabethan age."[8] The puppets grew in popularity during this latter era, and the increasing documentary evidence gives us a clear picture of the changes that took place in the years that followed. The puppet masters fell under the same interdictions as the actors, mountebanks, and other itinerant performers who were classified as "rogues and vagabonds" as they toured the countryside. Their subject matter consisted of parodies of classical legends and historical events interspersed with songs, bawdy and otherwise. Ben Jonson inserted the puppet play of *The Ancient Modern History of Hero and Leander* in his *Bartholomew Fair* in 1614, a comedy which epitomizes the playgoers' taste for the ribald, satiric, and grotesque. During the eighteen-year drought of the Commonwealth, "the puppet show was, for most people, the only form of theatre available, and it flourished accordingly. . . . Once again, as in the first centuries of Christianity, when the public playhouses were closed and the actors exiled, the drama was preserved in the puppet booths."[9] Shortly after the theatres reopened, the puppets achieved a new measure of respectability and added a new dimension to the English theatre.

An Italian puppet master, Signor Bologna, brought his theatre to

Covent Garden in 1662 and introduced the commedia dell'arte favorite Pollicenella to an English audience. Through many transformations
the character became the thoroughly Anglicized Punch, who with his
consort Joan (later designated Judy) established a native tradition.
Several months after his opening, Bologna was invited to play before
the king and was richly rewarded for his performance. Both Samuel
Pepys and John Evelyn attended the booths and made frequent and
laudatory comments in their diaries. By the turn of the century the
puppet theatre had grown far beyond its fairground patrons and was
catering to a new audience: "On a superficial view, few periods of
history can have been so sympathetic to the puppets as the eighteenth
century, and never before could the puppets so naturally hold up the
mirror of ridicule to their masters. Never before or since have the
puppets played quite so effective and so well publicized a part in
fashionable Society; never before or since have puppet theatres so
successfully made themselves the talk of the town."[10] Perhaps no better
proof of their pervasive influence and popularity can be found than
the map of London which George Speaight includes in his study and
which locates thirty-three sites used for the performance of puppet
plays during the century.

   We are now very close to George Alexander Stevens and only a few
additional puppet masters need to be mentioned before we allow him
to step into the mainstream. Martin Powell brought his string puppets
from Bath to London in 1710 and for the next three seasons his
"Punch's Theatre" was the third playhouse in town. Powell, who was to
become rich and famous, was a showman who "had an eye to the taste
of Society and an ear for the follies of the day and for five years he
caught fashion on the wing. Lords and ladies sat in his boxes, and wits
and writers put his name in books and poems."[11] His son briefly carried
on the tradition during the twenties and in 1738 Charlotte Charke, the
unhappy daughter of Colley Cibber, with a license from the Lord
Chamberlain, opened her "Punch's Theatre" in a converted tennis
court near the Haymarket. Included among her puppet adaptations
were three plays by Fielding, Shakespeare's *Henry IV* with Punch as
Falstaff, and various *divertissements*. As with most events in her life, the
venture was ill-fated, and in subsequent years she moved in and out of
the puppet world.

   Charke may have worked with Stevens at this time. She certainly
knew him and his personality had made a lasting impression. At the
beginning of her memoirs, written in 1755, she links their names. In a
mock preface, to herself, from herself, she writes: "nor can you be
match'd, in Oddity of Fame, by any but that celebrated Knight-Errant
of the Moon, G——E A——R ST——S: whose Memoirs, and yours

conjoin'd, would make *great Figures in History*, and might justly claim a
Right to be transmitted to Posterity; as you are without Exception, two
of *the greatest Curiosities* that ever were the incentives to the most
profound Astonishment."[12] While this does not give us very much to go
on it does shed a little light on some of the missing years; it suggests
Stevens's link with the puppet theatre and reinforces the notion that
Stevens had a curious, but strong, impact on his associates several
decades before he came into prominence with the *Lecture*. Stevens
provides some autobiographical clues about his puppet activity. In *The
Dramatic History* he says, "I have composed Drolls for Mr. Warner's
booth, (perhaps at Southwark Fair) and by his recommendation, I have
wrote several dramas for the proprietors of puppet-shows [could this
include Charlotte Charke?]."[13] One of the digressions in *Adventures of a
Speculist* provides a text. He writes:

> The person who was interrupted in his Song, (Stevens) was next desired to
> *do the Puppet show*; upon which, after some little preparation or preface, he
> began thus:

> The first figure, Gemmen and Ladies, I represent you with, is St. George
> and the Dragon: Observe and take notice of the richness of his dress, the
> lance in his hand, the rolling of the Dragon's eyes, and the sting in his tail.
> This figure, Gemmen, is the wonder of the world: it has been shewn
> before the *Riol Siety*, and those learned scholars cou'd not tell what to make
> of it; for some said it was a sea-monster, and some said it was a land-
> monster, and some said it was no monster, only a monstrosity; and some
> said it was a griffin, and some said it had ne'er a fin; and so, at last, they all
> agreed, that it was neither one thing nor another.[14]

The monologue continues for several pages as Stevens changes his
voice to represent the different characters. Speaight includes this passage in his study and explains the tradition of the "interpreter," usually
the author, who stood by the side of the booth and introduced the
figures.[15]

By 1764, then, Stevens, was a seasoned performer, satirist, pup-
peteer, and monologist, and these skills fell naturally and inevitably
into place.

Ticket Prices and Audiences

Tickets for the Haymarket premiere of the *Lecture* in 1764 cost 4s, 3s,
and 2s respectively for box, pit, and gallery. About a decade later box
seats were 5s and by 1785 the range was 5s, 3s, 2s, 1s, the latter price for

the second gallery which had been added. It is remarkable that during almost a quarter of a century there was an insignificant change in admission charges, particularly during an era of rapidly rising costs and inflation. In the various other halls, taverns, and smaller play-houses, where there was a much wider variety in the scale due to the size and configuration of the auditorium, it was possible to get a good seat at an average price of 2 shillings. In America the situation was considerably more complicated. At the John St. Theatre in New York and the Southwark in Philadelphia prices averaged 6s, 4s, 2s over the same period but other smaller locales were listing prices in colonial dollars, state dollars, and pound sterling and the equivalencies would vary from colony to colony and from year to year. There are several recorded occasions when the lecturers had difficulty getting audiences and were forced to cut their prices by as much as half. Sometimes tickets were sold as pairs, for two ladies, or a lady and a gentleman, and special reductions were occasionally made for children.

Since all prices are relative, these have little significance for us until they are set in some meaningful perspective. Let us examine the economic conditions that existed in London in 1767 to understand the relationship between wages and what they purchased. In that year a member of the working class—a skilled craftsman, laborer, clerk or servant—would earn an average of two to three shillings a day. A working day was generally eleven hours long for a laborer. While money wages (actual cash earnings) were not the same as real wages (earnings augmented by various perquisites—beer money, cast-off clothing, and so forth), many workers did not work a full six-day week. Indolence, drunkenness, boredom, lack of jobs, and poor weather conditions all affected the total earning power. Conversely, family income was frequently augmented by working wives and children. Despite these complexities, the average daily wage in London can be considered reasonably accurate. Outside the metropolis the average tended to drop in proportion to the distance from the city. Agricultural wages were notoriously lower. Prices were rising faster than wages, and in 1767 there was scattered rioting in England. The most telling picture is provided by the prominent British social historian M. D. George. She quotes a contemporary source which describes the economic conditions of a typical London clerk in 1767. Keep in mind the average daily wage and the average cost of a comparatively inexpensive theatre ticket at two shillings.

> From the great increase in expence in all necessaries of life, which is now
> more enormous than ever, I know the difficulties that people in a mid-

dling station must have laboured under for twenty years past. . . . I have made the following extracts:

[Food and drink per week] 8s/2½d. A ready-furnished room . . . containing . . . a bed and bolster . . . a small wainscot table, two old chairs . . . a small looking-glass . . . an old iron stove . . . [and such various items as poker, shovel, tongs, candlestick, pot, curtains, etc.] (per week) 2s/6d. [Other necessaries included] A suit of cloathes, second cloth, 4s/10d; A hat, 12d; Four pair of shoes, 1s; A wig, 18d, [etc. His total expenses came to £49/7s/3d for the year. The observer concludes]

I have now conducted your clerk thro' the expences of a year, in which, tho' some articles may have been omitted, none will be found superfluous, none over-rated. For the common entertainments of life, such as almost all people partake of, I have left him wholly dependent upon the bounty of others, not allowing him, at his own cost, one night at Sadlers-Wells, one drop of wine or punch, one dish of tea or coffee . . . one pipe of tobacco, or one pinch of snuff . . . and yet, with all this economy and penury, the wretch, at the year's end, has no more than twelve shillings and ninepence to lay by for sickness and old age.[16]

At these prices the lower classes were forced to choose carefully among the entertainments available to them. Generally they would frequent the minor theatres such as Sadler's Wells and the fairs, where prices were lower and the theatrical fare was more to their tastes because the managers provided bills of musicals, farces, variety shows, animal acts, pantomimes, burlettas, and so forth. The patent theatres staged similar entertainments, usually during the second half of the evening, and so the working class, laboring until about seven o'clock could come an hour later and enjoy the program at half price—until the managements eventually discontinued the practice. At Drury Lane and Covent Garden second gallery seats were available for one shilling, and the "heavens" were filled with an unruly and noisy audience.[17]

The eighteenth-century playhouse was, as we know, a mirror of class distinction. The boxes were taken by persons of class and privilege and the pit accommodated an affluent group of tradesmen, merchants, and varied professionals. It was common practice for the well-to-do to send their servants to the theatre in mid-afternoon to have their places saved for them so they could arrive by curtain time and avoid the inconvenience of standing in line to pay at the door. It gave them plenty of time to dine, dress, and come to the playhouse at their leisure.

These, briefly, are some of the conditions that prevailed at the time, but such conditions did not always exist for the kinds of audiences that attended the *Lecture on Heads* by Stevens and his imitators. Not only did

the higher prices tend to preclude a lower-class audience but performances generally started at an hour when it was inconvenient for most of
them to attend. With the exception of the matinees, curtain time was
usually announced for six or seven o'clock with hardly any performances ever starting later. Obviously, half-price tickets were not the
practice. The nature of the audience was governed, however, by a
more consequential factor, namely the nature of the material. While
there was a considerable amount of extravagance in the satirical treatment of the material, much of it relied on "haut-monde" allusions,
classical and literary references, and elaborate word play and witticisms
aimed at a reasonably well-read and sophisticated audience. The various broadsides, bills of the day, and contemporary comments (q.v.)
bear this out—"calculated for the entertainment of persons of understanding, education and taste," "a witty well bred satire," "for the
Amusement of the Polite and Gay," "served up to please the Palates of
the Judicious." Despite what may appear to be a limited and specialized
audience, the *Lecture* and its offspring had a phenomenal stage history.

Advertising

Advertising for the *Lecture* followed the same general practices used
for productions at the larger playhouses; bills were posted, paid advertisements were inserted in the newspapers, puffs were written and
published, occasional criticism was printed, and reliance was placed on
word-of-mouth publicity.

The newspaper ads and playbills bore the largest responsibility and
provide us with the bulk of our information. Impressed as we may be
by the prodigious number of recorded performances of the *Lecture*, we
can be certain that hundreds of others will never come to light, given
the ephemeral nature of the material and the lack of complete files,
particularly for the smaller cities. Newspaper advertising was expensive and chancy and occasionally created problems for the performer
(and in retrospect for us). I have encountered numerous errors of
omission and commission, improper matching of days and dates, in-
furiating typos, late insertions, and one curious exchange between the
publisher and Lee Lewes, then performing at Covent Garden, who was
agitated because his notice appeared in column two instead of column
one along with the intelligence for Drury Lane and the Haymarket.

George Winchester Stone, Jr., has provided us with a very useful
breakdown of the composition of a typical eighteenth-century theatri-

cal notice,[18] and we may see how it applied equally to the *Lecture* and to the more traditional fare. Stone's ten categories may be paraphrased as follows: "(1) The name of the theatre and date of performance; (2) The title of the mainpiece and other attractions; (3) The performers; (4) Any entr'acte pieces and its performers; (5) Ticket prices and relevant restrictive comments; (6) Curtain time and time for seat reservations; (7) Facts concerning benefit performances; (8) Background information about performers; (9) Apologies for deferments, substitutions, etc; and (10) Special conditions of performance." In addition, some notices, particularly for the smaller, non-patent houses, would also carry a synopsis of the entertainment. Following is a sample announcement, the details of which have been drawn from the entries in a later section of this book on the production history of the *Lecture*. This hypothetical composite will give a clear idea how the potential theatregoer was solicited and informed.

At the Desire of Several Persons of Distinction

At the New Theatre in the Haymarket this Evening

MR. GEORGE ALEXANDER STEVENS
Will deliver his LECTURE upon HEADS. divided into
Three Parts. The first Part, Contains an Exhibition of Men's
Heads, with the History of Nobody's Family, and a No-Head.
The second Part, An Exhibition of Ladies Head-Dresses, with
the History of Flattery and its Family. The third Part, Is a
Physical Dissertation upon Sneezing and Snuff-taking, with a
Dissection of Heads, viz. a Virtuoso's, a Stock-jobber's,
a Critic's, a Politicians's, a Wit's, and the Section of a
Methodist's, with a Methodistical Preachment.

Boxes 4s. Pit 3s. Gallery 2s. Doors to be opened at
Half an Hour past Five. To begin exactly Half an Hour past
Six. Places for the boxes to be taken at the Theatre.

For the Benefit of the SUFFERERS by the late Fire in
Bishopsgatestreet, &c.

N.B. The Lecture not being advertised yesterday in this
Paper for this Evening; was owing to a Mistake committed
by the Person who was to carry the Advertisement.

In the newspapers there was always a great variety in spelling, the use of capitals, italics, punctuation, mixed fonts, typefaces, spacing, and decorative devices. The key details, particularly the title of the work and the major performers, were most prominently displayed. The emphasis was on clarity, significant information, and economy. Compression prevailed rather than aesthetic composition.

The puffs, usually paid self-commendation, are sometimes difficult to distinguish from disinterested criticism. Both were usually anonymous or signed with those ubiquitous pseudonyms "Philotheatricus," "Impartial," "Dramaticus," and so forth. The actual criticism occasionally precipitated a response, and the newspaper would carry a spirited debate for several days. The greater the argument the greater the curiosity, and it is unlikely that the box office ever suffered as a result.

Paraphernalia and Stage Business

We will never be quite sure exactly how George Alexander Stevens presented his first *Lecture*. The early editions of the work are pirated, frequently abbreviated, and perhaps partly transcripts of performances by Stevens's imitators. Beyond a few parenthetical phrases they tell us next to nothing about the visual aspects of the performance.[19] When Stevens revived the *Lecture* at the Haymarket in 1772, the presentation coincided with another unauthorized London edition entitled "An Essay on Satirical entertainments. To Which is added Stevens' new Lecture on heads, now delivering at the Theatre Royal, Hay-Market."[20] The text of the *Lecture* includes numerous stage directions as well as detailed critical comments between the parts. Many of these comments provide additional information about the performance. This edition, coming as it does eight years after the premiere, contains sections and pieces which were not printed in the 1765 version selected for this study. Stevens himself has told us in intervening advertisements of the progress of the *Lecture* and how characters are "new dressed," how he has "furnished himself with a fresh Sortment of Goods of the newest Fashion," and how he contended with the pirates by exerting "his utmost Abilities toward enriching the Lecture with *new characters*, and by making such other Alterations, as appeared requisite for keeping Pace with the *Foibles* as well as the *Fashions* of the *Times*." While the material had changed to some degree, there is a strong possibility that his presentation was still substantially the same. If this is so, the anonymous editor of the *Satirical Entertainments* has left us with a wealth of valuable information. Following are some extracts describing the stage business of the 1772 performance. The physical aspects of the *Lecture* fall into four categories: the prepared caricature heads, probably fashioned from papier-mâché; neutral head blocks used to accommodate a variety of wigs; miscellaneous hand properties; and Stevens's own actions and business.

As the performance begins *"The Lecturer stands behind a long table covered with green cloth resembling a counter.* [On the front of it is the motto 'AS YOU LIKE IT'] *Two screens placed behind obliquely form his ambuscade, from whence he conveniently draughts his forces."* The editor describes the head of Sir Dimple Daisy—"From the affected languish of the eye,—The dress of the hair,—The delicacy of the complexion, etc. &c. the mechanic has in this bust, given us a striking resemblance of this race of *Insipids."* "The lecturer's personification of [the Broad-grinner] is highly entertaining; as we are here indulged with a display of his great comic powers." Stevens, describing Master Jackey, says of him: "His mother when she was of child with him, dreamt she was brought to bed of a pincushion." The editor observes: "Some years ago, in his first lecture, he was attached to this foolish pincushion, and with as much seeming propriety as in the present instance. The *head* then under inspection, was that of a *tea-table* critic. He was likewise *Mama's darling!* at that time however this pincushion, was made the *real child* of the young man's head, and not, as now, the *imaginary offspring* of a dozing woman." Upon imitating a Buck, Stevens *"puts on a dishevell'd wig"* and as act 1 comes to an end the *"Lecturer retires strip'd, and in a boxing attitude and the curtain drops."* "The various transactions are told in the different tones of voice, and expressed by distorted features." For the beginning of act 2 *"The portraits of* PAINTING—ARCHITECTURE—POETRY—MUSIC *and* ASTRONOMY *at whole length,* [are] *placed in view."* "This allegory, compiled from different parts of the former lecture, now carries with it the air of novelty, and has considerable merit." For the section on the origin of the shape and color of money, Stevens *"shews a golden apple"* and later *"exhibits some slices of it."* For the six virtues he presents "six antique medals (*painted on canvas*)." In the satire on the new conjuror, Stevens *"takes a broad piece of money between each finger and thumb, and conveys them dexterously out of sight."* Then *"taking up a pack of cards"* he performs a trick with one and "changes it imperceptibly."

The next section, dealing with distress, is assisted by *"a picture of a lame soldier and sailor, thrown down in the street by a Quack doctor's chairmen."* The editor writes, "The painting as a performance, is the most wretched ever held up for public inspection. The subject, ridiculous in itself, is assisted by the *ingenuity* of the artist." Stevens concludes act 2 with a satire of the opera maker but "not being able to hit upon any droll visage for that purpose, and concluding that no one could be more ridiculous than my own," he *"puts on an uncommon high tete, for a foretop"* and pantomimes playing on a harpsichord as he sings. The editor says that "the apology for offering his own head, instead of a bust, is sufferable," but he is displeased by Stevens's excuse for the lack of a musical instrument.

The section on female hats utilizes several head coverings: one "*with five or six rows of silver cording*," "*a hat with a broad gold band*," "*a court hat*," and a Nivernee, or Fantail, "*which he puts on*." The laughing and crying philosophers are represented by busts held in each hand, and they engage in a puppetlike dialogue. For the lady of ill-temper Stevens holds up a medallion "(*exhibiting a portrait*) of a lady in her natural sweetness of disposition" and then "*turning the canvas*" shows her in an ill mood. The editor says, "The paintings are not bad; and being here left, as in justice they ought, to speak for themselves, they have consequently more effect on the spectators, than all the oratory he could have spouted off to explain them."

The section on matrimonial tranquility is assisted by "*exhibiting a painting of the gentleman stretching across two chairs,—the lady three parts asleep upon a sopha*." The editor finds the painting "tolerable" and "being well-timed gives great satisfaction.—The observations [Stevens] makes upon it, holding it in his hand, are strong, and as they do not break upon the design of the painter, are agreeable." The head of Flattery is presented as "*half white, half black*" and then "by a sudden toss the mask falls back, and *exhibits the head of Reproach*."[21] The editor is very impressed with the material, particularly "when it received the additional graces, from the mode of representation, it may be stiled a masterly performance."

Stevens concludes act 4 with another satirical attack on the law, this time with the extremely popular case of Botum vs. Bullum, wherein he presides over the mock trial and "puts on the wig, and personates a judge." The fifth act of the *Lecture* ends with Stevens's most famous impersonation. He takes a wig of lank locks "*puts them on, places part of a tub before him, and imitates a methodist teacher*" concluding with "you shall be scalp'd of all your iniquities, as easily as I pull off this peruke."[22] Then the "Lecturer comes forward on the stage" to deliver the final quatrain.

The Rhetorical Structure

Stevens's *Lecture* neatly suits the satiric spirit of the times. His method is unique; the work does not fit any traditional mode, nor does it limit itself to any single style or technique. His subjects are, with the exception of the Methodist Parson, generalized and unidentified types or classes of society, each reflecting some excess of behavior which is subjected to his scorn and ridicule. His tone is incisive, bantering, and derisive but seldom contemptuous or malevolent. The targets are venial sins rather than deadly ones: hypocrisy, extravagance, flattery, folly, ostentation, and pomposity.

Later editions of the *Lecture* were supplemented by *An Essay on Satire* written by a Mr. Pilon. In order to put Stevens's work in perspective, Pilon delineates three types of satire: (1) narrative satire describes characteristics of an individual or the general manners of a society, people, or nation in verse or prose (Horace and Juvenal); (2) dramatic satire contains perfect resemblance, which is described by comedy, or caricature, which is described by farce (Aristophanes and Foote); and (3) picturesque satire exercises the painter, engraver, and sculptor (Hogarth). Pilon points out that all of these types of satire have their limitations, and he concludes: "Thus it is evident that a species of satire, which could blend all the advantages of all the three, can only be that which is adequate to the idea of perfect satire. This kind of satire is the Lecture on Heads. We cannot, therefore, be surprised that it should have been the most popular exhibition of the age."[23]

Stevens, as we have seen, had a knowledge of classical literature, and many allusions and figures of speech are utilized in the *Lecture*. Note his use of rhetorical figures such as aposiopesis, or suppression: "a woman of the town or a ———"; alliteration: "a true classical conjugating countenance and denotes dictionary dignity"; metaphor: "Life is said to be a lottery"; simile: "Law! it is like fire and water"; pun: "The word brethren comes from the Tabernacle, because we all breathe there—in"; and numerous others. He invents comic jargon when needed: "The kitchen is Camerero necessaro, in uso cookeraro." Specific references are made to well-known figures of the past: Alexander the Great, Midas, Medea, Solomon, Semiramis, Homer, Minerva, Cleopatra, and Shakespeare. We also hear parodic echoes of Shakespeare: "What importance is now seated on these brows" reminds us of Hamlet in the closet scene telling his mother, "See what a grace was seated on this brow"; and the pun-ch line to the long story about the landlord and the soldier, when the latter is dismissed as one of the catter-pillars (of the nation), is almost surely a subtle reference to Bushy, Bagot, and Green, those "caterpillars of the commonwealth" in *Richard II*. There are scattered proverbs ("good wine needs no bush"); Latin tags ("imprimis," "secundum artem"), and extended narratives based on personification (i.e., Wit, Flattery, and Justice). It is remarkable how this diversity of devices and techniques results in a singular and identifiable style.

The earliest versions of the *Lecture* comprised three separate sections. There is no apparent thematic unity within or among the parts. The treatment of the individual subjects varies in length and style, and one gets the distinct impression that any of the units are dispensable or replaceable. Some, like Alexander the Great, Daniel vs. Dishclout, and the Methodist Parson were perennial favorites and remained in the *Lecture* during its long history. Within two years of its premiere the *Lecture* was being presented in four or five parts, old material was rewritten, new heads were introduced and old ones were dropped. It was constantly revised to appeal to jaded audiences, to capitalize on the popularity of current events or personalities, or to exploit the particular talents of individual performers.

Selected Targets

WIGS

Stevens's decision to include the wig as an object of his satirical jibes was logical and expected. It was a clever theatrical stroke for it reduced the necessity of having many prepared heads; a variety of wigs could be placed sequentially on a single wig block or he could use his own head as the model. Stevens had had his fun with the wigs earlier, particularly in the *Beauties of All the Magazines Selected* and *The Adventures of a Speculist*, and their appearance in the *Lecture* was predictable.

In our own age, when the male wig is generally used for ceremonial purposes (the British barrister and judge), as an isolated joke (the circus clown), or as the only sure cure for baldness, it may be difficult to appreciate fully its pervasiveness in Stevens's day. Wigs were worn by servants, farmers, and royalty alike and "indicated status, social class and beliefs and were taken so seriously that a good barber would offer a choice of twenty or thirty styles."[24] More precisely, at least 111 individual styles have been identified for the century.[25] Many of the modes came from France and frequently were Anglicized and elaborated in preposterous variety. The dandies Ambrose Phillips ("Namby Pamby") and "Beau" Nash ("King of Bath") put their own particular stamp of elegance on fashion, and the excesses were most prominently displayed by the Macaronis, those super-exquisite fops who gave a new word to the language.

Stevens's timing was propitious. Shortly after 1764 wigs began to go out of fashion and men took to having their own hair dressed. There was a temporary revival of their popularity, but during the 1790s wigs were seen as a symbol of the aristocracy in France and in England heavy taxes were levied on the powder used to dress them. They were soon to become a thing of the past. Thus, when Stevens talked of a "full frizzel bob" or "Caxons," he was referring to actual current styles so ludicrous that he could scarcely avoid satirizing them.

NOBODY AND SOMEBODY

An early literary reference to Nobody and Somebody appears in an English play of the same name dated about 1606. The characters belong to the underplot of a political satire and are depicted in two woodcuts in the printed edition (see plate 5). Nobody is a figure with almost all legs and no body and Somebody is shown with almost all body and no legs. The title page tells us that the printer, John Trundle, used the figure of Nobody on the sign over his shop. Shakespeare and his audience were familiar with the character: in the third act of *The Tempest* Trinculo declares, "This is the tune of our catch, played by the picture of Nobody." Speaight tells us that in 1748 Madame de la Nash had given a puppet show for a fashionable audience the advertisements of which referred to a "pacifick dance between Somebody and Nobody." He suspects a political satire and concludes, "Somebody and Nobody were stock figures of popular legend . . . they must have lent themselves to interpretation by puppets."[26]

THE QUACK DOCTOR

The quack doctor has been a satirical target from the earliest days of the theatre. Philip W. Harsh states that "of all the galaxy of comic characters none perhaps surpasses the medical quack in age. He is listed in accounts of early Greek improvisations," and although the passage in Plautus's *Twin Menaechmi* "is the only one in Roman comedy where he has survived, he must have been a stock figure."[27]

As the Dottore he is a central figure in many of the commedia dell'arte scenarios. Frequently appearing as either a lawyer or a physician, his humor is based on grandiloquent monologues filled with abstruse jargon, garbled phrases, mangled Greek and Latin, neologisms, extravagant pretensions, and, for the physician in particular, ludicrous cures for the horrendous diseases that have beset mankind. A seventeenth-century Dottore speaks: "I am not only an avalanche of medicine, but the bane of all maladies whatsoever. I exterminate all fevers and chills, the itch, gravel, measles, the plague, ringworm, gout, apoplexy, erysipelas, rheumatism, pleurisy, catarrh, both wind-colic

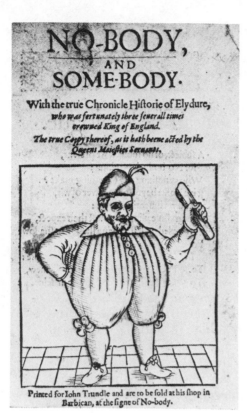

Plate 5: Nobody and Somebody. Reproduced from *Nobody and Somebody*, Tudor Facsimile Texts, vol. 113 (New York, 1970).

and ordinary colic, without counting those serious and light illnesses which bear the same name. In short, I wage such cruel and relentless warfare against all forms of illness that when I see a disorder becoming ineradicable in a patient I even go as far as to kill the patient in order to relieve him of his disorder."[28]

Hope springs eternal, and the quack is still with us peddling his nostrums to a gullible public for underdeveloped busts, overdeveloped buttocks, baldness, and declining virility. It was no different in Stevens's London. The extracts from the following advertisements are taken from the *Public Advertiser* of April 6, 1764, the month of the *Lecture*'s debut:

Walker's Patent Jesuits Drops . . . the most pleasant and infallible cure for all Weaknesses, in both Sexes, occasioned by Strains, Mercurials, &c. and in all Cases of a certain Disorder, and have no Mercurials in their Composition.

Montpellier Drops, for the Cure of a certain Disease in all its Stages, a Medicine very pleasant to take, and easy in its Operation, . . . the Dose is only from 12 to 20 drops on a Lump of Sugar; and is so efficacious, that the most inveterate Scurvy, Evil, or Leprosy, cannot stand before it, restoring Health, Strength and Vigour to the Body.

Restorative Cordial Drops, discovered by Mr. Beckett . . . A new Medicine. . . . it circulates the Juices, enlivens the Spirits, recreates all the Faculties both of Body and Mind, and efficaciously nourishes the whole Vital System, dissipates all Sorts of Weaknesses and imbicilities, and restores Strength and Vigour to a decayed Constitution. . . . And what still adds greatly to the Praise of this singular Medicine, is, that with the greatest Certainty, it removes the causes of Sterility or Barrenness. The Truth of its having this wonderful Effect is confirmed by the recent Informations the Author daily receives.

There is more on the same page, including notices of the publication of Dr. Becket's *Observations on the Nature and Cure of a Certain Disorder* . . . , which was distributed free of charge, and the third edition of *A Dissertation on the Properties and Efficacy of the Lisbon Diet Drink, in the Cure of the Venereal Disease and Scurvy* . . . by J. Leake, M.D., which sold for 1s. 6d.

Stevens's quack (see plate 6) is linked with Alexander the Great and the Cherokee Chief but is the greatest killer of the three. The dissertation on snuff-taking defines sneezing, or sternutation, in derisive medical terms, and the dissection of the Tea-table Critic's head does not reveal a cerebellum or "other hard words." From the Greeks to

QUACK DOCTOR.

G. A. Stevens in his Lecture on Heads.

Pub.ᵈ October 10 1793 by S.W. Fores; N 3 Piccadilly

S.W.F

Plate 6: Quack Doctor. (Harvard Theatre Collection.)

twentieth-century American burlesque, the doctor has always been fair game. Stevens was astute enough to know a surefire audience pleaser.

The final sketch of the Methodist Parson with the accompanying tabernacle harangue was one of the most popular and frequently repeated sections of the *Lecture*. Religious and moral opposition to the theatre in England began with the papal fulminations of the Middle Ages and became a cause célèbre for the Puritans during the Renaissance and the Commonwealth. During the eighteenth century, however, the antitheatre forces were dominated by the Methodists. Despite their attacks, the theatres remained full as the opposing factions exchanged vociferous and often vituperative volleys. In addition to hundreds of defensive tracts, letters, and other literary missiles, over two dozen theatrical works of this period have been identified which either depict or satirize the Methodists.[29] They are presented as "hypocritical, avaricious, drunken, gluttonous, uneducated, and coarse. They are mimicked and mocked for their personal appearance, their style of preaching, and their supposedly bad character."[30]

Tate Wilkinson's "principal charge against the Methodists ... [in his *Memoirs*, 1791] is that they were hypocrites. He contends that the Methodists attacked the stage because they were actually competitors with the stage who vied for audience support and financial return."[31] Robert Mansel, in his *Free Thoughts*, found the Methodist criticism of the stage largely undeserved and cataloged many of their indictments: "The PLAYHOUSE!—That tabernacle of the Devil!—The pit of Hell— Boxes for the train of Lucifer!—Galleries for the high throne of Satan!—The castle of Belzebub!— ... A trade of wickedness which leads to Hell!—The Devil's solemnities, or pomps!—Mammon's vineyard, where Satan's labourers work for the wages of sin and iniquity!—The toy-shop of vanity, supported by the Devil's buffoons!— Roisters, brawlers, ill-dealers, boasters, stallions, ruffians!"[32] Samuel Foote joined forces with his play *The Minor* (1759) in which he satirized the prominent Methodist preacher George Whitefield, as Dr. Squintum, with barbed references to Whitefield's severely crossed eyes and their symbolic connotation of hypocrisy.

Stevens, then, had ample precedent for his target. The parson is the only character identified by name—"The motives of our deeds the same with Whitefield" he says in the epilogue. But Whitefield is identified earlier—"with one eye he looks up to Heaven ... and with the other eye he looks down to see what he can get." And the deformity is confirmed by the pictorial evidence (see plates 6 and 7). Stevens saved the Methodist Parson for last, and evidently it was the high point of the recital. But his satire became uncharacteristically vicious. The genial, bantering style was replaced by meanness and vilification. He was no longer laughing; his images turned gross and the attack was relentless. Consider "My great bowels, and my sm——all guts groan," "gripe of compassion," "belly-ache of pity," "full of filth," "preaching scow'rs the belly," "pinching to the human tripe," and the other near-scatological images. Then, as the diatribe concludes, Stevens shifted his ground and returned his audience from the tabernacle to the more comfortable environs of the playhouse.

Notes

1. *B.D.* (1812), p. 689.
2. Again I resort to the generic use of a term. Without quibbling over a specific definition of satire, the word is also used to include such blood cousins as irony, burlesque, lampoon, ridicule, caricature, parody, and so forth. Better minds than mine have addressed themselves to the distinctions, but I am still not convinced that they are all mutually exclusive.
3. *Speculist*, vol. 2, p. 94.
4. Ibid., p. 91.
5. Foote "presented the first matinee in English dramatic history" (*The London Stage*, pt. 3, vol. 1, p. clxxxiii).
6. *B.D.* (1812), p. 689.
7. James Roose-Evans, *London Theatre: From the Globe to the National* (Oxford, 1977), p. 36.
8. George Speaight, *The History of the English Puppet Theatre* (New York, 1955) p. 54. Much of the following information on the puppets and marionettes in England has been taken directly from Speaight. Readers are directed to this remarkable book for a thorough account of the development of the genre.
9. Ibid., p. 72.
10. Ibid., p. 92.
11. Ibid., p. 101.
12. *A Narrative of the Life of Mrs. Charlotte Charke . . . Written by Herself* (London, 1755). Quoted from the first American edition, (New York: Richard R. Smith, 1930), pp. 13–14.
13. *Dramatic History*, p. 134.
14. *Speculist*, vol. 2, pp. 32–33.
15. Speaight, p. 173. In appendix B, "Plays Performed by Puppets in England," Speaight attributes the following to Stevens: *The Creation of the World; Solomon and the Queen of Sheba; The Children in the Wood; St. George and The Dragon; The Gunpowder Plot; Fair Rosamond; Whittington, thrice Lord Mayor of London, and his Cat.*
16. M. D. George, *English Social Life in the Eighteenth Century* (London, 1923), pp. 76–78.
17. For a fuller discussion of the economics and the audiences, see Harry William Pedicord, *The Theatrical Public in the Time of Garrick* (New York, 1954).

18. *The London Stage*, pt. 4, vol. 1, pp. lxxiiff.
19. Important clues, however, can be discovered from several of the illustrations reproduced in this book.
20. See the section entitled *Bibliography of the Works of George Alexander Stevens* in this book.
21. If the illustrations are accurate, the earlier representations of Flattery were painted on canvas.
22. Conversely, it seems that the early Methodist was a modeled bust.
23. *A Lecture on Heads by Geo. Alex. Stevens, with Additions, by Mr. Pilon . . . to Which Is Added an Essay on Satire.* (London, 1812), pp. 105–07.
24. John Woodforde, *The Strange Story of False Hair* (London, 1971), p. 1.
25. Ibid., pp. 46–47.
26. Speaight, pp. 109–10.
27. Philip W. Harsh, *A Handbook of Classical Drama* (Stanford, 1944), p. 357.
28. Pierre Louis Duchartre, *The Italian Comedy* (New York, 1966), p. 202.
29. Terence X. McGovern, "The Methodist Revival and the British Stage" (Ph.D. diss., University of Georgia, 1978), p. 312.
30. Ibid., p. 353.
31. Ibid., p. 293.
32. Robert Mansel, *Free Thoughts upon Methodists, Actors, and the Influence of the Stage* (Hull, 1814), pp. 171–72.

III

The Lecture on Heads:
A Text

THE FOLLOWING TEXT of the *Lecture* is taken from the 1765 Dublin edition. It is among the earliest of the versions and was published without Stevens's approval or permission. A year had elapsed between the premiere and the first printing—plenty of time for the pirates and copyists to put together what must have been a reasonably accurate version. As the years went by the text underwent numerous changes; the editions of the 1770s and 1780s are noticeably different.

It has often been pointed out that the real success of the *Lecture* was due to Stevens's special talents as a performer in this particular genre. Very few playscripts convey the immediacy of the actual production, and the *Lecture* is an even more pertinent example since there are few stage directions and much of the business is implied and even improvised. It would help the reader to refer to the two plates reproduced in section 4 even though a number of the heads are later additions.

The text is reproduced here almost verbatim: with the original format, spelling variations, and obvious typographical errors. If nothing else, they preserve the sense of haste and carelessness that accompanied the printing of an unauthorized version of a work that had captured the public's imagination and promised to be a very marketable commodity.

THE CELEBRATED

would have been better if annotated

LECTURE

ON

HEADS

Which has been exhibited upwards of one hundred
successive Nights, to crowded Audiences, and
met with the most universal Applause.

By

G. ALEXANDER STEVENS.

DUBLIN:

Printed for J. HOEY, sen. in *Skinner-row*,
J. HOEY, jun. in *Parliament-Street*, and
J. WILLIAMS, in *Skinner-row*, 1765.

The Introduction

PART I.

Alexander the Great—Cherokee Chief—Quack Doctor—Cuckold—
Lawyer—Humourous Oration in praise of the Law—Horse Jockies—
Nobody—Lottery of Life—Nobody's, Somebody's, Anybody's, and Ev-
erybody's Coats of Arms—Family of Nobody—Vanity—Wit—Judg-
ment—Genius—Architecture—Painting—Poetry—Astronomy—Music
—Statues of Honesty and Flattery.

PART II.

Ladies Heads—Riding Hood—Ranelagh Hood—Billingsgate—Laugh-
ing and Crying Philosophers—Venus's Girdle—Cleopatra—French
Night Cap—Face Painting—Old Maid—Young Married Lady—Old
Batchelor—Lass of the Spirit—Quaker—2 Hats contrasted—and 2
Heads contrasted.

PART III.

Phisical Wig—Dissertation on Sneezing and Snuff-taking—Life of a
Blood—Woman of the Town—Tea Table Critic—Learned Critic—

City Politician humorously described—Gambler's 3 Faces—Gambler's Funeral and Monument—Life and Death of a Wit—Head of a well known Methodist Parson with a *Tabernacle Harangue.*

The Celebrated Lecture on Heads

PART I.

Ladies and Gentlemen,

By all the laws of laughing, every man has an undoubted right to play the fool with himself; under that licence this Exhibition is attempted.— Good wine needs no bush;—the bad deserves none:—If what I have to offer meets with your approbation, you will applaud it; if otherwise, it will meet with the contempt it deserves.—Some of these heads are manufactured in wood, and others in pasteboard, to denote, that there are not only Blockheads, but Paper Sculls.

This is one of those extraordinary personages called Conquerors. He was called Alexander the Great, from the great number of people his ambition had cut to pieces, he was a most dexterous slaughterman, and thought mankind only made for him to cut away with; he was a great hero, warrior, and mankiller.—Formerly. And—This is the head of a Cherokee Chief, called Sachem-Swampum-Scalpo-Tomahauk;— He was a great hero, warrior, and man-killer—Lately. And

This is the head of a Quack-Doctor:—a greater man-killer than either of the other two. This head of the quack-doctor is exhibited to shew the weakness of Wisdom, and the strength of folly; for if wisdom was not so weak, would such fellows as Carmen, Coblers and Potters be permitted to vend their unwholsome mixtures, under letters patent;— and if folly was not too strong, wou'd any body swallow their compositions!—The madness of * this head, made him a conqueror.—The folly of the town dubb'd † this a doctor.—The exploits of Alexander are celebrated by half the great writers of the age; and yet this Alexander was nothing more than a murderer and a madman; who ran from one end of the world to the other, seeking whom he might cut to pieces;— and ** this copper-complexioned hero wants nothing to make him as great as Alexander, but the rust of antiquity to varnish over his crimes, and the pens of writers to illustrate his actions.—The Quack-doctor is his own historian; and publishes, in the Daily Advertiser and Gazeteer,

*Alexander.
†The Quack Doctor.
**Cherokee Chief.

accounts of cures never performed, and copies of affidavits never sworn to.

Here is the quack-doctors coat of arms;—three ducks proper, and Quack, Quack, Quack, for the motto.—'Tis charg'd round with death's-heads; and by way of crest, a number of quack puffs, and bills of mortality.—It was made up for him by the worshipful company of Undertakers, and presented to him by the Sextons and Gravediggers; to denote, that these people look upon Quack-Doctors as their greatest benefactors.

The ornaments of ‡ this head, are not for what the wearer has done; on the contrary, he bears about with him the constant memorial of the faults of others, and is, by the ill-judging part of the world, condemned for crimes he could not commit, and the very commission of which constitute all his unhappiness. These horns, like the cornucopia of the ancients, signify plenty; and denote, that this head hath abundance of brethren in affliction; they are gilt, to shew, that there are wretches base enough to accept the wages of dishonour, even in a point the most delicate.—This brass Buck's head, we all well know, is made use of both in public and private houses; nor had it been made in this shape, but to accustom mankind not only to the sight of horns, but to the use of hanging their hats upon them.

From the ancient custom of adorning the temples, came the modern custom of embellishing the whole head. Hence arose the wig manufactory—the consequence of which we shall endeavour to illustrate.

*Here is a head, and only a head; a plain simple, naked, unembellished appearance; which in its present situation, conveys to us no other idea, than that of a bruiser, preparing to fight at Broughton's. Behold how naked, how simple a thing Nature is! But, beho'd, how luxuriant is † Art! What importance is now seated on these brows! What reverence the features demand! What dignity is diffused on the whole countenance!—This is a compendium of law.—Special pleadings in the fore-top, pleas, rejoinders, replications, and demurs in each turn of the head—the knotty points of practice in the twist of the tail—the depth of the full bottom, denotes the length of a chancery suit, while the back coif at top, like a blister plaister, seems to tell us, that the Law is a great irritator, and never to be used but in very desperate cases.—But as it is not enough to suppose a resemblance, and as we have more blocks than one to try our wigs upon, we will make an exchange, and attempt an oration in praise of the law.

‡The head of a Cuckold.
*A Counsellors head.
†A large tye wig upon the head.

Law! law! law! is like a fine woman's temper—a very difficult study—
Law; law! is like a book of surgery;—a great many terrible cases in
it.—Law! it is like fire and water; very good servants; but, very bad,
when they get the upper hand of us;—'tis like a homely genteel woman,
very well to follow;—'tis also, like a scolding wife, very bad when it
follows us;—and again, it is like bad weather, most people chuse to
keep out of it.—In law! In law there are four parts; the Quidlibate, the
Quodlibate, and quidproquo, and the Sinequanon.—Imprimis; the
Quilibate; or who began first? because, in all actions of assault, the law
is clear, that pribis jokis, is absolutis maris, sina jokis; which, being
elegantly and classically rendered into English, is, that, whosoever he
be that gave the first stroke, it was absolute ill, and without a joke.

Secondly, the Quadlibate, or the damages, but that the law has
nothing to do with, only to state them; for whatever damages ensue,
they are all the client's perquisites, according to that antient Norman
motto;—If he is cast, or castandum; he is semper idem, ruinandum.

Thirdly, the Quidproco; seeing council.—Giving words for money,
or having money for words: according to that ancient Norman motto,
"Si curat lex,"—We live to perplex.

Fourthly, the Sinaquanon; or, without something, what would any
thing be good for? Without this wig, what would be the outlines of the
law!

I shall illustrate this by a case in point (Peere Williams, p. 96) Daniel
against Dishclout:—Plaintiff Daniel was groom in the same family
where defendant Dishclout was cook. Plaintiff Daniel had been drinking, or, as Dr. Bibbibus in his dissertation on bumpers, he was Dupli-
cans, that is, he was a double man; he was not as he should be, ipse he;
but as he should not be, Tipse he.—Plaintiff Daniel made a forcible
entry on the cook's premisses, the kitchen.—Now the kitchen, according to Serjeant Plodding, as he has it in his 149th vol. folio, of the
abridgment of the statutes, page 1296, there he says, that the kitchen is,
Camero necessaro, in usu cookeraro, where she has the overlooking,
the conduct, the management, the impervising, the seeing to, the
superintendance, and the speculation of all the sauspannis, stewpan-
nis, frienpannis, et stovis smokejacko and where our cook was at this
time employed in all the duties of her office; where she was rostandum,
boilandum, fryandum, frigaseyandum, et plumb-puddingandum,
mixandum. At this time Plaintiff Daniel made a forcible entry, &c. and
demanded a sop in the pan; defendant Dishclout insisted on her right
of refusal;—(a sop in the pan, gemmen, is a very serious thing;) and
without perquisites. what are all honours and places good for? Nothing
more than an embroidered button-hole; and if we consider a minister

of state as the nation's cook, then perquisites are the sop in the pan to the minister of state, with which omnium gatherum choose to grease their fingers.—Well, Plaintiff Daniel demanded a sop in the pan; Defendant Dishclout insisted on a right of refusal; Daniel seized Dishclout by the left hand, there was the Quidlibate, or the assault; Dishclout took Daniel by the right hand, and pulled him into the dripping-pan; there was the damages—the dripping pan.—Now, if the dripping-pan had not been there, he could not have fallen into the dripping-pan; and if he had not been there, the dripping-pan could not have received him. And this is Law; is the loquaciousness of the law is multi loquacious; forasmuch, nevertheless, moreover, likewise, and also.—The liberty of the Law is the happiness of the English: and it is very happy for us Englishmen, that we have the liberty to go to law.

Here is a wig, as stiff as if chisseled out by a stone cutter; and as unnatural as Chinese ornaments; and yet these wigs, and the wearers of them too, are in fashion in some parts of the town; and thus plaistered, like the top of a cabbage plant after a shower of snow, 'tis called the Journeyman's Jemmy. And

This is Sir Languish Lisping, these creatures adorn the outside of their heads to attack ladies hearts, and they are promoted to places in the service of the ladies, in proportion to their respective merits; they are tea-cups carriers, fan bearers, and snuff box holders. This is the He at the one end of the town, and this is the He at the other end of the town. It would perhaps give pain to any one of this audience, to have such a pomatum cake pasted to their heads; But the extreme delicate creatures these represent, seldom make any other use of their heads, than to have their hair or wigs dressed upon them. They smile, and simper, they ogle, they admire every lady, and every lady alike. Nay, they copy the manners of the ladies so closely, that grammarians are at a loss, whether to rank them with the masculine or feminine, and therefore put them down as the Doubtful Gender.—These wigs, from the quantity of powder that is lavished upon them, are called Ammunition Caxons; and thus sweetened over, like the sugar at the top of a twelf cake, may seem to denote, that the wearers must needs be very sweet fellows.

Here, is a full frizzell bob.—The wearer of this wig looks like an ostrich in a fright; as if he had run his head into a bush, and brought it away with him about his ears.—Wigs may be considered as bearing great analogy to books: this, then, will be an huge quarto in large paper; as this is a duodecimo in small print, and belongs to Mr. Donefirst, the long odds layer: and here is his man, "Cross and jostle in," sweated down to ride a sweepstakes; and thus dressed, in true turf taste, they are called a brace of "knowing ones."—The head of a horse jockey, and a jockey's horse, may be said to have great affinity: because the jockey's head can pull the horse's head on which side the post he pleases; but what sort of heads must those people have, who know these things are done, and yet trust their capitals with such sinking funds! but we shall forbear to say any more on this head, for fear of offending those high personages who chuse to resemble grooms and horse jockeys.—A conversation should have been formed for these heads, and they should have talked of various subjects; such as politics, religion, and cold cream, eau de luce, lavender water, demyreps, and French chicken gloves.—But as all that has been said is to no purpose, and as least said is soonest mended; and as those that say nothing cannot be blamed for speaking, we have chosen to exhibit these capitals as mutes; and hope the audience won't take offence at it.—Some heads are mute, because they have nothing to say: some, should be mute, because they say nothing to the purpose; some men say nothing at all to their wives; and some married men would be extremely happy, if their wives said nothing at all to them.

This is nobody's head; or, the head of nobody; because thus adorned with the fool's cap, nobody chuses to own it.—Historians have left us in the dark with respect to these hood bonnets; but it is, however, supposed, that the first who wore them was, Judge Midas, who had the inimitable art of turning every thing he touched into gold; and now touch some people with gold, and you may make anything of them; money getting, consisting in the art of making fools wise; or, of properly suffering ourselves to be made fools of.

Life is said to be a lottery; and folly concerned in the chances.—Now let us see if this fool's cap has any prizes!—This may appear as a satyr against card playing, but 'tis not a just one; on the contrary, most card players are said to belong to ** this family, and generally bear their name; they are called court cards, because when turned up trumps, they become honours.—Which shews, if you deal fairly you may gain honours, and that often, honours or no honours, depend entirely on a shuffle.

This crest belongs to those easy kind of mortals, who are said to be nobody's enemy but their own. They are divided into three classes;—there are your generous fellows,—your honest fellows,—and your devilish clever fellows.—As to your generous fellow; he is treat master; your honest fellow he is singing master, who is to keep the company

**Four knaves held up.

alive for four or five hours; and then, your devilish clever fellow is to drink them all dead.—They married into Folly's family, and got this crest.—"the fool's cap."—And which to this day nobody chuses to be known by.

If you ask why we so frequently use the term nothing, let this serve as a reason; from ten to twenty, we go to school to learn, what, from twenty to thirty, we are strangely apt to forget; from thirty to forty, we think things must needs be as we would have them; from forty to fifty, we find ourselves a little out in our reckoning; and from fifty to sixty, upon casting up life's debtor and creditor, we find ‡ this the certain ballance.—These are a number of nothings, which, in their present state, have no power or consequence; yet, by the addition of one, they take rank and precedence immediately; which shews, that in life, as well as arithmetic, nothing may be turned into something, by the assistance of any one lord of a golden manor; take away the one and they are nothing again.—To nothing we must all come; happy they, who, amidst the variations of nothing, have done nothing, to be ashamed of. If they have nothing to fear, they have every thing to hope—Thus, ends the dissertation on nothing; which the exhibiter hopes he has properly executed,—by making nothing of it.

From the dissertation on nothing, we come to Nobody's genealogical tables.—This is nobody's crest, because, whoever this may suit nobody cares to own it.—this is somebody's crest; "a screen," because in all political disputes, somebody is supposed to be behind the screen.— This coat of legs and arms belongs to those easy kind of mortals, who are always throwing their legs and arms about 'em; restless every where at home; no where; how they live, nobody knows; and how they die, no body cares. However insignificant this may appear, yet that is of no small importance; for the moment a man begins to fancy himself something, he assumes a big look; we have therefore given him a big belly, with a vast corporation; as for the absent members, let them be thus made out; let the mayor be the head; the two sheriffs the arms, as they execute the law; the aldermen the legs, as they support the chair; and as to the eyes, nose, mouth, &c. why let them be composed of a committee of common council men; and so, the corporation is made out.

This is any body's coat of arms; the shield is blank, a blank for the rest! it being as easy now-a-days to buy and bear a coat of arms, as any other coat.—

‡A board held up, with a parcel of noughts.

The Herald's office is the true Monmouth street in the parish of Pedigree. It is honour's piece broker's shop, where every remnant of reputation is to be purchased.—It should seem as if the Herald's office had the virtue of Medea's kettle, where every plebean vulgarity is boiled away, and out they come spick and span new gentlefolks.

This is every body's coat of arms;—a bag of money, and hands catching at it; money reaping being mankind's universal harvest work: we have given a death's head to every body's coat of arms, being the exact likeness of every body drawn after the life.

It may seem strange that we should exhibit such terms, as esteem, generosity, friendship, gratitude, public spirit and common sense; as belonging to nobody's family: but, the truth is, that these fine qualifications have been so ill used, that nobody cared to own them. The consequence of which was, that they were ordered into the workhouse: but the parish officers unanimously agreed, that they should, have no admittance there.—Mr. Overseer, standing up, and saying, that as how,—in the first place; imprimis; first of all, and foremost—Gemmen of the westry, Why what business have we with friendship! I take it, that as how the best friend a man has, is a man's own money in a man's own pocket: and friendship is nothing more or less, as I take it, in the whole versal world, but to borrow a man's money out of a man's pocket. I come now to your gratitudes. and I take your gratitudes to be a sort of a foreign lingo; which we English folk have nothing at all to do with;— and ye know my gemmen of the westry, since Self Interest was member of parliament, Gratitude has been turned out of doors.

Mr. Headborough, slowly rising from his chair, and gravely snuffing the candle, begg'd leave to be heard—and he said, that as how, where- of, and wherefore, not so much for the saying of the thing, as tho't it should be said, though to be sure no man should be certain sure of his own judgment; yet for his part; now as to your generosity, he look'd upon it to be a sort of something of a foreign plant, and we have nothing to do with it—And as to your public spirit, why ye know gemmen of the westry, I need not tell you, that is nothing more than a licence for publicans to sell spirituous liquors:—and as to your esteem wh——y some people esteem brandy punch; and some people esteem rum punch; for my part, give me a little sup of your rum punch: and if I was the people of Jamaica, if the people of England would not drink rum punch, why they should have no turtle, and then they would all be starved. And

Now my gemmen of the westry, I come to my imprimis, third and last; and that is your common sense; and as to your common sense, if I may be allowed to speak my reflexions about; I look upon it to be too common, and too vulgar a thing, for the gemmen of the westry to trouble their heads with, or be concarnd about.

All these fine qualifications must have perished in oblivion, had not Chance recommended them to the family of Ostentation. Here is the lady of Ostentation's manor, her name was Vanity. She had a sister named Wit, who ran away with Judgment, the house steward, from which two was begot Genius, but as it's very common to use genius ill, so, she suffered many and great hardships, till at length she was reduced to so low an ebb, as to be obliged to lodge in a garret with the Poet Oblivion, and his mother Necessity. In process of time Judgment, her father, found her out, and promoted a marriage between Genius and Science, and from that marriage were produced these five fine children, Architecture, Painting, Poetry, Astronomy, and Music. But the disturbance at that time between the Goths and the Vandals, having overturned the temples of the Arts and Sciences, these scientifics took shipping, and a storm a rising at sea, they were shipwreck'd on the inhospitable coast of Sussex, where, after being plundered of their wearing apparel, they were left to starve, by the inhumanity of the country people. The reason why our sea-side savages may rob and plunder shipwrecked passengers with impunity, is owing to a defect in the Game Act, which was made for the preservation of the game all over England, the gentlemen, who drew up that act, forgetting to make men, women, and children game, though it is so common, now-a-days, to make game of men, women, and children. They begged their way up to London on foot, where they were in hopes that the merit of their works would recommend them, poor creatures! 'Tis a sign they knew very little of the world, to imagine any such thing: however, (to prevent starving) Architecture turned bricklayer's labourer to a Chinese builder, Painting, was a grinder of colours to a paper stainer, Poetry, turned printer's devil, Music, sung ballads about the streets, and Astronomy, cried almanacks. In some little time lady Fashion found them out, and, as soon as lady Fashion found them out, all the world ran mad for their company.

This is a most curious exhibition, and very likely to make the learned look about them; for as there is no mark or sign to discover what it is, 'tis a sure proof of its being a genuine antique—It may, for ought we know, be a King Solomon, or Queen Semiramis; an Old Venus, or a New Nabob, a Methodist Preacher, or a Bottle Conjuror. It was intended to place the face of Probability upon it; but that motion was soon laid aside, as people, in our days are only fond of improbabilities: at length, a part of the bronze, or plaster, being rubbed off, a letter was discovered by which it appeared to be the remains of the statue of Honesty; thus maul'd and mutilated by the various inroads that had been made upon it.—Imagine not, spectators that this bust of Honesty is exhibited, as if the real face would be a stranger, to any one of this company;—No,—She is only shewn here, emblematically; the meaning of which is, that the manners of the times are such, as may put Honesty out of countenance.—Not as a companion, but as a contrast to the head of Honesty, is

This, the head of Flattery, exhibited. The ancients had days they called White, or Lucky days; thus it is with Flattery; to the fortunate she turns her white, her shining side; to the unfortunate, she is ever in eclipse. Upon the approach of any ill fortune, Flattery generally turns into reproach; the meaning of which is, that it is a reproach to our understandings to suffer Flattery, yet we continue to accept the injury, though we despise the hand that offers it; not remembering that the receiver is as bad as the thief.

This being, Flattery, was begot on Poverty, by Wit; which is the reason why poor wits are generally the greatest flatterers.

This Flattery was employed by the princes of the earth, to carry their congratulations one to another: but being at a certain time dispatched by the Dutch with a card of compliments to the Hottentots, the ship she went in was taken by a pyrate; the captain of which fell in love with Flattery, left off the sea for her sake, took an inn, set up, and made Flattery his barkeeper: a gentleman arriving in those parts in pursuit of an heiress, and having tried all efforts in vain, at last purchased Flattery of the inn-keeper; and, by her means gained the lady. But to see the ingratitude of mankind, he had not been married a fort'night before he kick'd Flattery out of doors; and from that time to this, she has had no settled place of abode, but is usually to be found at the beginning of courtship, and at the latter end of a petition. This being, Flattery, was the occasion of the very first duel that ever was fought: she was placed at the top of a pyramid in the middle of an highway, where four roads met: two knights, adventurers, the one from the north, and the other from the south, arrived at the pyramid at the instant; the hero from the south, who saw this white side, said it was a shame, that a white, a silver profile, should be trusted on the highway side. The hero from the north, who only saw this, said,—A white silver profile, why it is a black one! Flat contradictions produced fatal demonstrations: their swords flew out, and they cut and hued one another in a most unmerciful manner: till fainting with the loss of blood, they both fell down each of the opposite side to that on which the combat began; when looking up, too late they beheld their mistake. At this instant a venerable hermit coming by, bound up their wounds, and replaced them on their horses; giving them this piece of friendly advice, "That, henceforward, in all political disputes, and matters of a public nature, never to trust themselves till they had examined both sides of the question."

PART II.

In the first part of this lecture we considered men's heads; in this second part, we shall consider the head dress of the fine ladies: for as the world is round, and the world turns round, and every thing turns round with it; so no lunar, or sublunar revolution, hath caused greater alteration in the affairs of men, than hath from time to time taken place in the head dresses of the ladies.

From the Egyptians, from whom we derive all our arts and sciences, philosophy and fashions, our good dames of antiquity seem to have borrowed this riding hood. Behold the riding-hood! how the lappets fall down the side of the face, like the lappets on the side of the face of the Egyptian mummy: or like the cumbrous foliages of the full-bottom'd peruke: but our ancestors disliking the use of these full-bottoms, contrived a method of tying up their wigs behind; hence the origin of tye wigs!—The ladies, too, not to be behind hand with the gentlemen in their fashions, contrived a way to tye up their tails too; and from the riding-hood, they tuck'd up their tails and form'd the Ranelagh hood; as for example;

This is the hood in high taste at the lower end of the town: and while this is worn by lady Mary, lady Betty, lady Susan, and women of great distinction; this is wore by plain Moll, and Bess and Sue, and women without any distinction at all! This is the invariable mode or head dress of those ladies who used to supply the court end of the town with sea dainties, before land carriage for fish came into fashion! And there is not more difference between the head dress of these ladies, than in their mode of conversation; for while these fine ladies are continually making inroads upon their mother tongue, and clipping polysyllables into monysyllables; as, when they tell us they caant and they shaant, and they maant; these coarse ladies make ample amends for their deficiency, by the addition of supernumary syllables, when they talk of breakfastes, and tosteses, and running their fisteses against the posteses.

These are the ancient laughing and crying philosophers, perpetual presidents of the noble and venerable order of the Groaners and the grinners.—This the president of the dismal faction, is always crying for fear the world should not last his time out;—this the member of the Choice Spirits, egad, he don't care whether it does or not. This laughs at the times: this cries at the times; and this blackguard's the times; and thus the times are generally handled. Old people praise the times past which they neglected to use when they might; young people look forward with anxious care to the time to come, neglecting the present; and almost all people, treat the present times, as some folk do their wives,—with indifference, because they may possess them.

This was the fashionable mode, or head dress, in the times of our forefather's and foremothers; when a member of parliament's wife was jogged up to town once a year, behind John, just to see my Lord Mayor's shew, and have her gown cut to the court fashion, and then, with her pillion new stuffed, and her lap cramm'd with confectionary, she was hoisted back again, as fine as a gingerbread stall upon a fair-day. From Minerva's helmet, the ladies seem to have taken the custom of wearing bonnets; the pompoon, or egret, from the halfmoon that encircled the temple of Diana.

From the ancients, too, came the custom of giving lectures, Juno, that termagant of antiquity, being the first who ever gave her husband a lecture; and which, from the place where it was delivered, was called a curtain lecture! And philosophers are of opinion, that these curtain lectures are not yet entirely out of fashion.

Homer, the historian, from whom all these facts are taken, relates great things of the zone, or girdle of Venus;—and to it he ascribes great virtue; he says that whatever lady wears Venus's girdle, will infallibly possess the beauties of Venus. Now, ladies, I have that very girdle mentioned by Homer; and every lady will look lovely as long as she chuses to appear in it.*

This is a real antique, the morning head dress of that celebrated demi-rep, of antiquity, Cleopatra! this is what astronomers call the night rain, or shrouding the Moon in a cloud; and to this day the ladies of Edinburgh, when they go abroad in the morning, told a tarpin about their heads; or, as they express it, they heep their heads about in plaid. But our ladies in the south, disliking so cumb'rous a fashion, and imagining that something whimsically like it might be the invention of a new fashion, invented this French night cap, or cheek wrapper. A lady in this dress looks hooded like a horse, with eye-flaps,—to keep them from looking one way or the other; and perhaps that is the reason why most ladies in our days chuse to look forward! One would imagine

*Good-temper.

that this cap was invented by some surly duana, or ill-natured guardian, who being past the relish of beauty themselves, would deny even the sight of it to the rest of mankind!

Since we are on the subject of ladies faces, permit me a word on the pernicious practice of face painting, or rubbing of rouge and white wash on the complexion. Women of the town may be allowed the use of paint, because the dexterity of their profession, like that of pirates, consists of fighting under false colours. But, for the delicate, the unculpable part of the sex, to paint, looks as if they would fish for lovers, as men do for mackrel,—by hanging something red upon the hook; or as if they thought men were generally of the bull and turkey cock kind, and would fly at any thing scarlet. Exercise is the best face painter; innocence the best giver of complexion. There is, however, a certain period in life among the ladies, no less an enemy to the face, than the custom of face painting; 'tis called antiquated virginity; when elderly unmarried ladies are supposed to be condemned to lead apes about, because, when they were young and handsome, they made monkies of mankind. Shakespear has beautifully described the difference of the two states in a few lines; thus,

But earthly happier is the rose distill'd,
Than that which withering on the virgin thorn,
Lives, grows and dies in single blessedness.

We have here two heads taken from these lines of Shakespear. This is the married rose; and this is that withering on the virgin thorn. Disappointments bring on wrinkles: the wrinkles, therefore, of this face are no cause for wonder; the best wines, if kept too long, will turn to vinegar. But as this subject seems to grow serious, we'll dismiss it with a wish,

"May each married lady preserve her good man,
"And the young ones get good ones as soon as they can."

Not to be partial to either sex, this is exhibited as the head of an old batchelor. These old batchelors are mere bullies in love; continually abusing matrimony, without daring to accept the challenge. They tell you, if they were married, their wives should not go abroad, when they please; the children should never cry; the men should not kiss the maids: O! they would do mighty matters! But these lion-like talkers abroad, are mere balaambs at home; and continually under subjection to some termagant of a mistress, who makes them amply repay to her insolence, the contempt in which they pretend to have held the worthier part of the sex. As a punishment for their infidelity, when they are old and superannuated, they set up for suitors; they ogle through spectacles and they sing love songs, with catarrhs, by way of symphony. This lace coat, solitaire, and bag wig, shew what he would be, and this fool's cap, what he is.

As this is an head in ancient primitive simplicity; so here is an head, in modern simplicity; and belongs to a lass of the spirit, usually a Quaker. And

This is the head of one mov'd by the spirit. He wears this large umbrella like covering, to keep off the outward light, to strengthen the light within. As this is the hat of one moved by the spirit, so

This is a hat, in the true spirit of the mode. This is a Niverne; or a Nivernoise; or a Nivernoi se; or a Never enough: enough: (it's all the same in the Greek) a fellow with such a hat as this, looks like a man coming from market with a skimming dish on his head. The French, perhaps, have acted wisely in curtailing the size of their hats, because we have curtailed them of the fur trade; but, for Englishmen to wear such hats, is neither sound policy, or common honesty; yet we persist in copying the manners of the French, tho' we know they despise us for the imitation.—As there are two hats contrasted so here are two heads contrasted.

This a plain, honest, well meaning, manly sentiment speaking countenance. This, with a French grin, and simper, seems to say— "Entendez vouz Monsieur; "entendez vouz; Sire you have no complasance." To whom this replies, "But Sir, we have sincerity." "Sire, we have de gran monarch." "And we liberty." "Sire, we come over to England every year to learn you." "And yet sir, we are very much your masters" "Point de tout, Point de tout. Not at all, not at all. You beat us in one part, and we go to anoder. The French be de vise people, they go all over the world to get money." And, the English, go all over the world to spend it.

PART III.

In the first part of this lecture, we considered wigs lexonically; in this part we shall consider them physically; or rather, a physical wig: not as it relates to the faculty; but only with an intent to shew, how some of the faculty treat their heads. This wig, is charactura of both doctor and apothecary, according to the doctrine of topsy turvey; which supposes, that any apothecary may be a doctor, though no doctor can be an apothecary.

Presuming we may now look something like some of the faculty, we shall attempt a dissertation on sneezing and Snuff-taking; and this we shall endeavour to execute in the true secundum—artem—medicum phrase, which may serve either for doctor, or apothecary. Sneezing, otherwise, learnedly called sternutation, is occasioned by a violent, involuntary, impression, repression, compression, suppression, and oppression, of the animal spirits and nervous fluids; which acting on the nerves, which are subservient to the muscles and the diaphragma, communicate the same vibration, otherwise oscellations, of the medellary substance, of the nerves, and excite those impulses and concussion of the thorax which accompany sternutation, by which means, the patient is in such a sort of a kind of a situation, that—if he has a pocket handkerchief he may wipe his nose with it. There are several sorts of snuff; physical and metaphysical. With physical snuff the town has been sufficiently pestered. Let us consider metaphysical. And first,

The snuff, or Self-consequence: upon the sudden accession of any good fortune, pride usually presents the possessor with a box of the snuff of Self consequence. On opening the lid, the dust flies in to his eyes, and prevents his recollecting any of his old acquaintance. On these occasions, the eyes of the Snuff-taker are so injured, that he cannot recognize those very friends, whom perhaps (but the day before) he would have been glad to have received a dinner from—then,

There is the snuff of Contempt; this is sure to be taken by all well dressed persons, when they are in company with others with worse cloaths on than themselves: for though we know there is a material difference between real genius, and Monmouth-street finery, yet the Pantheon of Parade shall have crouded auditors, while the Temple of Merit stands open without a worshipper.—When the performance of an English artist is exhibited as the work of a master unknown, its merit will have due praise; but the moment his name is known, and he is found guilty of being an Englishman, admiration changes into disgust, and the club of connoisseurs take the snuff of contempt at him and his works immediately. Pshaw;—Paltry;—Damn'd bad, Vile, &c. &c.

Englishmen are supposed to be meer John trots; incapable of any thing, but halling a rope, or pulling a trigger: nor would merit have been allowed in this particular, had not our soldiers and sailors so very lately shewn all over the world such capital performances.

With these heads we intended to have begun our dissection. This is the head of a blood: he wears a bull's forehead, for a fore-top, in imitation of that blood of old, Jupiter, who turned himself into a bull, to run away with Europa: and to this day your bloods are mighty fond of making beasts of themselves; this is a fine fellow to kick up a dust; or to keep it up when it is kicked up: to chuck a waiter behind the fire; toss a beggar in a blanket; play at chuck with china plates; hop round the room with a red hot poker in his mouth, upon one leg; say the belief backwards; swallow red hot coals. Oh, he was qu——ite the thing. He was a wit, at Wetherby's a toastmaster, at Bob Derry's; a constant customer, at the Round-house; a terror to modest women, and a dupe to women of the town; as one of whom,

This portrait is exhibited. This is a man of the town, or a blood; and this is a woman of the town, or a——but by what other name the lady chuses to be called, we are not entitled to mention: suffice it to say, that when we attempted dissection, we found this head proof against our keenest instruments, and this so soft, that it mouldered away at the first touch.

This is the Tea table Critic; or master among the maids. He was mama's darling. His mama would never let him learn to read, for fear he should get a naasty custom of holding down his head; but he was a purdigious scholar for all that; he had got four pages of Hoyle by heart, which his mama's woman had taught him: and he could calculate, he could calculate, how much cream should be put into a codling tart. He died of a fit of despair for the loss of his lap-dog; who was poisoned with eating up the cold cream, that was prepared for his mama's next day's complexion. We divided the suters of his brain with an ivory bodkin; but instead of the cutis, and the cuticular; the cerebum, and the cerebellum, medula oblong, and other hard words; we found nothing of them; and, for brains, we discovered this pincushion. From the Tea-table Critic, we proceed to the Learned Critic, or Word-grubber.

This was an hunter after commas, semicolons, and underevatas. This is a true classical conjugating countenance and denotes dictionary dignity. He was one of those learned Doctoribus's, who always argue Propria quæmaribus. He has for a band a pair of horn books, to denote that he was a man of mere letters. He lost his best friend, in a dispute, relative to the pronunciation of a Word: as he was one day walking in his friend's garden, little miss came running to him, "Sir," said she, "my papa's horse Cicero has won the race;" foaming with rage, our grammarian bounces into the parlour, "Madam," says he, "Why do you bring up your children thus? How dare you suffer these violations of all grammar; you'll be the very destruction of all learning and of all common sense! for the pronunciation of the word is not Cicero, but, Kikero." Nature never does her works by halves; she proportions the parts of all animals, to the use for which they are designed; thus, the ears of this critic are immensely large; they are called trap doors to catch syllables! On the contrary; his eyes are half closed; that's called the Wifeman's Wink; and shews he can see the world with half an eye. He died of insanity of mind, occasioned by a dispute relating to the restoring of oiled butter; he said, butter once oiled, could never be restored; and he proved it from the Greek too, at the very same interim, in came Betty the cook maid, with a little sprinkling of flower, and no Greek, and restored it in a moment. When we came to a dissection of this head, instead of the hard terms used by anatomists, we found none of the parts thereby described! we found only large fragments of abuse! epitomes of indexes, and title pages: and all the brain covered over with a blotting paper. Before we opened,

This stock-jobber's head, we had a mind to make an experiment upon the ear: but, as to notes of music, the cries of distress, the praise of merit, and the demand of gratitude, the stock-jobber's head was like his stock, consolidated. We then ought of a method of striking one piece of money against another; we did so. We struck one shilling against another; the chink of the money alarmed the member; and on our striking one guinea against another, the ear expanded to its utmost extent: in other subjects, there are certain vessels that convey to the face a consciousness of guilt, or the glow of innocence. In the stock-jobber they were all petrified. In other subjects, there are certain vessels between the head and heart; called the nerves of humanity! in the stock jobber, they were all eaten up by the scurvy.

This is, Sir Full Fed Domine Double Chin; citizen, turtle, and venison eater. He was one of the common council of Farringdon within; he was a very good sort of a man; he was half brother to an alderman, and had been deputy of his ward: his time was taken up in the affairs of the state, and the affairs of a kitchen. He loved politics, and he loved venison. He thought a cook was the greatest genius in the world, except a news writer: he constantly read every political pamphlet that was published, and on both sides of the question, and always framed his opinion according to the writer he read last; and according to the humour he happened to be in: he would take his cap, and his pipe, and a glass of the righteous (as he called it) and he would be for setting the world to rights in an hurry. Ay! Ay! neighbour Costive; all for their own ends now a-days; all for their own ends; nobody do you see now a-days, loves their own country, since queen Semaramus, and she invented Solomon Gundy, and that's the best eating in all the versal world. If I was at the head of affairs, things should not be as they are now; that's all; they should'not indeed, I would shew them another of a manner of going to work: now I'll shew you my plan of operations: do you mind me now, mark what I say: suppose then these two or three bits of tobacco ashes, to be the main land continent.—Ve——ry well! And suppose now, neighbour Sprigins, this little drop of milk punch, (well come, here's the king, god bless him) suppose this little drop of milk punch, to be the main sea ocean: very well! very well! and suppose these three or four bits of cork to be all our great men of war: very well! But what shall I do now for fortified places? Oh, he——re I have it. Here's your Havannahs, and you Pondicherries, and your Tilbury ports, and your Tower Ditches; and all our damn'd strong places? there's a plan of operations for ye now: A——h, Well, and then our army all should wear a new uniform; all our horse infantry should wear air jackets, and all our foot cavalry should wear cork waistcoats; and then ye know why they'd be all over the sea before you could say Jack Robinson. Well, and where do you think I'd land them now? You don't know; now you don't know; how the devil should you know. You don't understand geometry. Why I'll tell you where I'd land them; I would land them under the line, close by the South Pole; there I'd land them; and then I'd ambuscade all the Spaniards back settlements; and take from them all their (—Pshaw.—You know what I mean well enough: all their—all them damn'd hard names mentioned in the news papers) all their Mexicos, and their Perus, and their Dimont Islands! and then I'd come with a circumvendibus on the Dutch, in flatbottom'd boats; (because ye know that is a flatbottom'd country) open the sluices—let in the water—drown all the poor Dutch, and then we should have the turtles, and the Spice Islands, for nothing; and there'd be living in Old England.

While our politician was thus going on with his plan, censuring men and measures he knew nothing about, and it happening at a time when our army lay encamped on one side of the river, and the French on the other; an officer in company with his stick, gave our politician a rap on the knuckles: What's that for? A——y? Only, sir, replied the officer, coolly to inform you, that that commander who crosses a river, to attack an enemy in front, may chance to get a wrap on the knuckles: that's all!—The alteration is easy from politicks to cunning.

Behold here the head of a sharper. In Truth's dictionary, under the article Cunning, is the verb, to sharp; from whence the noun substantive sharper: that we may offend no countrymen by the birth of our hero, be it known that he was born at sea, on board a transport, in which, his mother was humbly requested, by a rule of court to take a seven years tour to America. At length, by his unshaken resolution, and matchless impudence, he acquired a fortune of forty thousand pounds.

This is his original face; a heavy, vulgar, incurious, down-looking, countenance: this was his holyday face, that he went into company with; and, under this mask battery he used to play off, all his flight of hand artillery; and this was his face that he awoke at midnight with; when Conscience assisted by Memory, commanded him to undergo a self examination; for, as there was nothing too base for him to commit, so neither was there any thing so dreadful, but he had reason to fear it. He lived in the utmost dread, and died in the utmost despair; putting a period to his existence with this: which, in the catalogue of medicines, bears this name.† He left all his fortune to the hospital for incurables, in Moorfields; that as he had got all his money by the incurables, so he was very willing, now he could make no farther use of it, to return it to the right owners.

Although he had lived a life so infamous, he was buried in all the to be purchased pomp: behold here the funeral of the gambler! and two of his torch bearers! Such is the partiality of fate, and such the different rewards of merit and infamy: that, that soldier and sailor, are employed at the price of a shilling, and glad too of that scanty pittance, to attend the gambler to his grave; the sailor lost his arm in one of the famous sea fights where Sir Edward Hawke commanded; and the soldier lost his leg, in one of the six regiments who so bravely fought on the plains of Minden. To shew, however how we treat our soldiers and sailors, when we have no occasion for them, we will just beg leave to relate a little story that happened in the year 1745; when our army was marching into the North, under the command of the gallant Duke of Cumberland. The landlord of the house where one of the soldiers happened to be, began to take great notice of him; and would say to him, why honest fellow, says he, you soldiers are the pillars of the nation; you are the bravest men in nature; without a standing army, we should have no standing corn; when you come home, pray come and see me, you, and your wife, and your children, and stay as long as you please, a week, a month, or a year, as long as you please, and make yourselves welcome to every thing you find here; and he always wound up his invitation with telling him that soliders were the pillars of the nation. When the affair at Culloden was happily over; our soldier called, rather to thank him for his kind invitation, than with any design to accept it. But, the danger being past, and peace being restored, he began to talk about large taxes, and standing armies; and he did not know what occasion there was for a pack of lobstering dogs to be crawling about the country, eating up peoples victuals and drink. He saw no occasion we had for soldiers now, not he, we had peace hadn't

†Suicide's Grand Specific.

we? Why, cried our soldier, with a generous disdain, I did not invite myself, did not you tell me to come, me and my family, and we should be welcome; and says he did not you always close your invitation with saying, that we soldiers were the pillars of the nation!—pillars of the nation?—Well, I believe I might say something about pillars; but I meant—catter-pillars.

Thus, while true merit is neglected and despised, to shew how Genius and Science can condescend to decorate unworthiness behold here, the monument of the gambler,—Justice and Compassion, and weeping over his medallion, and Honour descending with a crown of laurels, to reward his virtue; to the basso relief, are four little boys representing the cardinal virtues, or as weeping for his death; but we, who are apt to moralize on things, rather think they are four little boys whose parents the gambler has ruined; and that they are now turned out of doors, and crying for cloaths to cover them.—From the head of one who lived by his wit, we proceed to a real wit; as one mentioned by the famous Yorick, and Tristram Shandy; and he is supposed to have a good deal of the family likeness; when we came to a dissection of this head, we found one of the most capital parts of the brain quite worn out: he lived so long depending on what others would do for him, that he was at length reduced to the necessity of asking Charity: amongst others of his resting places, he one day set himself down at the door of a large mansion-house; some of the servants hearing he was a Wit, had him into the steward's parlour; and where, according to the notion some people have of wit, they desired he would be comical. One of them said, if he was a wit, to be sure he could run round the room with a red hot poker between his teeth.—The cookmaid said, to be sure if the gentleman was a wit, she hoped he would be so kind, and so civil, and so liging, and so condescending, and so complaisant, and so good, and so submissive, as to tell her fortune on the cards.—The butler was rather for a tune on the musical glasses.—The groom said, if so be as how the gentleman was a wit, why he could not do no less than ride upon three horses at once.—The laundry maid, she said to be sure he could swallow a box iron and heaters.—While they were thus debating, down came the French Mammeselle, and ordered him to be turned out of doors, saying, "he wondered vat English vit vas good for?"

Wit being thus turned out of doors, went to visit Hospitality; but it being election time, there was no room for him there. He then paid his addresses to Merit; but Merit could do nothing for him, being at that time pursued by Faction. He then addressed himself to Charity; and she would have done any thing in the world to serve him; but, as ill luck would have it, she was herself that very morning ran over by the bishop's new set of coach-horses. He died, at length, of mere hunger; and was interred in the poor's burial-ground, after his friends had raised money to pay for surplice fees:

And the modes of christianity are such in our days, that tho' any churchman may receive a large benefice, yet if any churchman be found guilty of giving away in charity, he would be thought guilty of being righteous overmuch.

Behold here one of the righteous over much—yet nought doth he give away in charity! No! no! he is the bell-wether of the flock, who hath broken down Orthodox's bounds, and now riots on the common of Hypocrisy.—With one eye he looks up to Heaven, to make his congregation think he is devout, that's his sprirtual eye; and with the other eye he looks down to see what he can get; and that's his carnal eye; and thus, with locks flowing down his face, he says, or seems to say, or at least, with your permission, we'll attempt to say for him—

Bretheren! Bretheren! Bretheren! The word bretheren comes from the Tabernacle, because we all breathe there—in—If ye want rouzing, I'll rouze you: I'll beat a tat-too upon the parchment cases of your consciences, and whip the Devil about like a whirl-agig.—Even as the cat, upon the top of the house doth squall: even so, from the top of my voice, will I bawl, and the organ pipes of my lungs shall play a voluntary among ye; and the sweet words that I shall utter, shall sugar candy over your souls, and make carraway comforts of your consciences.—Do you know how many taylors make a man?—Why nine—Nine taylors make a man.—And how many make half a man?—Why four journeymen and a prentice.—Even to have you all been bound 'prentice to misfortune the fashion-maker; and now you are out of your times you have set up for yourselves.—My great bowels, and my sm——all guts groan for you.—I have got the gripe of compassion, and the belly-ach of pity.—Give me a dram!—Give me a dram—Do give me a dram—A dram of patience I mean, while I explain unto you what reformation, and what abomination mean! Which the worldly wicked have mixed together, like potatoes and butter-milk, and therewith made a sinful stir-about.—Reformation, is like the comely froth at the top of a tankard of porter;— and Abomination—is like the dregs at the bottom of the tap-tub.—Have you carried your consciences to the scowerers? Have you bought any fullers earth at my shop? to take the stains out?—You say yes: you have! you have! you have!—But I say no: you lye! you lye! you lye!—I am no velvet mouth preacher; I scorn your lawn sleeves.—You are all full of filth; ye must be boil'd down in our Tabernacle, to make portable soup, for the saints to sup a sadleful of; and then the scum, and the scaldings of your iniquities, will boil over; and that is called the kitchen-stuff of your consciences, that serves, to grease the cartwheels that carry us over the Devil's ditch; and the Devil's gap— The Devil's ditch; that's among the jockeys at Newmarket; and the Devil's gap, that's among the other jockeys; the lawyers at Lincoln's-inn-fields.—And then there is the Devil among the Taylors, and the Devil among the Players; the players, they play the Devil to pay.—The play-house is Satan's ground, where women stretch themselves out upon the tenter-hooks of temptation.—Tragedy is the blank verse of Beelzebub;—Comedy is his hasty pudding; and—Pantomime is the Devil's country dance.—And yet, you'll pay the players for seeing plays; yes, yes; but you won't pay me: no; no; till Beelzebub's bum bailiffs lay hold of you; and then you think I will pay your garnish; but I won't, No; you shall lay on the common side of the world, like a toad in a hole that is baked for the Devil's dinner.—Do put some money in the plate—Put some money in the plate;—and then all your iniquities shall be scalded away, even as they scald the bristles off the hog's back; and you shall be cleansed from all your sins, as easily as the barber shaveth away the weekly beard from the chin of the ungodly.

> Do put some money in the plate,
> Or I, your preacher, cannot eat:
> And 'tis with grief of heart I tell ye
> How much this preaching scow'rs the belly:
> How pinching to the human tripe
> Is pity's belly-ach, and gripe:
> But that religion (lovely maid)
> Keeps a cook's shop to feed the trade.

> The motives of our deeds the same
> With Whitefield, I put in my claim;
> The pious thieves attack your purses,
> With cries, and tears, and pray'rs and curses;
> But, I more modest in the trade,
> Dare never damn the fools I've made.
> But will, if so your worships please,
> In future times, on bended knees,
> Say, sing, and swear, that those alone are right,
> Who crowd this tabernacle every night.

FINIS.

IV
Production History
of the *Lecture*

THIS SECTION traces the history of the *Lecture on Heads* from its initial performance in 1764 to the last discovered record dated May 1820. Included are performances of the entire *Lecture* as well as the numerous variations, spinoffs, and segments. In each case I have tried to include the date(s), city, location, lecturer, and number of performances as well as a substantial amount of additional relevant material including ticket prices, starting time, syllabi, puffs, commentary, benefits, and so forth. Wherever possible the data have been confirmed and documented by primary sources.

A reasonable attempt has been made to retain the flavor of the eighteenth-century typography, but not the physical format of the advertisements. The period spellings, with all their arbitrary variations, have also been kept. Obvious typographical errors have been corrected; a few are printed verbatim and are so indicated.

While these entries are comprehensive, they are certainly not complete. There must have been hundreds of performances given by itinerant lecturers in small provincial towns who announced themselves by heralds and broadsides which no longer exist, or who purchased advertisements in newspapers which are inaccessible. Any additional information or corrections would, of course, be most welcome.

John Genest's comment on the title page of his *Some Account of the English Stage . . .* is most appropriate and I take the liberty of quoting him: "If anything be overlooked, or not accurately inserted, let no one find fault, but take into consideration that this history is compiled from all quarters."

LONDON: HAYMARKET THEATRE.

April 30, May 1, 2, 4, 8, 10, 12, 15, 17, 19, 22, 26, 1764 (12 perfs.).

George Alexander Stevens gave the first performance of the *Lecture on Heads* at the New Haymarket Theatre on Monday, April 30, 1764, presumably at 12:30 P.M. It continued for a total of twelve performances,[1] most of the later ones from May 4 on starting at 1:00 P.M. with the final presentation taking place on

Saturday, May 26. The first printed notice appeared Thursday, April 26, and read:

"At the Little Theatre in the Hay-Market, on Monday Noon, the 30th of April, at Half an Hour after Twelve o'Clock precisely, will be given A LECTURE upon HEADS; And NO HEADS. Being a CAPUT-all Exhibition, with proper Apparatus, of Antique and Modern Sculptures, Bronzes, Pictures, &c. &c. With Observations on the LEXONICAL and PHYZICAL CONSEQUENCE of WIGS; wherein a Full-bottom Oration, and SECUNDUM ARTEM dissertation, will be CARICATURED, HORNS will be accounted for AB ORIGINE: And the Genealogical Table of NOBODY, properly explained. To conclude with a Dissection of THREE HEADS viz. 1st, a STOCKJOBBER's; 2d, An AUTHOR's; 3d, A CRITIC's. Attempted by G. STEVENS N.B. NO HEAD FOR POLITICS. Gallery 2s. Pit 3s. Boxes 4s."[2]

Subsequent notices (eighteen for the next eleven performances) contain interesting variations and interpolations. Selections are included here for the additional light they shed on the various circumstances of the lecture. On Saturday, May 5, the following was added: "Mr. Stevens takes this Opportunity to return the Public Thanks, for the Approbation with which they have been pleased to honour this his Attempt."[3] The addition for the following week was: "N.B. As there was a prior Engagement for the Use of this Theatre for the Remainder of the Summer, this Lecture cannot be repeated but three or four Mornings more."[4]

Stevens was running into contractual difficulties. On Monday, May 14, the notice began: "The SEVENTH DAY [actually this was the announcement for the eighth performance to be given the next day] And the LAST WEEK of Performing." It concluded with "The House by a prior Engagement, being lett for the Remainder of the Summer to others, the Lecture can only be continued TO-MORROW, THURSDAY, and SATURDAY next, this Season."[5] The engagement did not end as indicated above. The popularity of the lecture resulted in another performance on May 22: "BY PARTICULAR DESIRE. The TENTH DAY [actually an announcement for the eleventh performance to be given on the 22] . . . TO-MORROW, . . . A LECTURE upon HEADS, And NO HEADS, . . ."[6] The run concluded on Saturday, May 26, with a notice that day reading: "The TWELFTH DAY, [the correct performance number is given here] And positively the LAST MORNING. . . ."[7]

The first review, or puff, appeared on May 3:

"SIR,

For my own part, Mr. Printer, altho' an Enemy to all Sorts of Puffs, yet I must declare I never met with more original Humour and Novelty in any one Exhibition than there is in the Lecture upon Heads, now exhibiting at the Hay-Market. I do not know the Person who repeats the Lecture. His Name, I find, is STEVENS. But I congratulate him on his Success, and will say, that a piece so well constructed to entertain the Public does indeed deserve their Favor.

I am yours, &c.

<small>AN ENCOURAGER OF REAL MERIT."</small>[8]

On the same day the following quatrains appeared in another newspaper:

On hearing G. STEVENS's Lecture upon Heads, *in the* Haymarket.

> Quoth *Wit* to *Humour*, I'm undone,
>   Nor dare I shew my face once more;
> *Stevens*, in broad and open day,
>   Has rifled all my precious store.

> Said *Humour*—he's a double thief,
>   For not content with robbing thee,
> The rogue, in spite of all my care,
>   Has, *vi et armis*, plunder'd me.

> Then let's arrest him, *Wit* reply'd,
>   And lay the villain in a jail,
> Indict him ten—convict him next—
>   For want of *proof* we cannot fail.

> Tush, tush, quoth Humour, on that head
>   You need not argue or enlarge,
> He'll save th' expence of witnesses,
>   By pleading *guilty* to the charge.
>   W.[9]

As early as May 4 we find the first of many quotes drawn from the *Lecture*. Here the editor declines to publish what must have been a libelous letter: "The letter signed A *Constant Reader* is received; but, as a constant Reader, *may* (as Mr. G. A. Stevens, in his *Lecture on Heads*, says) be *Any Body, Every Body*, or *Nobody*, and contains a Charge on a Set of Persons in Office, (which we hope is not true) we must beg Leave to refuse it a Place . . ."[10]

On May 16 Stevens went for the puff personate only to have it backfire on him.

"INTELLIGENCE EXTRAORDINARY *Haymarket*. For some Days past that *Choice Spirit*, George Alexander Stevens, has entertained the Town at the Little Theatre with what he calls a *Caput-all* Exhibition, and Lecture upon Heads. They who have a relish for Tom Brown, will not be displeased with George Stevens: But those delicate Connoisseurs in Wit and Humor, whose Understanding have such weak Nerves, that they are apt to faint away at the Sound of a Pun, are warned not to venture into the House without Salts, *Eau de luce*, Hartshorn, or Sal Volatile. Being Friends to Good Humour and innocent Pleasantry, we are inclined to think favourably of the Exhibitor and his Exhibition, which we are apt to consider as a Rest of Wit played by a single Hand, where a Word is no more let fall, than it rebounds like the Tennis-ball, and,

then is bandied backwards and forwards, to and fro, here and there, and
kept-up for Half an Hour together; or as a Firework, whose Squibs are
whizzing, and Crackers bouncing, through the whole Course of these Lectures.
To speak of Wit somewhat in the Stile of the Lecturer, we shall indulge
ourselves, like him, in the familiar Use of the Prosopopoeia, and say, 'That Miss
FUN, one of the younger Sisters of HUMOUR, being seduced by a young Fellow of
the Town, called NECESSITY, eloped from Comus's Court, opened a House in
the Haymarket, and read *Curtain-Lectures*. Being a *new Piece*, she drew in
Customers. WHIM, an agreeable Romp, and one of FUN's first Cousins, was Bar
keeper; who, with the Seville Orange of Satire, the Sugar of Good Humour,
and the choicest Spirits, made Punch that pleased the *Taste* of most of those
who frequented the House. Each of these Girls were allowed to be possest of
some irregular *Beauties*, well adapted to the Meridian of the Haymarket,
though not equally calculated to shine in the Purlieus of Covent-Garden, or the
Hundreds of Drury.' "[11]

The newspaper was good enough to publish Stevens's reaction to the letter and
thus afforded him an additional piece of publicity.

"SIR,
    When I undertook to dissect a Critic's Head, I expected to have all those
Paper Bullets of the Brain vollied against me; for according to the old Song,
                    Each cries that was levell'd at me.
Some of my acquaintance advise me to begin first, and throw out some Squibs
against my own Exhibition: This they told me was true News-paper Policy.
Accordingly I sent that Intelligence Extraordinary inserted in the St. Jame's
Chronicle, and which you copied from thence; but the transcriber of my
Manuscript mistook what was wrote; I never was vain enough to compare
myself to *Tom Brown*; it was *Tom D'Urfy* in my Copy, And then again, I intended
indeed to be rather obscure in what I had drawn up; but he has made it quite
unintelligible. My Design was only to abuse myself; but he has, by committing
such a Blunder, made me ashamed of myself. However, I know he *meant well*;
therefore am his and yours,
                    G. STEVENS."[12]

Toward the end of the run Stevens performed for several distinguished
spectators: "Their Royal Highnesses Prince William and Prince Henry were on
Saturday last [May 19] at the Little Theatre in the Haymarket, at the *Lecture
upon Heads*, exhibited by George Stevens."[13]

And, shortly before closing, another quotation as found in the following letter
to the editor: SIR: Rambling on Saturday about Town and being of a thirsty
Disposition, I pop'd my Nose into an Ale-Shop where I had not sat long before
Mr. *Makeweight*, the Tallow-Chandler came in, and his Friend. They had scarce
seated themselves, when the Conversation turned upon *Tallow*; Mr. *Makeweight*
interrogating his Friend (who, to use George Stevens's Words, by his Caput-all

Exhibition, appeared to me a *Lump of Tallow*) . . ."[14] The remainder of the letter is irrelevant nit-picking over terminology concerning the price of tallow. The London engagement was now over and Stevens set out to tour the provinces.

1. The *Gazetteer and New Daily Advertiser* printed twenty-one notices for the *Lecture* between April 26 and May 27. On Thursday, May 3, the notice advertised the next day's performance (Friday the 4th) as the "THIRD DAY." Actually it was to be the fourth performance. This error was continued through the Wednesday, May 23 notice of the "ELEVENTH DAY" to be given Saturday, the 26th. The last notice, on the 26th, correctly publicized the "TWELFTH DAY, and positively the LAST MORNING." This was a common occurrence in the newspapers of the time. They lost track, occasionally reprinted the same ad for a later performance but eventually seemed to catch up. These same errors also appeared in different newspapers. Genest, over a half-century later, may have been confused by these errors when he wrote: "Prior to the opening of this Theatre for dramatic performances, Stevens had delivered his Lecture on Heads—the 11th and last morning was on May 23." See John Genest, *Some Account of the English Stage, from the Restoration in 1660 to 1830* (Bath: Printed by H. E. Carrington, 1832), vol. 5, p. 61.

2. *Gazetteer and New Daily Advertiser*, April 26, 1764. Notices for the *Lecture* also appeared (with minor spelling variations) in the *Daily Advertiser* and the *Public Advertiser*.

3. *Gazetteer and New Daily Advertiser*, May 5, 1764.

4. Ibid, May 12, 1764.

5. Ibid, May 14, 1764.

6. Ibid, May 21, 1764.

7. Ibid, May 26, 1764.

8. *Public Advertiser*, May 3, 1764.

9. *London Evening-Post*, May 3–5, 1764.

10. *Public Advertiser*, May 4, 1764.

11. Ibid, May 16, 1764.

12. Ibid, May 17, 1764.

13. Ibid, May 21, 1764.

14. Ibid, May 23, 1764.

DUBLIN: CAPLE STREET (?).

1764

Stevens's itinerary for 1764 is not entirely clear. One clue to his whereabouts is suspect.

"About this period [1764] Mr. George Alexander Stevens, for the first time, visited this kingdom with his celebrated Lecture upon Heads, and exhibited in the Little Theatre in Caple-street,[1] with infinite applause. The novelty of his undertaking drew the attention of the public.

"Though not possessed of much merit as an actor, yet he certainly delivered his lectures with vast humour, variety, and judgment; reputation and success attended him in both kingdomes, and in the course of a few years, he acquired an independent fortune, solely by the repetition of this then singular species of entertainment."[2]

1. LaTourette Stockwell in *Dublin Theatres and Customs, 1637–1820* suggests that this theatre was not in use at the time.
2. Robert Hitchcock, *An Historical View of the Irish Stage; from the Earliest Period down to the Close of the Season, 1788* (Dublin, 1788), 2 vols., vol. 2, pp. 152–53.

DUBLIN: SMOCK ALLEY.

June 23, 26, July 3, 1764 (3 perfs.).

Edward Shuter, earlier identified as the actor for whom Stevens might have written the preliminary version of the *Lecture*, did perform the piece in Ireland in 1764 and continued to be identified with it for several years.

June 23. "At the Theatre in Smock-Alley. This present Saturday will be presented . . . [*The Revenge* and other entertainments] To which will be added a New Theatrical Entertainment, called, A LECTURE UPON HEADS, . . . The Lecture to be delivered by Mr. Shuter."[1] The syllabus for the *Lecture* was essentially the same as that used by Stevens in April and May.

June 26. "This present Tuesday being the 26th instant."[2]

July 3. "On Tuesday next"[3]

"An Evening paper of last night says, that their correspondents in Dublin acquainted them that theatrical exhibitions still engross the attention of that city . . . The Lecture upon Heads has been pronounced with great success.[4]

1. *Dublin Journal*, June 19–23, 1764.
2. Ibid., June 23–26, 1764.
3. Ibid., June 26–30, 1764.
4. *Gazetteer and New Daily Advertiser*, July 25, 1764.

MANCHESTER: THE SWAN INN IN MARKET STREET LANE.

July 1764.

"In the summer of 1764, Mr Stevens humourously anounced a short stay at the Swan, in Market Street Lane, for the purpose of giving—at two shillings each person—his Lecture upon heads and head-dresses, being the first year of its delivery."[1] The broadside which Stevens issued for this performance read:

"Every person who possesses, or supposes he possesses, any rarity worthy the company of the curious, to gain the patronage of the public, puts forth a pompous advertisement, which every puppet show master, wire dancer, bear leader, and fire eater find their account in, declaring that as how their perform-ance have given perdigious satisfaction to London, to the nobility and the quality, and the ladies and the gentlefolks, and also to the royal family. Not to differ from any of his brother showmen in point of phrase, the exhibitor of this lecture upon heads and no heads takes the liberty to acquaint the ladies and gentlemen of this town, that the approbation with which the above-mentioned lecture was received at the theatre this year in London, by persons of the first distinction, encouraged him to perform it this summer in the country; and as it is calculated for the entertainment of persons of understanding, education, and taste, he hopes to have the favour of their company while he is here."[2]

1. Richard Wright Procter, *Manchester in Holiday Dress* (London and Manchester, 1866), p. 30.
2. Ibid., p. 32.

BATH: THEATRE IN ORCHARD STREET.

Late November to December 7 or later, 1764 (perhaps 10 perfs.).

Stevens had a successful and extended run in Bath. The records are incom-plete, but we know that he was performing prior to November 30. Mrs. Montagu was in attendance on December 5 and conveyed her enthusiasm in a letter to her husband the following day. It is possible that the *Lecture* was given after December 7, the date of the last notice I have found for this engagement.

"*Extract of a Letter from* BATH. 'Among the many Entertainments now in this City, calculated for the Amusement of the Polite and Gay, the Lecture upon Heads and Head-dresses, by George Alexander Stevens seems to be the Favourite Diversion.

"I have been every Time he has performed here, and, without Partiality, confess myself greatly pleased to see Taste do Such Justice to merit, as Mr. Stevens receives for his Exhibition from the most polite and crowded audiences.'"[1]

[Mrs. Montagu's letter to her husband.] "I was yesterday morning at a very singular entertainment calld a lecture upon heads. I found all people had been much entertained with it, but I expected little better than a drole kind of buffoonery; but on the contrary, it was a witty well bred satire. The man who

exhibits this amusement was a player, he has a fine voice and gracefull elocution, and he ran through the follies of some professions and characters with
admirable humour. He gave us a law pleading, a medical dissertation, a
politicians discourse, a presbyterian sermon with great humour, a very elegant
allegory of genius, jests on fashions, and in short an hour of the best theatrical
entertainment I have seen. He is infinitely beyond Mr. Foote, whose excellence
is mere personal mimicry."[2]

Wrote extempore on hearing the Lecture upon HEADS *by Mr.* STEVENS.

> Tho *Pope* and *Swift*, and *Churchill* are no more,
> And *Wilkes* alas! has left his native Shore;
> Yet think not Britons, Satire's Sting is dead,
> And Vice uncensur'd now may raise its Head,
> While STEVENS lives, Keen Satire will appear,
> And Villains, Knaves and Fools, must shrink with Fear.[3]

"By Desire For the Benefit of a *Public Charity*, The Lecture upon HEADS by
George Alexander Stevens Will be exhibited at the Theatre in Orchard-Street,
TOMORROW MORNING, December the 7th, 1764: *Divided into three Parts.* The First
Part contains, An Exhibition of MEN's Heads. with the History of Nobody's
Family, and a no-Head. The Second Part, an Exhibition of LADIES Head-
dresses; with the History of Flattery and its Family. The Third Part is, A
Physical Dissertation upon Sneezing and Snuff-taking, with a Dissection of
Heads, viz, a Virtuoso's, a Stock-jobber's, a Critic's, a Politician's, a Wit's, and
the Section of a Methodist's; with a Methodistical Preachment, To conclude
with a Mock Italian Cantata. The Doors to be opened at Eleven o'Clock, and to
begin exactly at Twelve . . . Boxes 3s, Pit 2s, 1st Gal 1s.6d, Upper Gal 1s."[4]

1. *Gazetteer and New Daily Advertiser*, November 30, 1764.
2. Reginald Blunt, ed., *Mrs. Montagu "Queen of the Blues": Her Letters and Friendships from
   1762 to 1800*, vol. 1, 1762–76, (Boston and New York, n.d., ca. 1923), p. 120.
3. *Pope's Bath Chronicle*, December 6, 1764.
4. Ibid.

BRISTOL: COOPER'S HALL.

December 17, 18, 20, 21, 1764 (4 perfs.).

Stevens then moved to Bristol.

December 17–21. "At the COOPERS-HALL in *King Street*, On MONDAY, TUESDAY,
THURSDAY, and FRIDAY EVENINGS next, The Lecture upon HEADS will be exhib-
ited, by *George Alexander Stevens*, Divided into THREE PARTS. The first Part,
Contains an Exhibition of Men's Heads, with the History of Nobody's Family,

and a No-Head. The second Part, An Exhibition of Ladies Head-Dresses, with the History of Flattery and its Family. The third Part, Is a Physical Dissertation upon Sneezing and Snuff-taking, with a Dissection of Heads, viz. a Virtuoso's, A Stock-jobber's, a Critic's, a Politician's, a Wit's, and the Section of a Methodist's, with a Methodistical Preachment. To conclude with a Mock Italian Cantata. The Doors to be open'd at Six, and to begin at Half after Six.—Admittance Two Shillings and Sixpence. ***As this lecture has been honour'd with the Company of Persons of Distinction, Education, and Understanding, and as it is calculated only for such, the Audience may depend on their not being detain'd one Minute after the Time specified for the beginning."[1]

1. *Bristol Journal*, December 15, 1764.

LONDON: LITTLE THEATRE IN THE HAYMARKET.

March 4, 5, 6, 8, 9, 13, 15, 18, 20, 22, 25, 27, 29, April 1, 8, 9, 11, 13, 15–20, 25, 27, 30, 1765 (27 perfs.).

Almost a full year after the premiere, Stevens began an extensive run of the revised *Lecture* at the New Haymarket.

"BY DESIRE LITTLE Theatre, Haymarket, This Evening next will be delivered The LECTURE Upon HEADS. With ADDITIONS By GEORGE ALEXANDER STEVENS. To conclude with the Section of a Methodist's Head, and Harangue. A Syllabus of the Lecture will be delivered gratis that Night at the Theatre. The Doors to be opened Half an Hour past Five. To begin exactly Half an Hour past Six. The Characters all new dressed in the Habits of the Times. Boxes 4s. Pit 3s. Gall. 2s. Places for the boxes to be taken at the Theatre."[1]

April 8. "To conclude with a NEW HEAD."[2]

April 11. "To conclude with the CONJURER'S HEAD."[3]

April 15. "As Mr. STEVENS must very soon quit the Haymarket, his Lecture will be repeated every Night at the usual Time, until farther Notice."[4]

April 20. "Being positively the LAST."[5]

April 22. "To the PUBLIC By whom the Lecture upon Heads has been so greatly patronized, THE EXHIBITOR hopes he may be allowed to address his grateful Acknowledgments, and subscribe himself, With the utmost Respect, Their most obliged, And most humble Servant, GEORGE ALEXANDER STEVENS Haymarket Theatre Saturday, April 20, 1765."[6]

April 24. "We can assure the Public, that Mr. Stevens has received an Order to

Plate 7: The Heads. From "The Universal Museum and Complete Magazine of Knowledge and Pleasure" (September 1765). (British Library.)

Frontispeice to the Celebrated Lecture on Heads.

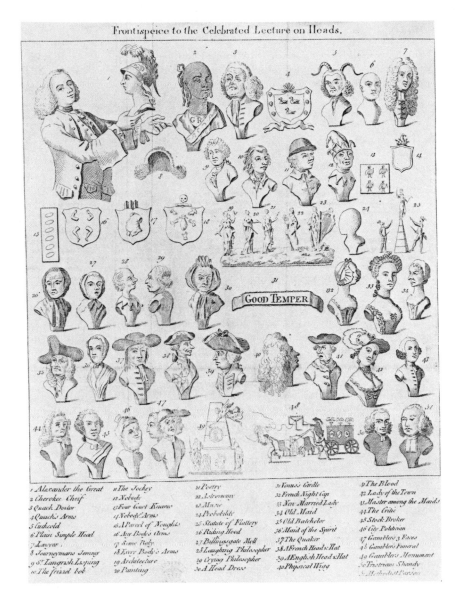

1 Alexander the Great	11 The Jockey	21 Poetry	31 Venus's Girdle	41 The Blood
2 Cherokee Cheif	12 Nobody	22 Astronomy	32 French Night Cap	42 Lady of the Town
3 Quack Doctor	13 Four Court Knaves	23 Music	33 New Married Lady	43 Master among the Maids
4 Quack's Arms	14 Nobody's Arms	24 Probability	34 Old Maid	44 The Critic
5 Cuckold	15 A Parcel of Noughts	25 Statute of Flattery	35 Old Batchelor	45 Stock Broker
6 Plain Simple Head	16 Any Body's Arms	26 Riding Hood	36 Maid of the Spirit	46 City Politican
7 Lawyer	17 Some Body	27 Billingsgate Moll	37 The Quaker	47 Gambler's 3 Faces
8 Journeymans Jemmy	18 Every Body's Arms	28 Laughing Philosopher	38 A French Head & Hat	48 Gambler's Funeral
9 St Langrish Lisping	19 Architecture	29 Crying Philosopher	39 A English Head & Hat	49 Gambler's Monument
10 The frizzel bob	20 Painting	30 A Head Dress	40 Physical Wigg	50 Tristram Shandy
				51 Methodist Parson

Plate 8: Another version of the Heads. Note the variations. From *A Lecture on Heads* (London, ca. 1767). (British Library.)

exhibit his *Lecture upon Heads, Three* more Evenings for the Entertainment of some Persons of Distinction, which will be To-morrow, Saturday, and Tuesday next and no longer."[7]

1. *Public Advertiser*, March 4, 1765.
2. Ibid., April 8, 1765.
3. Ibid., April 11, 1765.
4. Ibid., April 15, 1765.
5. Ibid., April 20, 1765.
6. Ibid., April 22, 1765.
7. Ibid., April 24, 1765.

LONDON: COVENT GARDEN.

March 18, 1765 (1 perf.).

Edward Shuter, whose name has occasionally been linked with the origin of the *Lecture*, presented the work as an afterpiece on the same night Stevens was performing at the Haymarket. These circumstances raise several interesting questions. Was Shuter's performance an authorized one? Was Stevens able to get to Covent Garden in time to see it? How did the audiences react to the opportunity of seeing two different presentations in the same week? "For the BENEFIT of Mr. SHUTER . . . This Day will be Presented The WAY of the WORLD . . . After the Play Mr. SHUTER will deliver The LECTURE upon HEADS; As originally given at the Theatre in the Haymarket, by G. A. Stevens."[1]

1. *Public Advertiser*, March 18, 1765.

ISLINGTON: THE LONG ROOM OPPOSITE SADLER'S WELLS.

Before June 10; September 2; September 16–18, 1765 (74? perfs. plus 3 perfs.).

The earliest notice of this engagement that I have been able to locate is dated June 10, but the run obviously started earlier since the June 15 notice is listed as the eleventh performance. By August 30 we are advised of the seventy-third performance. As we have seen earlier, it is very difficult to trust the accuracy of these statistics, but there is little question that this was a very substantial engagement. The few clues we have indicate that the performer was Mr. Gibson, who moved to Goodman's Field in late September and October (q.v.). The first advertisement quoted below was printed late in the run but is used here since it resolves several earlier printing errors. The extracts of the *Lecture* that were published in the September 1765 issue of the *Gentleman's Magazine* are prefaced by "The Lecture Upon Heads, that has been lately read near Islington." The reference is almost certainly to this engagement.

"This and every Evening during the SUMMER SEASON, at the Long Room, opposite to Sadler's Wells, will be delivered the celebrated LECTURES on HEADS. The following are Part of the Contents of the Evening's Entertainment. Part 1. Introduction. Alexander the great Cherokee Chief, Quack Doctor, Cuckold, Lawyer, humourous Oration in praise of the Law, Daniel against Dishclout, Horse Jockies, Nobody's, Somebody's, Anybody's, and Everybody's Coats of Arms, Family of Nobody, Architecture, Painting, Poetry, Astronomy, Music, Statues of Honesty and Flattery. Part 2. Ladies Heads, Riding Hood, Ranelagh Hood, Billingsgate, Laughing and Crying Philosophers, Venus's Girdle, Cleopatra, French Night Cap, Face Painting, Old Maid, Young Married Lady, Old Batchelor, Lass of the Spirit, Quaker, two Hats contrasted, Spitalfields Weaver. Part 3. Physical Wig, Dissertation on Sneezing and Snuff-taking, Life of a Blood, Woman of the Town, Tea Table Critic, Learned Critic, City Politician humourously described, Gambler's three Faces, Gambler's Funeral and Monument, Life and Death of a Wit, Head of a well-known Methodist Parson, with a Tabernacle Harangue. Conclusion. The doors to be opened at Five, and begin exactly at Six. Front Seats ls. 6d. Back Seats ls."[1]

June 13. "The Lecture on Heads which is delivered every Evening at the Long Room opposite Sadler's Wells, is, perhaps, the highest Ragout of Wit and Humour ever served up to please the Palates of the Judicious;—and the Applause with which it is received is adequate to it's uncommon Merit.   To say that it is *witty, sensible,* or *humourous,* is saying nothing:—It is *Wit, Sense,* and *Humour* itself."[2]

July 23. "On Tuesday last an august personage, attended by a noble duke and marquis and a foreigner of great distinction, went incog. to hear the Lecture on Heads at Islington, and testified their great satisfaction at the performance by the most unbounded marks of applause."[3]

August 2. "The fashionable Amusement of the Politer Part of the Town, is an Evening's Walk to Islington, to hear the LECTURE on HEADS, which is not less the entertainment of the Gentlemen than the Ladies, who express the highest Satisfaction at the Ridicule of many of their own most favourite Follies."[4]

September 2. "The LAST TIME of performing in this Place. This present Monday, at the Long ROOM, opposite Sadler's Wells, will be delivered the LECTURE on HEADS ... After the first act, by particular desire, Mr. GIBSON will give a LECTURE on a SCOTCH HEAD. WRITTEN BY HIMSELF."[5]

Gibson returns two weeks later for a three night stand: "*Nemo ne impune lacessit.* A SCOTCH HEAD, in the Lecture on HEADS To be delivered This, and the two following evenings at Six o'Clock, At the Long Room, opposite to Sadler's Wells, Mr. GIBSON will give, between the first and second Acts, A Lecture on a SCOTCH HEAD, Written by Himself. Front seats 1s 6d, Back Seats 1s."[6]

The popularity of the *Lecture* is further confirmed by the following entry: "A List of NEW BOOKS. A Lecture upon wrong Heads, read by Common Sense, for the Benefit of Politicians *without* Doors, and especially within Temple-Bar."[7] This is the first of ten satirical titles which also includes the typical "*Much ado about nothing*, a Comedy as it is lately revived at the old Playhouse in Lincoln's-Inn Fields."

1. *Public Advertiser*, August 13, 1765.
2. Ibid., June 13, 1765.
3. Ibid., July 25, 1765.
4. Ibid., August 2, 1765.
5. *Gazetteer and New Daily Advertiser*, September 2, 1765.
6. *Public Advertiser*, September 16, 1765.
7. Ibid., September 14, 1765.

RICHMOND: THE OLD THEATRE.

August 1, 6, 1765 (2 perfs.).

"*At the Desire of several Persons of Distinction* At the Old Theatre in Richmond, This Day Mr. GEORGE ALEXANDER STEVENS, will deliver his LECTURE upon HEADS, The Doors to be open at Six and begin exactly at Seven, At the usual Prices. Tickets to be had and Places taken at the Rising-Sun, the Three Compasses; and Mr. Stevens's Lodgings on Richmond Hill, opposite to the Star and Garter. The House is new fitted up."[1]

The *Lecture* was announced in the August 2 *Public Advertiser* for a performance on August 6. It was not advertised on that latter date. It was probably done.

1. *Public Advertiser*, August 1, 1765.

GOODMAN'S FIELDS: OLD WELLS.

August 31, September 4, 5, 6, 9, 12, 13, 1765 (7 perfs.).

"BY PARTICULAR DESIRE THIS PRESENT EVENING At the OLD WELLS, the bottom of Leman-street, Goodman's Fields, will be delivered the celebrated LECTURE on HEADS By a GENTLEMAN, being his first attempt. Boxes 2s. 6d. Pit 1s. Gall. 1s. The doors to be open at six, and begin at seven."[1]

September 4. "With Additions."[2] This advertisement identifies the performer as Mr. Rogers.

September 13. "N.B. Any gentleman that can exhibit well, may meet with encouragement, if he applies as above."[3]

The advertisements alternated between pages 1 and 3. Apparently Mr. Rogers could not always afford the best space. The September 13 note is very curious. Mr. Rogers may have needed help with the performance or was unable to meet his contractual obligations, or perhaps he was yielding to pressure from Stevens. There is also the possibility that he sought someone to perform the *Lecture* at Goodman's Fields while he, if indeed he is the person, alternated with the Proteus variant during September and October (q.v.). In any event, Mr. Gibson came to the theatre thirteen days later and presented the *Lecture* for almost half of the month of October.

1. *Gazetteer and New Daily Advertiser*, August 31, 1765.
2. Ibid., September 4, 1765.
3. Ibid., September 13, 1765.

WEST SMITHFIELD: BARTHOLOMEW FAIR.

September 4 + ?, 1765, (several perfs.).

Anonymous. Probably not Stevens: "AT BARTHOLMEW FAIR. The Public are requested to observe that the celebrated LECTURE on HEADS, Will be delivered in a large and commodious Room, near the End of of Hosier Lane, West Smithfield, During the short Time of BARTHOLOMEW FAIR. Front Seats 1s. Back Seats at 6d. To begin each day at Twelve o'Clock."[1]

1. *Public Advertiser*, September 4, 1765.

GOODMAN'S FIELDS: OLD WELLS.

September 23, 1765 (1 and more until October 21).

An early spin-off. Perhaps by Mr. Rogers.

"This evening will be delivered an Oration, called PROTEUS; being an Exhibition of Pictures, taken from the life, of the most remarkable Hearts of the age, interspersed with other subjects, viz. a humourous and deep Dissertation of the seat and colour of the Heart, undiscovered, till now, either by the ancient or modern philosophers. The seat of Paradise discovered, A Fop's Heart. The first Fop. The first Coquet's Looking-glass. The first Gallant; and a great variety of other Hearts of several important personages, set forth in their most lively colours. The whole concluding with some beautiful antiques, real ones, being the finest Hearts of the ancients, viz. Adam's Heart, A Roman Vestal's, Pilades and Orestes' Hearts joined together, Elosia's Heart, and many others, equally beautiful, too tedious to mention. Attempted by the Author, a gentleman who never appeared on any stage, but whose attitudes are taken from the finest painters and statuaries such as Raphael, Corregio, Guido, the Carracci's, Carlo Moratti, Michael-Angelo, Bernini, etc. The doors to be open at six, and to begin exactly at seven o'clock. Boxes 3s. Pit 2s. Gallery 1s. To be continued every evening. Tickets to be had next door to the Wells, at the Rainbow coffee-house, and at Lloyd's."[1]

1. *Gazetteer and New Daily Advertiser*, September 23, 1765.

GOODMAN'S FIELDS: OLD WELLS.

September 30, October 2, 3, 10, 14–16, 21–24, 28–31, 1765 (15 perf.).

Mr. Gibson resumes at Goodman's Fields. His disclaimer on October 21 was occasioned by Stevens's October 17 notice (see next entry): "A SCOTCH HEAD at the Old Wells, Goodman's Fields, this present Evening, the LECTURE ON HEADS will be once more attempted by a person, who hopes, through the indulgence of the public, to retrieve the credit of the exhibition, by a due attention to decency and propriety. At the end of the first part, Mr. Gibson, by particular desire, will exhibit a SCOTCH HEAD, and display the peculiar characteristics of a North Briton."[1]

October 10. "THE LECTURE ON HEADS will be continued at the Old Wells, Goodman's-Fields, till further notice. Any person or family in distress, desirous of having a benefit, may apply as above, especially if Members of the ancient and honourable Society of Free and accepted Masons."[2]

October 14. "At the end of the second part will be introduced a WEAVER'S HEAD, with a Descant, written by the Exhibitor."[3]

October 21. "A WEAVER'S HEAD . . . this and the three following Evenings the LECTURE on HEADS, will be repeated, as delivered by the last Exhibitor, who, to exempt himself from some late Aspersions, declares he was not accessary to the Publication of any Lecture; and presumes that notwithstanding a late modest Advertisement, he has some Claim to Education, Common Sense, and COMMON HONESTY."[4] This advertisement adjoined the one for Stevens's performance!

October 28. "Admittance (Benefit nights excepted) 1 shilling."[5]

October 30. "For the Benefit of a Brother FREEMASON under Confinement and other Distresses, through various Losses by unavoidable Incidents. . . . With an additional Character written by the Exhibitor."[6]

1. Gazetteer and New Daily Advertiser, September 30, 1765.
2. Ibid., October 10, 1765.
3. Ibid., October 14, 1765.
4. Public Advertiser, October 21, 1765.
5. Gazetteer and New Daily Advertiser, October 28, 1765.
6. Public Advertiser, October 30, 1765.

ALDERMANBURY: PLAISTERER'S HALL.

October 21–26, 28–31, November 1, 11–16, 18–23, 25–30, December 2–7, 1765 (35 perfs.).

The last quarter of 1765 was a period of special distress for Stevens. The *Lecture* was in its period of greatest popularity and prosperity, but Stevens reaped very few of the benefits. The piece was mercilessly pirated, burlesqued, and modified, and was published in unauthorized versions in several bound editions as well as in the newspapers and magazines of the day. The worst was still to come. Stevens would continue to be plagued by the pirates until he eventually sold his property to Lee Lewes in 1780. In late October Stevens would be performing simultaneously with Mr. Rogers, his most serious competitor at the time. Stevens began early to prepare the public for his own authorized version of the *Lecture.* On September 10 he announced in the *Public Advertiser* that performances were to be given "the Beginning of next Month" at the Plaisterer's Hall in Aldermanbury. They were described as

"his Lecture upon HEADS, Brains, Faces, Necks, Stocks, Necklaces, &c. &c. in FOUR DIVISIONS. In which will be introduced Variety of new CHARACTERS. [It took Stevens almost six weeks to prepare the Lecture and when it finally appeared it was presented in five parts.] As several things have lately been shewn at Alehouses and in Fairs, and inserted in Magazines, to which the Name of the LECTURE UPON HEADS have been given; to prevent such counterfeits for the future, the Proprietor of the REAL Lecture having now compleated his original Plan, has furnished himself with a fresh Sortment of Goods of the newest Fashion. He hopes therefore for the Continuance of the Favours of his former Customers, as the Public may be assured his Manufactures are genuine, being exhibited by the maker. G. A. STEVENS."[1]

The above ad was run frequently, but the *Lecture* did not open the "beginning of next month" as planned. Some time later the notice read "in a few days"[2] and continued in that manner until the eventual opening.

"At Plaisterers-Hall ON Monday Evening next. exactly at Six o'Clock Mr. GEORGE ALEXANDER STEVENS, Will deliver His LECTURE upon HEADS compleat.

As never before exhibited. Divided into Five PARTS. Price of Admittance Three Shillings. * * A spurious Piece having lately been inserted in Magazines &c. &c. and repeated in Alehouses and at Wells, and printed as a Pamphlet, to which the Name of Lecture upon Heads has been given, the Author of the Lecture declares, that he is in no way accessary to such a contemptible Publication and Performance, but that it is a most scandalous Piracy; and by which those who are concerned in it have shewn themselves as deficient in Education and common Sense as they are in common Honesty."[3]

How aggravated Stevens must have been to find immediately following his notice an advertisement for the publication of the fifth edition of the *Lecture*!

November 2. "MR. GEORGE ALEXANDER STEVENS does not exhibit his Lectures upon Heads any more until the Theatres Royal open again."[4]

November 14. "For the Benefit of the SUFFERERS by the late Fire in Bishopsgate-street, &c."[5]

November 26. "N.B. As the Hall cannot be lett any longer than next Tuesday, December 3, the Lectures will conclude that Night for this Season."[6]

December 4. "Last Night."[7]

December 5. "The GENTLAMEN, [*sic*] to whom by a Prior Engagement, the Hall was to have been given up, postpone their Business, on Account of so much Company being disappointed hearing the Lecture last Night for Want of Room; therefore (by particular Desire) . . . This Evening, and the two or three following ones, . . ."[8]

December 7. "PEREMPTORILY the LAST NIGHT."[9]

1. *Public Ledger*, September 10, 1765.
2. Ibid., October 1, 1765.
3. *Public Advertiser*, October 17, 1765.
4. Ibid., November 2, 1765.
5. Ibid., November 14, 1765.
6. Ibid., November 26, 1765.
7. Ibid., December 4, 1765.
8. Ibid., December 5, 1765.
9. Ibid., December 7, 1765.

LONDON: LITTLE THEATRE IN THE HAYMARKET.

December 2–7, 1765 (6 perfs.).

"THIS present Evening, and every Evening till farther Notice, at the Little Theatre in James-street, near the Haymarket, Mr. POTTINGER will deliver his

LECTURE on HEADS: The Doors to be opened at Five, and to begin exactly at Six
o'clock. Boxes 4s. Pit 2s. Gallery 1s. Vivant Rex et Regina. N.B. The Theatre is
fitted up in an elegant Manner and at a great Expense. Mr. Pottinger takes this
Opportunity of making his most grateful Acknowledgements to the Candour
of the Public, by whom he has been so warmly patronized; and, whereas Mr.
Stevens sometime since advertised that his Plan was compleat, Mr. Pottinger
declares, that his Plan will never be compleat, but that as fast as new Characters
of Vice or Folly make their Appearance on the Human Stage, their Heads shall
be carefully handed up to Notice, by the Public's Most devoted Servant 1.
POTTINGER".[1]

December 5. "N.B. Constant Fires are kept in order to make the House agreeably warm."[2]

Dibdin wrote that "POTTINGER was a sober bookseller, till STEVENS's lecture on
heads set him literally mad for lecturing and writing plays."[3]

This curious notice was printed during Pottinger's run and may relate to his
performance: "In a few days will be published, neat as imported. A LECTURE for
HEADS, if no bigger than a pin's. Dedicated to Mr. I—— P——. By Peter
Egerton, Heir of Sir Ralph Egerton, Standard-Bearer to King Henry VIII. and
not of Sir Thomas Egerton, the Duke of Bridgewater's Ancestor, as Mr. P——
had printed before."[4]

1. *Public Advertiser*, December 3, 1765. A very abbreviated notice was printed the
   previous day.
2. *Public Advertiser*, December 5, 1765.
3. Charles Dibdin, *A Complete History of the Stage* (London, 1800), vol. 5, p. 307.
4. *Gazetteer and New Daily Advertiser*, December 7, 1765.

LONDON: LITTLE THEATRE IN JAMES STREET NEAR THE HAYMARKET.

January 6–March 12, 1766 (76? perfs.).

"This and every Evening till Farther Notice, the LECTURE ON HEADS will be
delivered by a YOUNG LADY, who never appeared in public. The Doors to be
opened at Five, and to begin exactly at Six o'clock. Boxes 4s. Pit 2s. Gallery 1s.
6d. To the PUBLIC. After several of our Lords and Masters, the Men, have with
various Success made wry Faces for the Amusement of the Town; permit a
Woman to attempt the arduous Task of laughing the Men out of their Follies;
declaring, however, that while she attempts the Ridicule of Vices peculiar to the
Other Sex, she will by no Means spare the slightest Foible of her Own."[1]

This presentation was advertised for thirty-six performances between January
6 and March 12.[2] The March 10 notice designates the seventy-third performance, and the one for March 12, the seventy-sixth![3] The performer remains

anonymous. This is the earliest record of a woman doing the *Lecture*, and for one who had never before appeared on the public stage she had a remarkable run. Other notices of interest include:

January 7. "The Theatre is fitted up in an elegant manner, and constant fires are kept to make the house agreeably warm."[4]

January 9. "Every Tuesday, Thursday, and Saturday, till farther notice."[5]

January 10. "This, and every evening till farther Notice."[6]

March 6. "For the BENEFIT of the DOOR-KEEPERS." [For this night only, several new pieces were added between the acts.] "To which will be added The CRIES OF LONDON, for the last time."[7]

1. *Public Advertiser*, January 6, 1766.
2. *The London Stage*, vol. 2 [entry is incomplete when it states that the "lecture continued to March 6"], pp. 1145–46.
3. *Gazetteer and New Daily Advertiser*, March 10 and 12, 1766.
4. Ibid., January 7, 1766.
5. Ibid., January 9, 1766.
6. *Public Advertiser*, January 10, 1766.
7. *Gazetteer and New Daily Advertiser*, March 6, 1766.

BRISTOL: COOPER'S HALL.

February 10, 17, 18, 1766 (3 perfs.).

February 10. "George Alexander Stevens's Lecture on Heads by Rogers from the Haymarket, Where he gave great Satisfaction . . . ***After the Lecture (by Desire) Mr. ROGERS will mimic the Players of London; the Particulars of which will be express'd in the Bills. . . . admission 2s6d."[1]

February 17, 18. "***Mr. ROGERS thinks 'tis a Duty incumbent upon him, thus publickly to return Thanks to those Ladies and Gentlemen (who have honour'd him with their Presence) for the kind Indulgence they gave him, and humbly solicits a Continuance of their Favors. A good Fire will be kept in the Room.

"To the PRINTER. AS I am fond of every rational Amusement that is offered to the Publick, I went one Evening last week to see the *Lecture on Heads* exhibited at the Coopers-Hall in this City; and having heard Mr. Stevens, I must own I was so prejudiced in his Favour, that I expected but little Satisfaction from the present Exhibitor. In some arts I was agreeably deceived, for Mr. Rogers discovers a true Comic Genius, without Affectation; and goes through the

Whole with such a Vein of Humour, as not only to do Honour to the original Performer, but reserve a particular Share of Applause to himself. Yours, &c. IMPARTIAL."[2]

1. *Bristol Journal and Felix Farley's Bristol Journal*, February 8, 1766.
2. Ibid., February 15, 1766..

PHILADELPHIA, PA.: CHRIST CHURCH SCHOOL HOUSE; ASSEMBLY ROOM, LODGE ALLEY; GARNER'S ACADEMY, SECOND STREET.

February 13 +, March 31, April 2, 4, 17, 28, 29, May 5, 6, July 4 (+ 2 earlier perfs.), 1766; January 15, 20, 22, 27, 1767 (15 + perfs.).

Despite David Douglass's subsequent claim that his presentation of the *Lecture* on April 30, 1766 (q.v.) was "wholly new in this Part of the World" [presumably America and not Charleston], the earliest discovered performance in America took place two months earlier in Philadelphia. We are told that "the next public evening at said School [Christ-Church, School-House] will be on Thursday, the 13th of this Instant, on which will commence the first Part of that celebrated Lecture on Heads, which gained universal Applause in England, to be expounded by Master Joseph Redman each succeeding Evening until finished."[1]

Garrett points out that the young Redman was a scion of an important Philadelphia family and his schoolmaster sponsor, Joseph Garner, was a distinguished educator in that city as early as 1761. The *Lecture* seemed to be popular, and Garner was anxious to have it heard by larger audiences. He avoided a performance on Good Friday, devoting that evening to a lecture and hymn suitable to the "Solemnity of Easter" and announced:

March 31, April 2, 4. "As the season is so far advanced, as to render the finishing the LECTURE ON HEADS impracticable, if continued but once a Week, it is proposed to have three public Evenings in Easter Week, viz. Monday, Wednesday and Friday, by which means those who have not yet attended, may have an Opportunity of seeing the whole exhibited. Tickets as usual, at One Shilling each."[2]

Although the performer is not specified, it seems certain that Master Redman again delivered the *Lecture* and that he had also done so on several other unrecorded occasions since February 13. He probably continued performing through mid-April for we learn:

April 17. "THIS Evening will be continued the Lecture upon HEADS."[3]

His performance ran through the remainder of the month and into May, now at the Assembly Room in Lodge Alley, when the season ended.

April 28, 29, May 5, 6. "By particular desire of several gentlemen and ladies, on Monday and Tuesday the 28th and 29th inst. and on Monday and Tuesday the 5th and 6th of May, will be a concert of music on each of the above evenings, the much applauded lecture on heads began and completely finished on the first two evenings; and continued on the two last, if desired, by Master JOSEPH REDMAN . . . Mr. Garner is determined to render every particular of each entertainment as agreeable as possible. Tickets at half a dollar each . . . To begin each evening at half after seven o'clock. Note, Each Ticket admits the bearer two evenings."[4]

The Assembly Room was again the site for the *Lecture* when, on July 4, it was given for at least its third presentation by an anonymous performer who advertised:

July 4 (+ 2 earlier perfs.). "A LECTURE on HEADS. Written Originally by G. A. Stevens; altered and improved by the present Exhibitor."[5]

This particular Philadelphia connection came to an end during January of the following year. Garner, whose Academy had now moved to Second Street near Walnut, announced four benefits for the poor. The performer was not specified.

January 15, 20, 22, 27. "Mr. Garner, from frequent solicitations, and a readiness to contribute as much as in his power, to alleviate the deep distresses of many indigent families and prisoners in this city, many of whom the inclemency of the season and want of the common means of supporting life, have been reduced to unutterable calamities; proposes to have four publick evenings for the benefit of those indigent persons, viz. on Thursday the 15th; on Tuesday the 20th; Thursday the 22nd; and Tuesday the 27th instants. On these evenings will be exhibited, the celebrated Lecture on Heads. . . . Tickets at Two Shillings each. . . ."[6]

Douglass, who had given the *Lecture* in Charleston the previous April and May, was in Philadelphia at the time, and we are tempted to speculate if he attended the benefits or had anything to do with the presentations particularly since Garner, in February, was able to persuade "Douglass to loan actors for a charity concert of vocal and instrumental music."[7]

1. *Pennsylvania Gazette*, February 13, 1766. I am particularly indebted to Kurt Garrett, whose correspondence and article, "Palliative For Players: The Lecture on Heads," *Pennsylvania Magazine of History and Biography* (April 1979), pp. 166–76, first called my attention to these early performances.
2. *Pennsylvania Gazette*, March 29, 1766.
3. *Pennsylvania Gazette*, April 17, 1766.
4. *Pennsylvania Journal*, April 24, 1766, and *Pennsylvania Gazette* for the same date with minor variations.

5. *Pennsylvania Gazette*, July 3, 1766.
6. *Pennsylvania Journal*, January 8, 1767.
7. Garrett, p. 169.

LONDON: LITTLE HAYMARKET.

February 25–28, March 1, 3, 1766 (6 perfs.).

When the time arrived for Stevens's third annual stint at the Haymarket, he had prepared a new version of the *Lecture*, called the *Supplement*, to counter his imitators including the young lady who was performing at this time at the James Street Theatre. Much of his irritation over the piracies and his inability to gain redress is expressed in the prologue printed below. The *Supplement* did not do well. It ran six nights with indications that new scenes needed to be added. Stevens reverted to the 1765 version of the *Lecture* while he worked on the revisions. On April 3 he opened a twelve-night run of the *Supplement* with the additions: "GEORGE ALEXANDER STEVENS Proposes to Deliver, At the THEATRE in the HAYMARKET, THIS DAY being the 25th of February, An ENTIRE NEW LECTURE UPON HEADS, PORTRAITS, AND WHOLE LENGTHS called The SUPPLEMENT. Boxes 5s. Pit 3s. Gallery 2s. The doors to be opened at five, and begin exactly at half an hour past six o'clock. Vivant Rex & Regina. *** Places to be taken at the Theatre."[1]

"PROLOGUE to the new Lecture, called the SUPPLEMENT, wrote by GEORGE ALEXANDER STEVENS, now performing in the Haymarket.

"*The Curtain rises and discovers a Picture, on which the Lecturer is painted sitting at a table writing, and several people picking his pockets of his Papers*: then

"Enter *Stevens*, meeting a man who gives him some bills—(*Reads*)—A Lecture upon Heads, &c.—A Lecture upon—Well, Sir, I can't help it: in every business there will be interlopers. Some people will take advantage of other People's Heads, which is not at all surprising. But bid them prepare to begin the Lecture, while I endeavour to address this audience with a prologue."

> *Ladies and Gentlemen,*
> As if, or how, or so, or so may be,
> A Prologue should begin with a simile.
> So then—but what can then, or now be said,
> I know no simile to suit my Head.
> 'Twas here the town confirm'd me a Projector,
> Held up my head, upholding my Head-Lecture.
> Some poaching Curs, lurching behind that name,
> Cross'd the fair chace, and meanly stole my game.

Scorning to enter into altercation,
Redress I sought from act association;
And Counsel ask'd—But Counsel disagree,
Except in one thing—to accept the Fee.
When the first I attended, I bow'd, put my Case;
He open'd his snuff-box and star'd in my face:
Then in Law-Latin Lectur'd, *that Primus Jacobus,*
And Secundus were two, and that two were duobus,
That the statute in force against gaming prevails,
And to game was to play, or to toss up Heads or Tails.
Then told me *in my case, costs might be obtain'd*
By proving what damage my Head had sustain'd.
Had you seen by my face when I heard that suggestion,
My Head!—I sneak'd off, without answering the question.
The next Counsel gruffly demanded my name,
And ask'd me to how many Heads I lay'd claim?
And if I cou'd make Heads, or if I cou'd mend 'em?
And mention'd *a capiasad satisfaciendum.*
Then shaking full-bottom, and nodding his head,
Hemm'd, cough'd, strok'd his chin, and sententious thus said:
On an *Action of Tresspass,* or *Action of Trover,*
Or *by filing a Bill,* I don't think you'll recover.
A writ of *Quod Damnum* won't give satisfaction,
But for hurting the Head, there's a *Crown-Office Action.*
My answer was, Sir, that's not what I'd be at,
Concerning my own Head—there's not much in that.
'Tis for stealing my other folk's Heads I wou'd try 'em—
Your other folk's Heads! Friend! pray how came you by 'em?
I pick'd them up, Sir, as they laid in my way,
And 'pounded them as they do cattle astray.
Then made proclamation, gave each Head a name,
But no body appear'd to put in a claim.
Then to his desk turn'd, and down some books tumbling,
Ope'd one, then another—in this manner mumbling—
Henricus Tertius, Edwards Quartus, Carolus Primus,
Gulielmus, Georgius—this way of expressing,
Was like a school boy in haste to get over his lesson.
Then he laid down his spectacles, shut up his book,
And to me turns his head with a wisdomish look.
You're right to a Head, friend, your first proof must be,—
Interrupting, I said, Sir, *That won't do for me.*
He surlily answer'd, *why then I've no other,*
So I left him as wise as I went from his brother, However,
Since others with my Heads make free,
Repraisal sure's allowed to me;

My Heads they've parcell'd out in shares,
May I not make as free with theirs?
And since once more I've turn'd Projector,
And open shop with a new Lecture;
A shew-board must my trade make known,
As all the signs are coming down.
This-out-lined coloured manufacture,
Exhibits how I lost my Lecture;
When game gives hounds the slip, they say,
In Sportsman's language stole away.
Here 'tis reversed, the pack you see,
Sad curs! they steal away from me.
The Picture shown, with your permission,
We'll now begin the Exhibition.[2]

LONDON: LITTLE HAYMARKET.

March 5, 7, 12, 14, 1766 (4 perfs.).

"THIS DAY, by particular desire, GEORGE ALEXANDER STEVENS will repeat HIS
FIRST LECTURE UPON HEADS, As he delivered it Last Season. Boxes 4s. Pit 3s.
Gallery 2s."[3]

[He does this in the same theatre as above. There is a reduction in the price of
the boxes. Note this revival is being done by particular desire.]

March 7. "N.B. There being two benefit concerts next week at the Theatre in
the Hay-market, Mr. Steven's Lectures will not be repeated after this evening
until Wednesday next."[4]

On March 10 Stevens petitioned the Lord Chamberlain:

"If it should not be looked upon as an impertinent Request, May I beg his
Grace's Permission for Mrs. Stevens to repeat part of my Lecture with me. I
hope this Intrusion may not offend.

> I am &c. With great respect
> Your most Humble Servant
> G: Alexander Stevens."[5]

I have found no record of her performance.

March 12. "N.B. G.A. Steven's new Lecture, called The SUPPLEMENT, is deferred, until the ADDITIONAL SCENE (as desired) is prepared"[6]

March 14. "(Being positively the last)"[7]

LONDON: HAYMARKET THEATRE.

April 3, 5, 7, 9–12, 15, 19, 22–24, 1766 (12 perfs.).

"GEORGE ALEXANDER STEVENS at the Theatre in the Haymarket, Will deliver his NEW LECTURE With the ADDITIONS as desired This Evening . . ."[8]

April 15. "N.B. On account of some prior engagements, the Lecture can only be repeated in town, this season, This Evening and Saturday next."[9]

April 22. "Positively the Last Evening. By PARTICULAR DESIRE."[10]

April 23. "By PARTICULAR DESIRE"[11]

April 24. "By PARTICULAR DESIRE"[12]

1. *Gazetteer and New Daily Advertiser*, February 25, 1766.
2. *Public Ledger*, March 3, 1766.
3. *Gazetteer and New Daily Advertiser*, March 5, 1766.
4. Ibid., March 7, 1766.
5. P.R.O. L.C. 7.3. March 10, 1766.
6. *Gazetteer and New Daily Advertiser*, March 12, 1766.
7. Ibid., March 14, 1766.
8. *Public Advertiser*, April 3, 1766.
9. *Gazetteer and New Daily Advertiser*, April 15, 1766.
10. Ibid., April 22, 1766.
11. Ibid., April 23, 1766.
12. Ibid., April 24, 1766.

CHARLESTON, S.C.: THE THEATRE AT QUEEN STREET.

April 30, May 6, 8, 1766 (3 perfs.).

"Mr. Douglass returns the Public his most sincere Thanks for the many Favours he received this Winter as an actor; he assures them, he will ever retain a most grateful Sense of the Oligations he has to this Province, which have so amply rewarded his imperfect, though well-meant, attempts to contribute to their Entertainment.

"He purchased, when in London, a genuine Copy of the *Lecture on Heads* written by Mr. Stevens, and provided himself with the necessary Apparatus for delivering it: He has made some alterations and Improvements, which he flatters himself will be a considerable advantage to it, as many Strokes of Satire have escaped the author, which Mr. Douglass imagines to be directed at, rather, improper Objects, and in some Place the Sense was so obscure, that it was absolutely necessary to elucidate it, in Order to convey, with Precision, his Meaning to the audience.

"In this State he intends to exhibit it to the Town: But as an Undertaking of this Kind, is wholly new in this Part of the World, and the Success uncertain, he is advised by his Friends (that he may be enabled to form a Judgment of the Encouragement it is likely to meet with, before he engages in any further expence) to propose a subscription, for *Three Nights only*, at Three Pounds for the Three Nights. As soon as a competent Number have subscribed Tickets will be issued, and proper notice given of the night on which he will deliver the Lecture."[1]

The May 6 announcement reduced the price of the tickets to 20s. for the boxes and pit and 15s. for the gallery. At the same time Douglass announced his forthcoming departure from the colony and requested his debtees to come to him for payment.[2] Hugh Rankin gives an interesting and valuable account of this engagement but introduced some unnecessary complications. He writes: "It would seem that this was a pirated edition of this rather popular lecture, for it was not published in London until the following year. Quite possibly, he had secured a script from some unscrupulous actor in London or had heard the lecture and memorized the words, a practice not uncommon at the time."[3] Actually, J. Pridden had published and offered for sale at least six editions of the *Lecture* by January 1766. And there were others available.

1. *South Carolina Gazette and Country Journal,* April 15, 1766.
2. Ibid., May 6, 1766.
3. Hugh F. Rankin, *The Theatre in Colonial America* (Chapel Hill, 1960), p. 107.

LONDON: HICKFORD'S ROOM.

July 16, 1766 (1 perf.).

Look at this spin-off! "At Mr. Hickford's Room, in Panton-street, near the Hay market, This Day, the 16th instant, will be delivered A LECTURE on TAILS, called The FALL OF HEBE. The prologue and epilogue spoken by a dumb Lady and an Indian Gentleman born dumb. Tails of ancient and modern beauties; the mimick mimicked, who has been taken off; a Lecture on Tails by Mrs. Cole's Ghost. Prologue and epilogue spoken by a Mermaid.—Front seats 3s. Middle seats 2s. 6d. Back seats 1s. 6d. The doors to be opened at six, and to begin exactly at seven. Tickets to be had at the Hole in the Wall, next to the Room."[1]

1. *Gazetteer and New Daily Advertiser,* July 16, 1766.

LONDON: FOUNTAIN TAVERN, LUDGATE HILL.

August 4, 1766 (1 perf.).

"By PERMISSION For ONE NIGHT only. This present Monday Mr. POTTINGER will deliver The LECTURE on HEADS, at the Fountain-tavern, Ludgate-hill. To which will be added variety of Entertainments, as appear by the following Bill of Fare. Prologue, by Mr. Pottinger. The Early Horn, by a Gentleman. Lecture on Heads, Act I. Song, by a Lady. Mock Minuet. Cries of London, by Mr. Franklin. Lecture, Act II. Water parted from the Sea, by Signora Leoni. Dutch Story, by Mr. Franklin, Song, by a Lady. Lecture, Act III. Medley, by Mr. Franklin. Song, by Signora Leoni. Epilogue, by Mr. Pottinger.—Admittance 2s. 6d. Tickets may be had at the bar of the tavern."[1]

1. *Gazetteer and New Daily Advertiser*, August 4, 1766.

MANCHESTER: MARSDEN STREET THEATRE.

August 19, 20, 21, 1766 (3 perfs.).

"... in August Manchester was treated to three performances at the theatre of Stevens's 'Lecture Upon Heads.'"[1] The performances were given by Mr. Collins, whose later presentation of the *Evening Brush* was a variant of Stevens's work. Stevens was in Manchester at this time and may have attended Collins's performance with great displeasure. We are told that "two years having elapsed, [since the 1764 performance] Stevens paid us a second visit, on which occasion he railed, with all the bitterness of Tim Bobbin, against imitators and robbers."[2]

1. J. L. Hodgkinson and Rex Pogson, *The Early Manchester Theatre* (London, 1960), p. 43.
2. Richard Wright Procter, *Manchester in Holiday Dress* (London and Manchester, 1866), p. 31.

WHITEHAVEN.

1766?

The year cannot be confirmed but much of the evidence indicates that Stevens played Whitehaven during the spring or summer while he was on tour.

LONDON: HICKFORD'S GREAT ROOM.

September 22, 1766 (1 perf.).

"At HICKFORD'S GREAT ROOM, near the Hole in the Wall, Panton-street, THIS EVENING will be exhibited, by Mr. PALMER, Mr. STEVENS's celebrated LECTURE upon HEADS. Part I—Alexander the Great, Cherokee Chief, Quack Doctor, Cuckold, Lawyer, Horse Jockey, Nobody, Lottery of Life, Somebody's, Nobody's, any Body's, and every Body's Coat of Arms, Variety, Wit, Judgment, Genius, Architecture, Painting, Poetry, Astronomy, and Music, Heads of Flattery and Honesty. Part II. Ladies Heads, Riding Hood, Ranelagh Hood, Billingsgate, Laughing and Crying Philosophers, Married Lady, Old Maid, Old Batchelor, Lass of Spirit, two Hats contrasted, and two Heads contrasted. Part III.—Physical Wig, Dissertation on Sneezing and Snuff-taking, Life of a Blood, Woman of the Town, Tea-table Critic, Learned Critic, City Politician, Gamblers three Faces, Gamblers Funeral and Monument, Life of a Wit, Head of a well-known Methodist, with a Tabernacle Harangue.—Pit 2s. Gallery 1s."[1]

1. *Gazetteer and New Daily Advertiser*, September 22, 1766.

LONDON: HAYMARKET THEATRE.

October 30, November 6, 1766 (2 perfs.).

The performer and subject matter are unspecified, but some relationship to the *Lecture on Heads* is reasonable considering the date and place.

October 30. "This Day, Oct 30, At the Theatre in the Haymarket will be delivered, a new serious and comic LECTURE On various interesting and diverting SUBJECTS. Boxes 4s. Pit 2s. 6d. Gallery 1s 6d. . . . Places for the Boxes to be taken of Mr. Sewell, at the Theatre."[1]

November 6. Repeat.[2]

1. *Public Advertiser*, October 30, 1766.
2. Ibid., November 6, 1766.

ALDERMANBURY: PLAISTERER'S HALL (LATER GREAT ROOM OVER EXETER EXCHANGE).

December 12, 16, 19, 20, 26, 27, 29–31, 1766; January 1–3, 8, 10, 12, 13, 15–17, 19, 20, 22, 24, 27–29, 31, February 2–7, 9–14, 16–21, 23, 26, 1767 (47 perfs.).

An extensive run of the *Lecture on Hearts* and later *Noses* by Mr. Dodd.

"By Permission (of the Right Honourable the Lord Mayor) THIS DAY, December 12, at PLAISTERER'S HALL, in Addle-street, Wood-street, A New, Moral, and Satyrical LECTURE on HEARTS Will be delivered (in Three Parts) by the AUTHOR.

(Being the 1st Appearance in Public) With an Occasional Prologue. Boxes 3s. Pit 2s. Gall. 1s."[1]

*December 16.*On this date the advertisement also includes "N.B. The Author returns his sincere Thanks to his very polite and numerous Audience, for the uncommon Applause with which he was honoured."[2]

December 18. "N.B. The Author fearing, from the wet appearance of the beginning of last night, that there would be but little company, postponed the Lecture till TOMORROW NIGHT (the Hall being engaged to-night for a concert) when it will be *positively* delivered, with the addition of a *new Heart*."[3]

December 19. The following notice contains the full particulars. "THIS EVENING, (and every Tuesday, Wednesday, (except Christmas Eve) Friday and Saturday, till further notice . . . PART I An Upright Royal Heart—A Deformed Royal Heart—A Sailor's Heart—An Agent's Heart—A Coward's Heart—A real Captain's Heart—A Light Heart—An Userer's Heart—A Dutchman's Heart—A Frenchman's Heart—A Pedant's Heart—and an Attorney's Heart. PART II FEMALE HEARTS A Tender Heart—A Stoney Heart—A Bloated Heart—A Good Heart—A Termegant's Heart—A Giddy Heart—A Proud Heart—A Notable Heart—A Wavering Heart—An Old Maid's Heart—A Coquette's Heart—and a Prude's Heart. PART III A Faithful Heart—A False Heart—A Beau's Heart— A Foxhunter's Heart—A Jealous Heart—A Confident Heart—An Atheist's Heart—An Hypocrite's Heart—A Pious Heart—A Physician's Heart—A Quack's Heart—and a Clerk's Heart."[4]

December 26. "AT a GREAT ROOM over EXETER-EXCHANGE . . . (with alterations and additions) . . . N.B. At the desire of a number of Ladies and Gentlemen, the exhibition is removed from Plaisterers- hall to the above place. The entrance is up the great stair case from Burleigh-street."[5]

January 8. "To which will be added A CRITICAL DISSERTATION on NOSES. . . . N.B. The Room is *now* properly fitted up, at a large expence, for the *more convenient* accomodation of the Ladies, and such of the Nobility and Gentry as may chuse to honour this Lecture with their preference. Proper care is also taken to keep the room warm.—The Author hopes to be favoured with the company of *his Brethren* of the most Ancient and Honourable Order of *Free and Accepted* MASONS."[6]

G. Kearsley announced publication of the *Lectures on Hearts and Noses*, and the public was advised that copies could be obtained from the printer as well as the lecturer himself at the time of the exhibition.[7]

February 9. "Mr. Dodd humbly presumes to acquaint the public, that by the sudden fall of the house on Snow-hill last Saturday night (where he lived) the greatest part of his furniture and effects are destroyed. He has no hopes of retrieving his misfortune, but from the success of his Lecture, and appeals to the well known humanity of the British nation, for their benevolent encouragement thereof."[8]

February 21. "By ORDER of The GRAND of the ALBION LODGE . . . N.B. The Most Noble Grand, Vice Grand, Past Grands, and other Officers, will attend in their respective REGALIA. The company of the Brethern of other Lodges is requested."[9]

1. *Gazetteer and New Daily Advertiser*, December 12, 1766.
2. Ibid., December 16, 1766.
3. Ibid., December 18, 1766.
4. Ibid., December 19, 1766.
5. Ibid., December 26, 1766.
6. Ibid., January 8, 1766.
7. Ibid., January 28, 31, 1766.
8. Ibid., February 9, 1766.
9. Ibid., February 21, 1766.

WILLIAMSBURG, VA.: GREAT ROOM OF THE RALEIGH TAVERN.

January 12, 13, 1767 (2 perfs.).

"The celebrated LECTURE upon HEADS, so much admired and applauded by all who have heard it performed, will be delivered, on Monday and Tuesday next, at 6 o'clock in the evening, in the Great Room of the Rawleigh tavern, by Mr. William Verling, who is just arrived in this city. He does not intend to exhibit but these two nights."[1]

1. *The Virginia Gazette* (Purdie & Dixon), January 8, 1767.

NEW YORK, N.Y.: MR. BURNS'S ASSEMBLY ROOM.

July 15, 17, 21, 24, 28, 31, August 4, 7, 1767 (8 perfs.).

The notice for the second night gives the full details.

"At Mr. Burns's ASSEMBLY ROOM, To-Morrow, being Friday the 7th of July, Mr. DOUGLASS Will Deliver A Lecture on HEADS. The Syllabus of which follows; PART Ist.   Introduction—Alexander—Cherokee—Quack-Doctor—Arms—Cuckold—Cornucopia—Lawyer—Oration in Praise of Law—Case, Daniel versus Dishclout—Journey Man's Jemmy—Sir Languish Lispey—Frizzl'd Bob—Jockey—Nobody—Arms of Nobody, Somebody, any Body, and every Body—Fate of Esteem, Generosity, Friendship, Gratitude, Common Sense, and Public Spirit—Genealogy of Genius—Sciences—Honesty—Flattery. PART IId. Physical Wig—Dissertation on Sneezing and Snuff taking—Blood—Woman of the Town—Tea Table Critic—Stock Jobber—Alderman Double Chin the Politician and Turtle-Eater—Gambler—his Funeral—his Monument—Anecdote of a Landlord and a Soldier—Yorick—Methodist. PART IIId. Riding Hood—Ranelagh Hood—Billingsgate—Laughing and crying Philosophy—Origin of Ladies Bonnets, Pompoons, Egrette's, and Curtain Lectures—Night Rail—Cheek Wrapper—Face painting exploded—Young Wife and Old Maid contrasted—Old Batchelor—Quaker Man and Woman—Nevernois Hat—Englishman and Frenchman—Virtuoso—Learn'd Critic. Between the Parts, and at the End of the Lecture, Singing by Mr. WOOLLS. To begin exactly at Seven o'Clock.—Tickets to be had at the Bible and Crown in Hanover-Square, and at Mr. Burns's Bar, at a Dollar each."[1]

" ***Mr. DOUGLASS proposes to deliver the Lecture on *Tuesdays* and *Fridays*, for the short Time he has to stay in Town."[2]

"—The Price of Admittance having been objected to, as rather too high, the Exhibiter has, by the Advice of his Friends lowered it to Half a DOLLAR." The following notice appeared in the same column: "The celebrated Lecture upon HEADS, Which has met with universal Applause, where ever it was delivered, in all Parts of Great Britain, Ireland and America, having in London been exhibited upwards of an Hundred Nights successively (Sundays excepted) to crowded Audiences, may be had, Price, One Shilling, At the Printing Office, at the Exchange."[3]

"To conclude with the DISSECTION of The Heart of a British SAILOR. AND, The Heart of his AGENT, for Prizes."[4]

"This will positively be the last Time of Performance."[5]

1. *New York Journal*, July 16, 1767.
2. *New York Mercury*, July 20, 1767.
3. Ibid., July 27, 1767.
4. Ibid., August 3, 1767.
5. *New York Journal*, August 6, 1767.

PHILADELPHIA, PA.: SOUTHWARK THEATRE.

September 9, 24, 1767 (2 perfs.).

"Messieurs DOUGLASS and HALLAM will deliver A Lecture on HEADS, &c. In Three Parts. To conclude with a DISSECTION of the HEART of a BRITISH SAILOR, and the HEART of his AGENT, for PRIZE MONEY. Between the Parts of the Lecture, SINGING by Mr. WOOLS and Miss HALLAM, accompanied by the BAND of His Majesty's EIGHTEENTH REGIMENT. To begin exactly at SEVEN o'Clock . . . Boxes

5s. Pit 3s. Gallery 2s."[1] The program was repeated on September 24. The starting time was changed, and we learn that the entertainment was also to include "A Humorous Scene of a *Drunken Man*, by Mr. Hallam . . . To Conclude with A Picture of a Play-House, or, Bucks, Have at ye All! by Mr. HALLAM."[2]

1. *Pennsylvania Chronicle*, August 31–September 7, 1767.
2. *Pennsylvania Journal*, September 24, 1767.

BRISTOL: COOPER'S HALL.

April 25, (26, 27?), 1768 (3? perfs.).

A Lecture on Hearts.

"FOR THREE NIGHTS ONLY . . . On MONDAY next, the 25th of April, A satyrical Lecture on HEARTS, With a PROLOGUE, Will be delivered by Miss ADCOCK, Who performed last Season at Bath, and has exhibited it 3 Months in Dublin, with universal Approbation. Part I.—Hearts more valuable than Heads—Heart-Turners, who—An upright Heart—A deform'd Royal Heart—The Heart of a British Sailor—The Heart of an Agent—A White Heart—The Heart of a Real Captain—A Light Heart—The Heart of an Usurer—The Heart of a Frenchman—The Heart of a Philosopher—And the Heart of an Attorney. Part II. FEMALE HEARTS.—A Tender Heart—A Stony Heart—A Bloated Heart—The Woman's Royal Heart—The Heart of a Virago—A Giddy Heart—A Coquette's Heart—A Frozen Heart—And the Heart of a Prude. Part III. A Beau's Heart—A Fox-hunter's Heart—An Atheist's Heart—A Double Heart—A Pious Heart—The Heart of a Physician—And the Heart of a Quack-Doctor. To conclude with a PARAPHRASE on Shakespear's Seven Ages. Written by G. A. STEVENS, Author of the Lecture on Heads. N.B. The Lecture will be delivered by Miss ADCOCK, in Boy's Cloaths.—Admittance 2s. . . . To begin at Seven o'Clock."[1]

1. *Felix Farley's Bristol Journal*, April 23, 1768.

NEW YORK, N.Y.: JOHN STREET THEATRE.

August 22, 29, 1768 (2 perfs.).

"And here is the very theatre itself opening, in hottest summer, mind you, . . ."[1]

"By permission of his Excellency the GOVERNOR. . . . Will be Delivered by Mr. DOUGLASS, and Mr. HALLAM, A serio comic satirical LECTURE, On HEADS, COATS of ARMS, WIGS, HORSE JOCKIES, SCIENCES, HONESTY, FLATTERY, LADIES HEAD DRESSES, &c. &c. Between the several Parts of the LECTURE, Singing by Miss

HALLAM. To begin exactly at Half an Hour after Seven o'Clock . . . Boxes, 5s. Pit, 3s. Gallery, 2s."[2]

1. George C. D. Odell, *Annals of the New York Stage* (New York, 1927), vol. 1, p. 145.
2. *New York Journal*, August 18, 1768.

BRISTOL: COOPER'S HALL.

December 20, 21, 23, 26, 28, 30, 1768 (6 perfs.).

December 20, 21, 23. [By Permission of the Right Worshipful the Mayor] "Next MONDAY, TUESDAY, and FRIDAY Evenings, at the Coopers-Hall, beginning exactly at Six o'Clock GEORGE ALEXANDER STEVENS, Will repeat His LECTURE upon HEADS, With all the Additions, &c. for the Years 1767–1768. N.B. Some time after the Author had been favoured with the Approbation of the Public, a most wretched Compilation appeared in the Magazines, and was sold as a Pamphlet, call'd *George Alexander Stevens's Lecture upon Heads*; and Head Lecturers immediately spread over England; some of them taking his Name, some gave out he had taught them for a Sum of Money, some published in their Bills he was a Partner with them in the Profits, and others advertised they had bought his Apparatus, and were his Successors, as he had left off Lecturing upon receiving from them a large Premium.

"Thus he has been most iniquitously Pilfer'd, not only of his Property, but even of his Reputation, as a man of either common Sense, or common Education (as far as the Lecture upon Heads, as Printed, may be supposed to be his Writing) In Justification of himself, he has ever since exerted his utmost Abilities towards enriching the Lecture with *new Characters*, and by making such other Alterations, as appeared requisite for keeping Pace with the *Foibles* as well as the *Fashions* of the *Times*."[1]

December 26, 28, 30. ". . . LECTURE upon HEADS, WILL BE REPEATED At the COOPERS-HALL, On MONDAY, WEDNESDAY, and FRIDAY Evenings next Week, Being the 26th, 28th, and 30th of this Instant, *And positively no longer.*"[2]

1. *Felix Farley's Bristol Journal*, December 17, 1768.
2. Ibid., December 24, 1768.

PHILADELPHIA, PA.: SOUTHWARK THEATRE.

December 30, 1768, January 6, 1769 (2 perfs.).

Mr. Wall does the Noses: "POSITIVELY THE LAST PLAY. Never acted in America. By AUTHORITY. By the AMERICAN COMPANY. At the THEATRE in *Southwark*,

To-morrow, being *Friday* the 30th of *December*, will be presented, a TRAGEDY, called ALEXANDER THE GREAT, OR THE RIVAL QUEENS. [Followed by singing by Mr. Woolls and Miss Storer, a satirical oration on the Cock-Lane Ghost] ... After which Mr. WALL will deliver a Critical Dissertation, upon NOSES: In which will be Exhibited; A turn-up nose; A ruby Nose; A Roman Nose; A blunt Nose, and a hooked, or parrots-beak Nose. . . ."[1]

And the following week: "By AUTHORITY. The Company, in order to perform the Play for the Benefit of the Debtors, having been detain'd, beyond the Stage to which they had appointed to go to New-York, have now an Opportunity of gratifying those Ladies and Gentlemen, who could not get admittance on Monday: . . . [the bill is repeated]."[2]

1. *Pennsylvania Journal*, December 29, 1768.
2. Ibid., January 5, 1769.

BATH: MR. SIMPSON'S CONCERT ROOM.

January 4, 6, 11?, 13, 1769 (4? perfs.).

A few days later Stevens was in Bath. "At Mr. SIMPSON's Concert-Room, On Wednesday and Friday Mornings, the 4th and 6th of *January* next, GEORGE ALEXANDER STEVENS, By Particular Desire, will repeat his LECTURE UPON HEADS, With all its Additions, &c. The Lectures will begin exactly at TWELVE o'Clock each Morning, and end precisely at TWO. Tickets to be had, at Half a Crown each . . ."[1] The advertisement was repeated twice with minor variations, i.e., the starting time was moved to half past twelve and, as with the previous Bristol notice, the "Alterations and Additions, for the Years 1767, 1768" were noted.[2]

1. *Bath and Bristol Chronicle*, December 29, 1768.
2. Ibid., January 5, 12, 1769.

LONDON: HAYMARKET THEATRE.

March 28, 30, April 4, 6, 7, 10, 12, 14, 17, 19, 22, 24, 26, 28, May 2, 4, 1769 (16 perfs.).

"By PARTICULAR DESIRE At the Theatre Royal in the Haymarket, This Day, March 28, GEORGE ALEXANDER STEVENS will deliver his LECTURE upon HEADS With all the Additions, Alterations, &c. For the Years 1767 and 1768. It will be divided into five Parts, beginning exactly at Seven o'clock. And the Lecture concludes precisely at Half past Nine."[1]

March 30. "N.B. The Lecture not being advertised yesterday in this Paper for this Evening; was owing to a Mistake committed by the Person who was to carry the Advertisement."[2]

April 8. "The Theatre being engaged for a Play and Oratorio is the Reason of the Lecturer altering his Nights."[3]

May 4. "Positively the LAST TIME . . . As Mr. Foote will open for the Summer Season very soon, several necessary Alterations must be immediately made in the Haymarket Theatre Royal. Mr. Stevens therefore humbly presumes to acquaint the Ladies and Gentlemen who intend to honour him with their Company, that he can only repeat his Lecture This Evening."[4]

May 9. "For the Public Advertiser A CARD The Author and Exhibitor of the Lecture upon Heads takes the Liberty to present his Duty to the public, and hopes, for the Honour and Approbation so lately granted him, he may be permitted to subscribe himself with the utmost respect. Ladies and Gentlemen Your most obliged and Most Humble Servant, G. A. STEVENS. Haymarket Theatre May 6, 1769."[5]

1. *Public Advertiser*, March 28, 1769.
2. Ibid., March 30, 1769.
3. Ibid., April 8, 1769.
4. Ibid., May 4, 1769.
5. Ibid., May 9, 1769.

NEW YORK, N.Y.: JOHN STREET THEATRE.

April 24, 1769 (1 perf.).

"By Permission of his Excellency the Governor. By the AMERICAN COMPANY. For the benefit of Miss Cheer . . . After the Play, [ALEXANDER THE GREAT] Mr. WALL will deliver a Critical Dissertation on NOSES: In which he will exhibit, *a turning up Nose, a Ruby Nose, Roman Nose, Gluttons Blunt Nose, and an hook'd Nose,* . . ."[1]

1. *New York Mercury*, April 24, 1769.

NEW YORK, N.Y.: JOHN STREET THEATRE.

May 25, 1769 (1 perf.).

This benefit for Mrs. Douglass, which Odell called "truly a colossal bill",[1] began with *Richard III*, was followed by various entertainments, and concluded with *Love a-la-Mode.* For one of the entertainments Mr. Douglass presented: "(From the Lecture upon Heads) The HEAD of a LAWYER, and pronounce an Oration in Praise of the Law; with a humourous LAW-CASE, DANIEL VERSUS DISHCLOUT."[2]

1. George C. D. Odell, *Annals of the New York Stage* (New York, 1927), vol. 1, pp. 150–51.
2. *New York Mercury*, May 22, 1769.

NEW YORK, N.Y.: JOHN STREET THEATRE.

June 29, 1769 (1 perf.).

"By Permission of his Excellency the Governor . . . Mr. HENRY Will deliver a moral, satirical, and entertaining *Lecture*, on HEARTS, (Being the first Time of its Exhibition in America) The Original Prologue, by Mr. HENRY. With Entertainments, viz. End of the Lecture . . . N.B. As several Ladies and Gentlemen, have complain'd of the Late Hours of the Theatre; in order to endeavour at making the Entertainment as agreeable as possible, the Lecture will begin precisely at 8 o'Clock, and to be over by half after Ten; for which Intention the Audience may depend there will be no Delay between the different Parts . . . Boxes 6s. Pit 4s. Gallery, 2s."[1]

1. *New York Journal*, June 29, 1769.

BOSTON, MASS.: A LARGE ROOM IN BRATTLE STREET (FORMERLY GREEN AND WALLER'S STORE).

July 24, 31, August 2, 4, 7, 9, 11, 14, 16, 18, 1769 (10 perfs.).

"Mr. Douglass Will THIS EVENING, Deliver a Moral, Satirical, and Entertaining LECTURE, On various Subjects; among which are, THE HEADS of Alexander the Great;—a Cherokee Chief; a Cuckold;—a Quack Doctor;—a Lawyer, with an Oration in Praise of Law, illustrated by a Law-Case, *Daniel versus Dishclout*;—Nobody;—The Arms of Nobody, Somebody, Anybody, and Everybody;—The Sciences;—Esteem;—Generosity;—Public Spirit;—Gratitude and Common Sense;—Honesty;—Flattery;—Physical Wig;—Sneezing and Snuff-taking;—Gamester;—Yorick;—Ladies Head-Dresses; Pernicious Custom of Painting;—Eulogium on the Ladies of America, &c. &c. &c. &c. &c. *To begin precisely at Eight o'Clock*. Tickets for Admission may be had at the Bunch of Grapes in King-Street, and at Green & Russell's in Queen-Street, at a DOLLAR each."[1]

July 31. "This present Monday, July 31st, 1769 And on WEDNESDAY and FRIDAY next, and *No longer:* . . . at HALF-a-DOLLAR each."[2]

August 7. "(By particular Desire) . . . To conclude with the Head of a Learned Critic, or Book-Worm."[3]

August 14. "(Positively the last Week) . . . Mr. Douglass, Will deliver the LECTURE on H E A D S, Coats of Arms, Wigs, Ladies Head-dresses, &c.—After which he will read some Select Pieces from POPE, DRYDEN, ADDISON, and other celebrated English POETS. Among the Pieces intended for this Evening, an ODE for St. Cecilia's Day, called ALEXANDER'S FEAST, or the Power of MUSIC, will be pronounced."[4]

Slight changes in the program were made during this extended run, and the ticket price was cut in half after opening night. The practice of scaling ticket prices, common in the larger theatres, was not used here.

1. *Boston Post-Boy and Advertiser*, July 24, 1769.
2. Ibid., July 31, 1769.
3. *Massachusetts Gazette*, August 7, 1769.
4. Ibid., August 14, 1769.

CHARLESTON, S.C.: MR. HAWES'S LONG ROOM.

August 2, 1769 (1 perf.).

In July 1769 John Henry (with Miss Ann Storer) came to Charleston to negotiate the construction of a theatre in that city. He arrived at a bad time. Charleston was in the midst of various political and economic disruptions, and Henry was forced to abandon his plans.[1] He wrote a long letter of appreciation to the citizenry and in the same column of the newspaper stated: "HENRY intending to depart the Province in about Ten Days, proposes to entertain the Public for a Couple of Nights, with LECTURES on DIFFERENT SUBJECTS; and by Permission of his Honour the Lieutenant-Governor, *Wednesday next, being the 2d Instant, at Mr.* Hawes's Long-Room *on the Bay, will deliver,* LECTURE on HEADS. With SINGING between the different Parts, by Miss STORER . . . TICKETS, at a Dollar each . . ."[2] No other reference to a performance subsequent to August 2 has been found. The "Couple of Nights," therefore, remains unconfirmed.

1. See Mary Julia Curtis, "The Early Charleston Stage, 1703–1798" (Ph.D. diss., Indiana University, 1968), pp. 88–92, for an extended and lucid account of the difficulties. Curtis suggests that Henry presented the *Lecture* "in order to defray expenses before returning to Douglass," p. 90.
2. *South Carolina Gazette and Country Journal*, August 1, 1769.

PORTSMOUTH, N.H.: MR. STAVERS'S LARGE ROOM.

September 8, 1769 (1 perf.).

"By AUTHORITY. This Evening, . . . Mr. Douglass, WILL DELIVER A LECTURE ON HEADS, Coats of Arms, Ladies Head-Dresses, &c. &c. &c. IN THREE PARTS . . . To begin exactly at Seven o'Clock . . . HALF A DOLLAR EACH."[1]

1. *New Hampshire Gazetteer*, September 8, 1769.

PHILADELPHIA, PA.: SOUTHWARK THEATRE.

September 14, 1769 (1 perf.).

"BY AUTHORITY . . . Mr. HALLAM and Mr. HENRY WILL DELIVER A LECTURE on HEADS. With Entertainments of Singing by Miss HALLAM . . . An Occasional Prologue by Mr. HALLAM. To CONCLUDE with the CAMERA OBSCURA; As introduced with great applause in HARLEQUIN'S INVASION, at the Theatre Royal, Drury Lane,—Being the first time of its exhibition in America. . . . To begin precisely at *Seven* o'clock. BOXES 7s. 6d. PIT 5s. Gallery 3s."[1]

1. *Pennsylvania Journal*, September 14, 1769.

BRISTOL: MERCHANT-TAYLOR'S HALL.

December 1, 1769 (1 perf.).

An anonymous performance of Hearts: "THE LECTURE ON HEARTS, with the Recital of Mr. Garrick's ODE in Honour of Shakespeare, will be performed (by particular Desire) at the Merchant-Taylor's-Hall, in Broad-street, next Wednesday Night (instead of Cooper's-Hall) to begin at Six o'Clock.—Admittance 2s. 6d. N.B. Good Fire in the Hall."[1]

1. *Felix Farley's Bristol Journal*, November 25, 1769.

PHILADELPHIA, PA.: LODGE ROOM, SOUTHWARK THEATRE (?).

June 6, 1770 (1 perf.).

". . . Mr. WALL will deliver A RHAPSODY, Compiled from the works of George Alexander Stevens, Esq; author of the much admired lecture on heads. Part the first. Fate of Genius; general opinions; toad eaters; virtue; self-conceit; the commedians; puppet shew; chimney sweeper; fortune of war, and charms of peace; prodigies; elopement; and physical account of snoring. Part the second. History of the human mind; honour; duellist; originality of ghosts, and anatomy of phantoms; story of Phelim O'Monaghan; charity; Squeezum's monument; advice to eloping ladies; the tumbler; female opinions; private balls; grief; card playing; gambler; and advice to authors. Part the third. Feathers of the turf; race week; a fool; origin of fools; woman of pleasure; dungeon; and a jackass. Tickets, at half a dollar each . . . To begin at seven o'clock. After the exhibition, ladies and gentlemen who may choose to dance, the musick will attend them for that purpose. Mr. Wall begs leave to assure the public, that, as his sole design in this exhibition, is to present them with a New Evening's Entertainment, no party, sect, or denomination whatsoever is aimed at; folly is ridiculed, vice exposed, and virtue applauded; and he flatters himself, that those ladies and gentlemen, who may honour him with their company, will find an entertainment, not altogether unworthy their notice."[1]

1. *Pennsylvania Chronicle*, May 28–June 24, 1770.

N.P.

1772?

Elizabeth Farren, one of the most talented and popular actresses of the period, seems to have performed the *Lecture* at a very early age: "[Joseph Younger, later co-manager of the Liverpool Theatre] met with her, when barely entering her teens, in a barn, where she was delivering GEORGE ALEXANDER STEVENS'S Lecture upon Heads, to supply the necessities of herself, her mother, and her sister. YOUNGER was struck with the *toute ensemble*, and prevailed upon Mrs. FARREN to article her daughter to himself (it being a condition to maintain the family till the articles expired), and brought her out at *Covent Garden*, at which Theatre he was Prompter."[1]

Another source states that she performed the *Lecture upon Hearts*: ". . . Elizabeth made one of her earliest appearances in public, when she gave a 'Lecture upon Hearts', but, whether as a member of some itinerant company of players, or in what place, it is difficult to determine. At that time her age could not have exceeded eleven years. The enterprise was doubtless suggested by George Alexander Stevens' popular lecture on heads."[2]

1. James Winston, *The Theatric Tourist: By a Theatric Amateur* (London, 1805), p. 51.
2. R. J. Broadbent, *Elizabeth Farren, Countess of Darby* (reprinted from the Transactions of the Historical Society of Lancashire and Cheshire), vol. 61, p. 6.

LONDON: HAYMARKET, THEATRE ROYAL.

March 26, 31, April 2, 7, 9, 11, 21, 23, 25, 28, 30, May 2, 5, 7, 9, 11, 1772 (16 perfs.).

This run is the basis of the aforementioned edition of "An Essay on Satirical Entertainments" (q.v.), which tells us that "the one shilling gallery has never been opened during this exhibition at the Haymarket."[1] Stevens, in the notices, indicates a possible reason for restricting the size of the house. He may also have discovered that the apparatus was ineffective when projected such a great distance: "By PARTICULAR DESIRE THIS DAY at the Theatre Royal in the Haymarket, GEORGE ALEXANDER STEVENS will deliver his Original Lecture upon Heads. With new Decorations; beginning precisely at Seven o'Clock, and ending at Half an Hour past Nine. The Doors to be opened at Six, Places and Tickets for the Boxes to be taken at the Theatre. The great Exertion requisite to support this Lecture by a single Person in so extensive a Place as a Theatre Royal, deters the Exhibitor from attempting it oftener than twice a week. G. A. STEVENS therefore begs Leave to acquaint Ladies and Gentlemen, that it will be repeated only on Tuesday and Thursday Evenings in the ensuing Weeks. Boxes 5s. Pit 3s. Gall 2s."[2]

April 11. "The last Time 'till Easter Tuesday."[3]

May 11. "POSITIVELY the last ... N.B. As the Lecturer quits the Theatre Tonight, he thinks it is his Duty to thank the Town for the generous Reception he has met with this Season, which has exceeded his most sanguine Expectations: All the Return in his Power is thus to subscribe himself, the Public's very much obliged And very grateful humble Servant, GEORGE ALEXANDER STEVENS."[4]

1. "An Essay on Satirical Entertainments," (London, 1772), pp. 42–43.
2. *Public Advertiser*, March 26, 1772. Stevens also performed on Saturdays during the run and closed on a Monday.
3. *Public Advertiser*, April 11, 1772.
4. Ibid., May 11, 1772.

PHILADELPHIA, PA.: THE LONG ROOM IN VIDELL'S ALLEY.

July 27, August 1, 4, 6, 8?, 18, 1772 (6 perfs.).

The American Company left Philadelphia in 1770 for the southern colonies and did not return until 1772 when it reopened the season at the Southwark on

October 28. During the interim the *Lecture on Heads* was presented on six occasions by Mr. Foy during July and August of 1772.

July 27. "By PERMISSION. The LADIES AND GENTLEMEN, WHO intend to honour the EXHIBITION of the LECTURE on HEADS, with their presence, are requested to take notice, that the first time of performing will be this evening, the 27th instant, at the Long-room in Videll's Alley, between Chestnut and Walnut streets, in Second-street.*** . . . Tickets to admit two Ladies, or a Lady and a Gentleman at Ten Shillings each; single tickets at One Dollar each. No money taken at the door."[1]

August 1. "By PERMISSION. (SECOND NIGHT) THE LADIES and GENTLEMEN Who intend to honour the Exhibition of the LECTURE on HEADS, with their Presence, are requested to take Notice, that THIS EVENING the following SYLLABUS will be delivered, in Three Parts; PART I. Alexander the Great—Cherokee Chief—Quack Doctor—Cuckold—Lawyer—Humourous Oration in praise of the Law—Horse Jockies—Nobody—Lottery of Life—Nobody's—Somebody's—Anybody's—and Everybody's Coats of Arms. With a Song called the Highland Queen; by the same Gentleman who met with universal Approbation on Monday Night. PART II. Ladies Heads—Riding Hood—Ranelagh Hood—Billingsgate—Laughing and Crying Philosophers—Venus's Girdle—Cleopatra—French Night Cap—Face Painting—Old Maid—Young Married Lady—Old Batchelor—Lass of the Spirit—Two Hats contrasted—and Two Heads contrasted. With the Heroines or Modern Memoirs of some well known (English) Ladies of Fashion. PART III. Physical Wig—Dissertation on Sneezing and Snuff-taking—Life of a Blood—Woman of the Town—city politician humourously described—Gambler's Three Faces—Life and Death of a Wit—with a Tabernacle Harangue—to conclude with an occasional Epilogue—and a Song called Kate of Aberdeen. It is needless to say any Thing in favour of these well known and much admired Lectures, but to assure the Ladies and Gentlemen, that the Exhibitor has spared no Cost or Pains to render them agreeable; by which means, he has not only made the Room commodious, but elegant for their reception. He further begs Leave to acquaint them, that he has provided the best Band of Music the City can produce. The curtain to be drawn up precisely at half past Seven o'Clock . . . Every Precaution shall be taken to prevent improper Company, and the Room from being crowded."[2]

August 4. Same as above with very slight variations.[3]

August 6. "BY PERMISSION. Fourth Night . . . The curtain to be drawn up precisely at half past seven o'clock."[4]

"*** On account of the intense heat of the weather, the exhibition of the Lecture on Heads, is obliged to be deferred until further notice. The Exhibitor begs leave to acquaint the Public, that the next time of performing will be for the benefit of the Hospital."[5]

August 18. Note the change in curtain time and ticket prices: "By PERMISSION. For the Benefit of the Hospital. The Public are requested to take Notice, that the sixth time of exhibiting the LECTURES on HEADS, will be on Tuesday Evening, the 18th Instant . . . Price Half a Dollar each . . . The Curtain to be drawn up precisely at 8 o'Clock."[6]

At the conclusion of the run, this notice appeared:

"The Exhibitor of the LECTURES on HEADS, returns his most grateful thanks to the Ladies and Gentlemen who have honoured his exhibition with their presence, and takes this opportunity of acquainting them, and the public in general, that he intends to open his DANCING SCHOOL on the first of October next, with a Ball, at which time some of the scholars, whom he has already taught since his residence in this city, will perform some new dances: He further begs leave to acquaint them, that the method he intends teaching is the newest and most approved, now practised in all the polite assemblies in Europe. Exclusive of the minuet, country dance and Scotch reel, he teaches (such of his pupils as he finds has a capacity) the Allemande, Cotillon, and Leuvre, and takes particular care with respect to their dancing a proper country dance step, without any extra charge; and he humbly submits to the candid public, how to determine between him and others of the profession with respect to their abilities. The conducting his school with the utmost decorum shall be his constant study. N.B. He also teacheth FENCING."[7]

1. *Pennsylvania Packet,* July 27, 1772.
2. *Pennsylvania Chronicle,* July 25–August 1, 1772.
3. *Pennsylvania Packet,* August 3, 1772.
4. *Pennsylvania Gazette,* August 5, 1772.
5. *Pennsylvania Packet,* August 10, 1772.
6. *Pennsylvania Chronicle,* August 8–15, 1772.
7. Ibid. August 22–29, 1772.

NEW YORK, N.Y.: ASSEMBLY ROOM IN THE BROADWAY.

August 31, September 3, 7, 1772 (3 perfs.).

Less than two weeks later Mr. Foy was in New York, where he performed the *Lecture* three times and presented a concert and ball before returning to Philadelphia to open his dancing school.

August 31. "By PERMISSION: The Gentleman who lately arrived from London, and has had the honour of exhibiting (by permission) in Philadelphia, Mr.

George Alexander Steavens's [*sic*] celebrated lecture on Heads; Presents his most humble and respectful compliments to the Ladies and Gentlemen of this City, and acquaints them, that he intends (under their patronage) to exhibit for three nights, in the Assembly Room, in the Broad-Way, the following Syllabus in three parts, with a concert of vocal and instrumental music. [The syllabus which follows is almost identical to the one printed for his August 1 performance in Philadelphia.] The exhibiter thinks it needless to say any thing in favour of these well known and much admired lectures; but, begs leave to acquaint the Ladies and Gentlemen, that he flatters himself with being able to produce a musical genius, who, for his vocal abilities, is not inferior, (if equalled), to any publick performer on this side the atlantic—As Monday evening the 31st inst. is fixed for the first night, it is humbly requested, that those Ladies and Gentlemen who intend to honour him with their presence, will be so obliging as to subscribe their names at any of the following places, Mr. James Rivington, bookseller, in Wall-Street—Mr. Hugh Gaine, Printer, in Hanover-Square—Mr. John Holt, Printer, in Dock-Street—The merchant's Coffee-House, and at Mr. Hull's tavern, in the Broad-Way—Where tickets will be delivered—Price one dollar each."[1]

September 3. ". . . this Evening . . . to begin at seven o'clock."[2] The syllabus is the same as above.

September 7. ". . . this present Evening."[3] Same as above. Three days later Mr. Foy announced his preparations for a Concert and Ball (before his "departure from this City for Philadelphia").[4]

1. *New York Journal*, August 27, 1772.
2. Ibid., September 3, 1772.
3. *New York Gazette*, September 7, 1772.
4. *New York Journal*, September 10, 1772.

NEW YORK, N.Y.: MR. COX'S LONG ROOM, MR. DE LA MONTAGNE'S LONG ROOM.

January 19, 26, 29, 1773 (3 perfs.).

Mr. Foy returned to New York in January for a three-night stand performing at two different locations.

January 19. "At Mr. Cox's Long-Room, near the Liberty pole, to-morrow evening the 19th inst. will be exhibited, the celebrated LECTURE ON HEADS, with singing by the young man who has already been so justly admired. Tickets 5s. each."[1]

January 26. "The Exhibitor of the Lectures on Heads, returns his most grateful acknowledgments to the Ladies and Gentlemen who favoured him with their Presence on Tuesday Night Last; and takes this Method of acquainting them, that (by particular Request) he intends repeating them, at Mr. De La Montanye's Long-Room near the Liberty Pole on Tuesday Evening, the 26th Instant, with Singing, by the young Man, to conclude with a Ball—Tickets to be had of Mr. De La Montanye, Price 5 s. each."[2]

January 29. "(BY PERMISSION.) At Mr. De La Montagne's Long Room . . . The Exhibiter of the Lecture on Heads, returns his most sincere Thanks, to the Ladies and Gentlemen, who honoured him with their Presence on Tuesday Night last, and acquaints them, that on Friday Evening, the 29th Instant, (by particular Desire) he will deliver the following SALLABUS [*sic*], in three Parts, with a select Number of favourite Songs, between each Part, by the celebrated young Man who is so justly admired. [The syllabus for the *Lecture* which follows is the same as the one used for the July/August 1772 performances in Philadelphia.] . . .*** Mr. De La Montagne begs Leave to acquaint the Ladies and Gentlemen, that particular Care shall be taken to have all the Rooms well aired and properly illuminated, and every necessary Attendance given on his Part."[3]

Several New York booksellers took advantage of Stevens's popularity by advertising two of his published works during the month of January. The *Lecture*, "just published," was offered by Hodge and Shober, and by Samuel Dellap. The latter was a Philadelphia publisher and bookseller who was in New York for a short time on a book-buying trip locating himself at the shop of the merchant Thomas Nixon. Dellap had published an edition of the *Lecture* in September 1772. The bookseller James Rivington offered "Master George Alexander Stephens's Collection of Songs, jocund and satyrical, of which it were sufficient to add, that it is a genuine Publication of the pleasantest Professor of Comicality now alive, and will cost each Convivialist Seven Shillings—principal Money of New-York."[4]

1. *New York Mercury*, January 18, 1773.
2. *New York Journal*, January 21, 1773.
3. Ibid., January 28, 1773.
4. *New York Mercury*, January 11, 1773.

NEW YORK, N.Y.: BALL ROOM AT MR. HULL'S TAVERN IN THE BROAD WAY.

February 8?, 16, March 5, 1773 (2 perfs.).

February 16. "Mr. Hoar begs leave to acquaint the Ladies and Gentlemen of this city, that he has just received a copy of Mr. George Alexander Steevens's new Lectures (with charactura heads and dresses) as they are now delivered in London by that celebrated Genius; which Mr. Hoar proposes (under their patronage) exhibiting on Tuesday the 16th inst. in the Ball room at Mr. Hull's tavern in the Broadway; with a humorous epilogue, and a real representation of a married blood of the first rate, after he has been *keeping it up*. Between the acts, the young lad will sing a number of favourite songs, with proper accompaniments; the whole to conclude with a BALL, under the same restrictions of the concert and ball which he had the honour of conducting on the 5th of October last. Price of tickets one Dollar each."[1]

March 5. "Mr. HOAR Returns his most sincere Thanks to the Gentlemen who have honoured his Subscription with their Names, (for the LECTURE and BALL, to be given on FRIDAY EVENING, the 5th Instant, at Mr. Hull's Ball-Room, in the Broadway,) and humbly solicits those Ladies and Gentlemen (of Distinction) who have not yet subscribed, to honour him with their Presence on that Night. TICKETS one Dollar each, to be delivered by Mr. Hoar, and Mr. Hull; at whose House may seen a List of the present Subscribers."[2]

1. *New York Journal*, February 11, 1773.
2. Ibid., March 4, 1773.

NEW HAVEN, CONN.: YALE COLLEGE, MR. ATWATER'S HOUSE.

April 13, 1773 (1 perf.)

"At the anniversary celebration of 1773, Linonia [a Yale literary society] presented the first part of the *Lecture on Heads*, a form of entertainment frequently offered by Lewis Hallam and other early professional actors in America. This was followed after dinner (the meeting was held at the house of Thomas Atwater) by a performance of *The West Indian*, . . ."[1]

1. John L. Clark, "Educational Dramatics in Nineteenth-Century Colleges," *The History of Speech Education in America*, ed. Karl L. Wallace (New York, 1954), p. 527.

LICHFIELD.

Early October (?) 1773 (1 or more perfs.).

Evidence for this performance comes from a letter written by David Garrick to his brother Peter advising him of Stevens's forthcoming provincial tour. Garrick refers to Stevens as his "old Friend & Acquaintance," but I have not discovered any other documentary evidence to reinforce this. Garrick was a severe critic and not prone to unconsidered endorsements.

"Adelphi—Sepr 24. 1773 Dear Peter. I must recommend, (not with yᵉ usual form, & Spirit of recommendation), but with all my Pow'r & influence, if it extends so far as the City of Lichfield, my old Friend & Acquaintance *Mʳ George*

Alexander Stevens, a Name well known, & a Person deservedly applauded, for his Peculiarity of Genius, & Universal Love of Mirth & Letters—He has great Merit, & more than all he is a very honest, liberal-minded Man, & deserves Every Encouragement that has been given to him—As he is travelling Your Way with his heads, I must beg leave to introduce him to You, & yᵣ friends, not my dear Peter, that I think You & yᵣ friends want the least Amendment of Yᵣ Own, but that You may laugh with my Friend Stevens at yᵉ heads of other People—In short, I have so great a desire that he Should be well receiv'd, & approv'd at my own Native Place, (as I always call it, tho dropt at Hereford) that I beg You will let yᵉ whole Town know that I beg it, as a particular favour, that they will attend his Lectures—If any should be discontented with his Performance, I beg that I may treat them, & that You will pay for all the Malecontents, & draw upon Me for the Sum total—I need not desire You, to let him taste yᵣ Lichfield Mutton & best Ale, Your Own Heart always prevents my Wishes in these Matters. always in a hurry— . . . If the ladies expect a *Macaroni Player* in Master George, they will be dreadfully disappointed—"[1]

1. D. M. Little and G. M. Kahrl, eds., *The Letters of David Garrick* (Cambridge, Mass., 1963), vol. 2, pp. 899–900.

NEW YORK, N.Y.: THE BALLROOM AT MR. HULL'S TAVERN IN THE BROADWAY.

July 21, 28, 1773 (2 perfs.).

"By Permission of his Excellency the Governor. Mr. WALL, Comedian, Will exhibit, at Mr. Hull's great Room, on Wednesday Evening, the 21st of July, 1773, A NEW LECTURE Written by the Author of the much admired LECTURE ON HEADS. The Paintings, &c. are entirely new, and never before exhibited in America.

"SYLLABUS. FIRST PART. Introduction—Physical Imitation—modern Book Building—Bust of Sir Dimple Daisy—a broad Grinner—Sheep's Tail Macaroni—thick Stock ditto—turn down Collar—Master Jackey . . . Diana the Huntress—a Finnical—a Blood after he has kept it up—a modern Connoisseur—a Reasoner—Election Picture—Origin of Money—the Center of Friendship—Head of Somebody—and the whole System of modern English politics displayed in the various Heads of Busybody, Anybody, Somebody, Nobody, and Everybody.

"SECOND PART. Ladies Heads in high Taste—Mens Hats—Macaroni Thanet—corded Thanet—broad Band—Court Hat—a Fan Tail—Ladies Morning Head-Dresses—Head of a Jew Conjurer—ancient Conjurer—Dexterity of Hand.

"THIRD PART. Ladies high Head Dresses—artificial Candle-light Face, and the

Appearance of the same Face next Morning—the grand secret of Attraction—
two Portraits of the same Lady in a good and ill Humour—Courtship and
Matrimony—matrimonial Vis-à-Vis—the Laws considered, Case, Bellum versus Borum—compleat Macaroni—Conclusion.

"To begin at Seven o'Clock. Care will be taken to keep the Room cool. Tickets to
be had at Mr. Gaine's, Mr. Rivington's, Mr. Hull's, and of Mr. Wall, at Mr.
Pettit's for 5s. each."[1]

1. *New York Gazette*, July 19, 1773; *New York Mercury*, July 26, 1773.

ANNAPOLIS, MD.: THE THEATRE.

October 7?, 15, 1773 (2 perfs.).

"BY AUTHORITY. MR. WALL, COMEDIAN, On the evening after the last PLAY, Will
Present, At The THEATRE, A NEW LECTURE Performed with great applause to a
very polite and judicious audience at New-York, [see July 21, 28, 1773][1] and
likewise at Philadelphia: [I have not located a notice of an earlier performance
by Wall in this city] written by the author of the much admired LECTURE ON
HEADS. The paintings, &c. are entirely new, and never before exhibited in
ANNAPOLIS. . . . Tickets to be had of Mr. WALL at Mr. PHILIP MERONEY'S, of Mr.
REYNOLDS, and at the COFFEE-HOUSE.—Boxes Five Shillings—Pit 3/9. To begin
at Six o'Clock."[2]

1. The syllabus for this Annapolis performance was the same as the one used for the
   New York engagement.
2. *Maryland Gazette* (Annapolis), October 7, 14, 1773.

PHILADELPHIA, PA.: LONG ROOM IN VIDELL'S ALLEY.

November 22, 1773 (1 perf.).

Mr. Wall repeated the lecture a month later. Note that he does not refer to an
earlier Philadelphia performance here. The syllabus is the same as the one
used in New York and Annapolis: "BY AUTHORITY . . . Mr. WALL will exhibit A
NEW LECTURE, Performed with great applause to a very polite and judicious
audience at New-York, and, likewise in Maryland. Written by the author of the
much admired LECTURE on Heads. The paintings, &c. are entirely new . . . To
begin at Six O'Clock.—Tickets to be had of the bar-keeper at the Coffee-house,
and of Mr. Wall, at Mr. Marshall's, opposite the Theatre, for 3s. 9d."[1]

1. *Pennsylvania Journal*, November 17, 1773.

MANCHESTER: THE EXCHANGE.

Christmas 1773 (1 perf.).

"At Christmas, 1773 Mr Stevens lectured at our Exchange, to which building there was only one entrance; and as the lecturer was afraid, as he stated, that it would prove inconvenient for ladies and gentlemen 'to be detained at the door while money was weighed,' he hoped they would bring silver or tickets."[1] Although unconfirmed by the source, this was almost certainly the *Lecture on Heads*.

1. Richard Wright Procter, *Manchester in Holiday Dress* (London and Manchester, 1866), p. 31.

DUBLIN: MUSIC HALL, FISHAMBLE STREET.

1774 (? perf.).

This entry is based on an observation in John O'Keeffe's memoirs. The year of performance is implied but not confirmed. The assumption of performance is reasonable, however, since Stevens presented the *Lecture* in late 1773 and at the end of 1774. O'Keeffe may have been referring to an earlier performance, but it is unlikely that Stevens would have made the arduous trip to Dublin and not have offered his bread and butter piece.

"In 1774 I dined in company, at Mr. Heaphy's, with George Alexander Stevens; a short figure, round, good-humoured, ruddy face; he wore a wig, like his natural hair, in ringlets. The performance of his 'Lecture on Heads,' given by himself at the Music Hall, Fishamble-street, Dublin, gave me as much pleasure as any theatrical exhibition could; his powerful humour in delineating his variety of characters was such a vehicle for the excellent wit of the piece. When in private company with him, at my own house, I ventured to sing a whimsical song of my writing, and he prophesied I should yet cut a great figure as a dramatic author. This was a star of hope from such a bright fellow in that way, as the author of 'Once the Gods of the Greeks, at ambrosial feast.' "[1]

1. John O'Keeffe, *Recollections of the Life of John O'Keeffe* (London, 1826), vol. 1, pp. 302–3.

CHARLESTON, S.C.: CHURCH STREET THEATRE.

July 4, 6, 1774 (2 perfs.).

By mid-June 1774 the American Company had finished its Charleston season.

During the remaining weeks of the month its members set sail for New York, Philadelphia, and England. Richard Goodman remained behind.

July 4. "*** We hear that on MONDAY-EVENING the 4th of July, will be delivered at the THEATRE in Church-street, by Mr. GOODMAN, of the *American Company*, and Mr. ALLEN, from the *Theatre-Royal* in Edinburgh, *George Alexander Stevens*'s celebrated LECTURE on HEADS, which has been exhibited upwards of *Three hundred* successive Nights to crowded Audiences in LONDON, with universal Applause."[1]

July 6. "To the Lovers of *Novelty, Humour, Satire, Pleasure* and *Instruction*. For TWO NIGHTS only. On WEDNESDAY Evening, the 6th of July, will be delivered, at the THEATRE in Church-Street, by Mr. GOODMAN and Mr. ALLEN from the Theatre-Royal in Edinburgh; GEORGE ALEXANDER STEVENS'S Celebrated LECTURE ON HEADS, Which, at different Seasons since its first Exhibition, has been repeated, upwards of *Five hundred* Nights, [note the increase!] to *crowded Audiences* in *London*, and met with the most universal Applause. THE HEADS, which are the Subjects of this Night's Lecture, are the following: *Alexander the Great, Cherokee Chief, Quack Doctor, Cuckold, Counsellor, Horse-Jockey, Nobody, Flattery, Fine Lady, Billingsgate Moll, Laughing Philosopher, Crying Philosopher, Married Lady, Old Maid, Old Batchelour, Englishman, Frenchman, Drunken Buck, Woman of the Town, Sir Full-fed Domine Double-chin, Sharper,* and *Tristram Shandy*, With a great Variety of other Subjects, both Moral and Entertaining. . . . As Messrs. *Goodman & Allen* have been at great Expence in having the *Heads*, &c. executed in as masterly a Manner as possible, they humbly hope for the Encouragement of their Friends, and the curious in general. . . . BOXES, 32s. 6d. PIT & GALLERY, 20s. THE Doors to be opened at SIX, and the Lecture to begin precisely at SEVEN o'Clock."[2]

1. *South Carolina and American General Gazette*, June 17–24, 1774.
2. Ibid., June 24–July 1, 1774.

PHILADELPHIA, PA.: SOUTHWARK THEATRE.

September 19, 1774 (1 perf.).

By September 19 several of the company may have reassembled in Philadelphia to start a new season. On that date Goodman and Allen again presented the *Lecture*. On October 20, 1774, the Continental Congress passed its resolution against "Plays and other expensive Diversions and Entertainments" and the 1774–75 season never materialized. The American Company left these shores never again to return as a producing organization.

"For ONE NIGHT ONLY. To all lovers of Novelty, Humour, Satire, Pleasure, and Instruction. THIS EVENING, being the 19th inst. will be presented, at the Theatre in Southwark, AN ATTIC EVENING'S ENTERTAINMENT, Consisting of specimens of

Elocution, taken from the writings of the most approved English authors, by Mr. GOODMAN, of the American Company, and Mr. Allen, From the Theatre Royal in Edinburgh; Particularly an Introductory Address to the town, written upon the occasion, will be pronounced by Mr. GOODMAN; a humourous and satirical Oration will be spoken by Mr. ALLEN. In the course of this evening's Entertainment, Lectures upon a variety of subjects, moral and entertaining, selected from the celebrated LECTURE UPON HEADS, Written by *George Alexander Stevens*, will be delivered by Messrs. Goodman and Allen. . . . The doors to be opened at six o'clock, and to begin at seven. Box, Five Shillings, Pit, Three Shillings, Gallery, Two Shillings. No person to be admitted without tickets, which are to be had at the bar of the London Coffee House."[1]

1. *Pennsylvania Packet*, September 19, 1774.

BRISTOL: COOPER'S HALL.

November 24, 25, 28, 30, December 5, 7, 9, 1774 (7 perfs.).

"GEORGE ALEXANDER STEVENS *Presents his respects to the Ladies and Gentlemen* of Bristol, AND takes the Liberty to acquaint them that he intends to exhibit his LECTURE UPON HEADS, including the whole of his Improvements and Additions up to the present Year, 1774. It will be deliver'd at the COOPERS-HALL, on Wednesday next, the 23d, on Friday the 25th, Monday the 28th, and on Wednesday the 30th of this Instant. ***The Doors will be opened at *Six*— begins exactly at *Seven*—and concludes at *quarter past Nine*. Price of Admittance *Half a Crown*. Tickets to be had of Mr. STEVENS, at Mr. TAYLOR's close to the Theatre, and at the Printers. *N.B.* This is positively the last Time the Lecture ever will be exhibited in this Town. ***As it would be extremely Inconvenient for those *Ladies* and *Gentlemen*, who honoured the *Lecture* with their Company, to be detained at the Door while Money is weighed; it is hoped that no Person will take it ill if the Public (by this Address) are humbly requested to bring Silver or Tickets with them."[1]

December 3. "THE LECTURE UPON HEADS will be repeated by GEORGE ALEXANDER STEVENS, on Monday, Wednesday and Friday Nights of the ensuing Week. After which IT NEVER WILL BE EXHIBITED IN THIS CITY . . ."[2]

1. *Felix Farley's Bristol Journal*, November 19, 1774.
2. Ibid., December 3, 1774.

LONDON: LEBECK'S HEAD.

January 19 or earlier, 1775 (30 + ? perfs.).

Another long run of the *Lecture* was provided by Miss Rose, the child prodigy who had appeared as Tom Thumb at the Haymarket in September 1769. The newspaper files are incomplete, hence an accurate accounting has not been possible. The following extracts provide the features and subsequent changes in the *Lecture*.

"At the LEBECK's-HEAD, in the STRAND. To be continued every Tuesday, Thursday, and Saturday, THIS DAY the inimitable and justly celebrated Miss ROSE, A Child endowed with preter-natural gifts, and infinite retention, who with her Brother, has had the honour to perform before their Majesties . . . will (at the request of literary judges of her merit) deliver The ORIGINAL LECTURE on HEADS, Improved by the addition of Theatrical Capitals, introduced with a FAMOUS CONJURER as a familiar to the notorious DEVIL ON TWO STICKS: For these heads a sentimental conversation is formed. Between different parts of the Lecture (by desire) Miss ROSE will repeat various Theatrical Imitations; . . . . The doors to be open at Six, and begin at Seven o'clock. Admittance, front seats 2s. back seats 1s. Miss ROSE, as usual waits on the Nobility at their own houses, on receiving two days notice."[1]

February 16. "TWENTIETH NIGHT . . . THIS DAY, and SATURDAY next, Miss ROSE, Will deliver. as usual, the LECTURE on HEADS, with her Prelude, Epilogue, and various tragic and comic Imitations, the last time till Wednesday, March 1st when, by desire of many reputable Gentlemen, a LADY, who never appeared in public, will deliver the same Lecture improved by the addition of theatric capitals, for the benefit of Miss Rose, who between different parts of the lecture, will repeat variating Imitations of the first Actress . . . Tickets of admission to the Lecture and Imitations, 2s. 6d. each, which ticket will entitle either Lady or Gentleman to dance, on the purchaser's subscribing his name, for reasons obvious to the discreet. Children who only stay the Lecture, One Shilling."[2] [The price and time remained the same as earlier until the March 1st benefit.]

March 20. "The THIRTIETH NIGHT . . ."[3]

1. *Morning Post and Daily Advertiser*, January 19, 1775.
2. Ibid., February 16, 1775.
3. Ibid., March 20, 1775.

BOSTON, MASS.: PLACE UNCERTAIN.

April 11, 1775 (1 perf.).

Although the following entry does not make specific reference to Stevens's *Lecture*, it is included as a strong possibility. Antitheatre sentiment was still vigorous in Boston at this time and the free *Lectures* were an obvious subterfuge. Note also that the details of the entertainment are referred to as "proposals" rather than as a program or a bill: "Mr. [W. S.] *Morgan* requests Leave to acquaint his subscribers and the Public in general, that his first Evening's Entertainment will be on Tuesday the 11th Instant; when will be performed a CONCERT of Vocal and Instrumental MUSIC; between the Parts of which will be deliver'd (gratis) several Comic Lectures on various Subjects. Tickets at three shillings sterling each to be had at the British Coffee House, and of Mr. Morgan at his Chamber near the Mill bridge, where such Gentlemen as chuse to subscribe may be inform'd of the Proposals. N.B. No Person can be admitted without a Ticket. The Concert will begin at 6 and the Lecture at 7 o'Clock."[1]

1. *Boston Evening Post*, April 3, 1775.

BELFAST: MILL STREET THEATRE.

August 1775 (several perfs.).

Stevens "gave his Lecture on Heads several times in August 1775 at the Mill Street Theatre, Belfast, once for BT [benefit] of the Poor House, realizing receipts of 11. 2. 7½"[1]

1. W. J. Lawrence, MS 4291, National Library of Ireland. Cited on file card for the *Biographical Dictionary* at the Folger Library.

LONDON: CHINA HALL, LOWER ROAD, ROTHERHITHE.

October 9, 1776 (1 perf.).

This is almost certainly the Methodist-preacher segment. It was performed by the six (or seven?)-year-old Russell at the end of the second act of *The Minor*. Russell also played the title role in Fielding's *Tom Thumb* on the same bill. "An *Harangue in a Tub*, after the manner of the celebrated George Alexander Stevens, by Master Russell."[1]

1. *The London Stage*, ed. Charles Beecher Hogan (Carbondale, 1968), pt. 5, vol. 1, p. 24.

BRISTOL: TAYLOR'S HALL.

March 10–15? 17–22? 1777 (several perfs.).

An apparent spin-off.

"On MONDAY EVENING, *March the* 10*th, and every Evening next Week, but positively* no longer. AT the the TAYLOR'S-HALL, in *Broad Street,* will be presented, A *Comic, Satyric, Critical* and *Mimical* ENTERTAINMENT which was dubb'd at the University of *Oxford* with the Title of A LECTURE upon NO-HEADS, and which the Author has ever since adopted, as he has No-HEAD to exhibit besides HIS OWN, and has long been convinced that THAT is but a mere *Caput Mortuum*. In brief, the above is a *Humorous Exhibition*, in which is display'd the present Universal ABUSE OF SPEECH, with a few *Strokes* of *Satire*, and *Flashes of Merriment*, at those NO-HEADED BEINGS, who Rant it, Bellow it, Growl it, Whine it, and Mouth it, in the Regions of ORATORY, and wage continual War with Common Sense, both in READING AND IN SPEAKING. From him who *Thunders* from the *Rostrum*, to him who *Brawls* from the *Tub*; from the *Dionysius* of a *Reading-School*, to the *Boy* not out of his *Primmer*; from the learned *Lexicographer*, to the illiterate *Word-Grubber*; And from the *Macaroni Demosthenes* of the *Scavoir Vivre* Society, to the Plebeian Speechifyer of a Threepenny Porter Club. With several risible Examples of False Accent, False Emphasis, and False Pronunciation; Word-Clipping and Word-Coining; STAMMERING, LISPING, and SNUFFLING; *Scottish*, *Welsh*, and *Irish* Elocution, and the Laughable Dialects of *Somersetshire* and *Gloucestershire*, in a Conversation between a *Bath* and *Bristol* COLLIER. The Whole to conclude with a few Strictures on GESTICULATION; with Ocular Demonstration of Proper and Improper ACTION; and several ludicrous Specimens of the *Extravaganza* and *Burlesque*; the *Latter* particularly exemplified, in a METHODISTICAL PREACH-MENT. By the Author J. Collins. . . . The Doors to be opened at Six; the Lecture to begin at Seven.—Admittance *Two Shillings* . . ."[1]

1. *Felix Farley's Bristol Journal*, March 8, 15, 1777.

LONDON: HAYMARKET, THEATRE ROYAL.

March 11, 13, 15, 17, 19, 21, 31, April 2, 4, 7, 9, 12, 16, 21, 23, 25, 30, May 5, 1777 (18 perfs.).

"At the Theatre Royal, in the Haymarket, THIS EVENING, March 11, and the last season of its ever being done in London, GEORGE ALEXANDER STEVENS will deliver his LECTURE UPON HEADS in FIVE PARTS. Concluding with an Experiment upon the Human Face, with Two Wigs . . ."[1] The following puff appeared the next day.

"*George Alexander Stevens*, who was formerly a favourite among the Choice Spirits, a principal member of Comus's Court, and the fiddle of every company he sat in, last night renewed his acquaintance with the town in that more important, and truly *capital* character, the Lectures upon Heads. The Olio of Wit, Humour, Puns, Quibbles, and verbal Jests, which George last night delivered, is essentially the same as the same Lecturer has, within these ten years, repeated with equal applause and success, two different seasons, from the stage of the Haymarket Theatre; with some alterations in the form, and many additions, which the novel mode of head-dressing, in both sexes, ren-

dered necessary. For us, therefore, to commence a critical inquiry into the
merits of the Lecture at this day, and to set down with a cautious and wary eye,
to separate the grain from the chaff, and say decisively, which parts are
sterling, and which are counterfeit, would be ridiculous, suffice it therefore,
that we declare, upon the whole, the Lecture is exceedingly pleasant; the
humour of it is apposite to every man's mind; the Galleries may relish it as well
as the Boxes, and he that likes to laugh, grow merry, and fat, let him repair to
the *Head* Quarters of George Alexander Stevens, where he may enjoy more
than one *tete-a-tete*, and after all, come away without fear of an action for *crim.
con.*"[2]

March 13. "Including the whole of his Improvements and Alterations. In the
First Part is a Collection of MACARONIES. Second Part, upon the Sciences,
General Elections, &c. Third Part upon Ladies' Head Dresses. Fourth Part
upon Law. Fifth Part upon Politics and Physic. To conclude by way of Epilogue,
with an Experiment on the Human Face, with two Wigs."[3]

March 24–29. The theatre was closed for Holy Week during this period.

April 12. "For the Benefit for a Decay'd Tradesman."[4]

April 30. "N.B. The Lecture will be repeated only this day, Wednesday and the
Monday following, as Mr. Colman wants the house to be accommodated for his
meeting."[5]

May 5. "On account of the many necessary alterations wanted at the Theatre
for the ensuing season, the Lecture on Heads, can only be repeated the above
night."[6]

1. *Public Advertiser*, March 11, 1777.
2. *Morning Chronicle*, March 12, 1777.
3. *Morning Post and Daily Advertiser*, March 13, 1777.
4. *Morning Chronicle*, April 12, 1777.
5. *Morning Post and Daily Advertiser*, April 30, 1777.
6. *The London Stage*, ed. Charles Beecher Hogan (Carbondale, 1968), pt. 5, vol. 1, p. 80.

LONDON: COACHMAKER'S HALL, CHEAPSIDE.

March 14, 1777 (1 perf.).

The *Lecture on Hearts* by the child prodigy Russell six months later: "In Coach-
Maker's Hall, Foster-lane, Cheapside, This evening, March 14, Master
RUSSELL, (A child only Seven Years of Age) will attempt to give an Attic
Evenings Entertainment, Serious, Comic moral and entertaining in four Parts.

Part I and II. A selection of the most admired parts of the celebrated LECTURE on HEARTS, with a variety of Alterations and Additions, and an Introductory ADDRESS."[1]

1. *Morning Chronicle and London Advertiser*, March 14, 1777.

LONDON: GREAT ROOM, ST. ALBAN'S STREET.

May 6, 1777 (1 perf.).

The aging Miss Rose performs the *Lecture* two years later.

May 6. "A LAUDABLE EXHIBITION, In favour of the inimitable Young Lady, celebrated by the fictitious name of Miss ROSE, who at the Great Room, No. 24, St. Alban's-street, Pall Mall, this present Evening, will deliver a Lecture on many remarkable Heads in her own peculiar manner. . . . First seats 3s. Second seats 2s. Little Masters and Misses admitted at half price. Doors to be opened at six, will begin precisely at seven."[1]

1. *Morning Post and Daily Advertiser*, May 6, 1777.

BRISTOL: COOPER'S HALL.

May 20, 1779 (1 perf.).

Another variant: "*Positively the last Time of Exhibiting in this City.* ON THURSDAY Evening, the 20th Instant, at the COOPERS HALL in King-street, Mr. Collins purposes to deliver his new COMIC and SATYRIC Lecture upon LOGGER-HEADS. In Four Parts. The Doors to be open'd at Six, and the Lecture to begin precisely at Seven—Admittance Two Shillings."[1]

1. *Bristol Gazette*, May 20, 1779.

MANCHESTER: MARSDEN STREET THEATRE.

Summer 1779 (3 perfs.).

". . . he [Stevens] came to Manchester for the fourth time in the summer of 1779, when he thrice delivered his entertainment at the theatre."[1] Again, almost certainly the *Lecture on Heads*.

1. Richard Wright Procter, *Manchester in Holiday Dress* (London and Manchester, 1866), p. 31.

LONDON: LINCOLN'S INN FIELDS.

October 28, 1779 (1–3 perfs.).

"On 28 October 1779 *The Morning Chronicle* . . . carried the following advertisement: 'At the Old Theatre, No. 5, in Portugal Street, Lincoln's-inn-fields, this Day, the 28th instant, at Seven in the Evening, Mr. Cresswick's Third Lecture on Elocution will be exemplified in reciting part of . . . A few extracts from the Lecture on Hearts; . . . And Mr. George Stevens' remarks on the origin of Lectures, and the practice of snuff-taking. tickets for two people for 6d.' Creswick was said to be gratified at the response to two former lectures."[1]

1. P. Highfill, Jr., K. Burnim, and E. Langhans, *A Biographical Dictionary of Actors, Actresses, Musicians . . . in London, 1660–1800.* (Carbondale and Edwardsville, 1973–78), vol. 4, p. 44.

CHESTER: THEATRE ROYAL.

November 26, December 3, 1779 (2 perfs.).

"CHESTER, Nov. 16. On Monday next, the 22d Inst. and on the Friday following, at the Theatre-Royal, in this City, GEORGE ALEXANDER STEVENS will deliver his LECTURE upon HEADS, with all the Improvements and Alterations unto this present Year. The Doors to be open'd at Half past Six, and begin exactly at Seven.—Boxes, 3s. Pit, 2s. Gal. 1s."[1]

As the subsequent notice tells us, the first of these performances did not take place. The day after it was scheduled we learn: "At the Theatre-Royal, Chester on FRIDAY next, Nov. 26. *George Alexander Stevens* will deliver his LECTURE upon HEADS. . . . Mr. STEVENS respectfully hopes the Ladies, Gentlemen, &c. will excuse the Omission of his Performance on Monday (as advertised) a severe Cold having render'd him wholly incapable."[2]

The ad is repeated announcing "The LAST NIGHT" for December 3[3] and on that day two newspapers carried the following: "Positively the last Night. This present Evening, December 3, . . . N.B. George Alexander Stevens designs to be at Wrexham next week, where he hopes to have the honour of attempting to entertain the Ladies and Gentlemen for two nights only."[4]

1. *Adam's Weekly Courant*, November 16, 1779.
2. Ibid., November 23, 1779.
3. Ibid., November 30, 1779.
4. *Chester Chronicle* and *General Advertiser*, December 3, 1779.

WREXHAM, WALES: TOWN HALL.

December 8, 10, 1779 (2 perfs.).

"At the TOWN-HALL, in WREXHAM, For Two Nights only, On Wednesday and Friday next, the 8th and 10th Instant, December George Alexander Stevens Will deliver his celebrated LECTURE upon HEADS, With all the Improvements and Alterations, unto the present Year. The Performance will consist of Five different Parts, some Particulars of which will be express'd in Hand-bills. Admittance, Two shillings each."[1]

1. *Adams's Weekly Courant*, December 7, 1779.

LONDON: COVENT GARDEN AND GREENWOOD'S GREAT ROOM.

June 26, 29, July 3, 6, 12, 14, 17, 19, 20, 21, 22, 24, 1780 (12 perfs.).

June 26. "THIS DAY the 26th of June inst, 1780, MR. GEORGE ALEXANDER STEVENS'S LECTURE upon HEADS will be delivered by Mr. LEE LEWES. The whole revised and adapted to the TIMES. In which will be introduced the following new Characters: The Head of G. A. Stevens; the Debating Societies dissected, with the Heads of a Male and Female Moderator; a Fashionable Foreigner; Four National Characters, with the Heads of an English Sailor, a Frenchman, a Spaniard, and a Dutch Merchant. The HEAD of a Libeller. With a new Prologue. The Characters all new Dressed. . . . Boxes 5s. Pit 3s. Gal. 2s. Upper Gal 1s."[1]

The prologue for this performance, written by Frederick Pilon and spoken by Lee Lewes, was published several days after the completion of the run, in the *Morning Chronicle* of July 29, 1780. It is included in most of the subsequent "authorized" editions, which state that the prologue was first spoken on June 24, 1780. This is an apparent error since the best evidence indicates that the run began on June 26.

> "ALL's safe here, I find, though the rabble rout
> A few doors lower burnt the quorum out.
> Sad times, when Bow-street is a scene of riot,
> And justice cannot keep the parish quiet.
> But peace returning like the dove appears,
> And this association stills my fears;
> Humour and wit the frolic wing may spread,
> And we give harmless Lectures on the Head.
> Watchmen in sleep may be as snug as foxes,
> And snore away the hours within their boxes;
> Nor more affright the neighbourhood with warning,
> Of past twelve o-clock, a troublesome morning.

Mynheer demanded, at the general shock,
'Is the Bank safe, or has it lower'd the stock!'
'Begar,' a Frenchman cried, 'the Bank we'll rob,
'For I have got the purse to bribe the mob.'—
'Hoot awa, mon!' the loyal Scot replies,
'You'll lose your money, for we'll hong the spies:
'Fra justice now, my lad, ye shanna budge,
'Tho' ye've attack'd the justice and the judge.'—
'Oh! hold him fast,' says Paddy, 'for I'll swear
'I saw the iron rails in Bloomsbury-square
'Burnt down to the ground, and heard the mob say,
'They'd burn down the Thames the very next day.'
Tumult and riot thus on every side
Swept off fair order like the raging tide;
Law was no more, for, as the throng rush'd by,
'Woe to my Lord Chief Justice!' was the cry.
And he, rever'd by every muse so long,
Whom tuneful Pope immortaliz'd in song,
Than whom bright genius boasts no higher name,
Ev'n he could find no sanctuary in fame;
With brutal rage the Vandals all conspire,
And rolls of science in one blaze expire.
But England, like the lion, grows more fierce
As dangers multiply, and foes increase;
Her gen'rous sons, with Roman ardour warm,
In martial bands to shield their country arm,
And when we trembled for the city's fate,
Her youth stood forth the champions of the state;
Like brothers, leagu'd by nature's holy tie,
A parent land to save, or bravely die.
Did Britons thus, like brothers, always join,
In vain to crush them would the world combine;
Discord domestic would no more be known,
And brothers learn affection from the throne.
But know your Lecturer's awful hour is come
When you must bid him live, or seal his doom!
He knows 'tis hard a leader's post to fill
Of fame superior, and more ripen'd skill.
The blame will all be mine, if troops should fail,
Who'd lose their heads, but never could turn tail:
Who no commander ever disobey'd,
Or overlook'd the signals which he made.
Under your auspices the field I take,
For a young general some allowance make;
But if disgracefully my army's led,
Let this court-martial then cashier my head."[2]

Three reviews, not puffs, were printed the day following the opening of the run:

"Last night Mr. Lee Lewes delivered Mr. George Alexander Stevens's Lecture upon Heads, with many additional characters, for the first time, at Covent-garden Theatre. It was introduced by an occasional Prologue, abounding with many temporary strokes, drawn from the late alarming riots, and introduced as the dialogue of a Frenchman, Spaniard, Dutchman, and Irishman. It contained likewise a pleasing panegyric on a great Law Luminary, who had been so rudely treated by the mob, which was very warmly applauded.

"The new heads introduced were that of George Stevens, the three Turf Heads, or Students of the Stable, a French General, Female Moderator, Clerical ditto, Jonas the Juggler, British Tar, Frenchman, Spaniard, Dutchman, &c. The whole afforded a variety of original and entertaining matter, which was delivered with a great deal of comic humour, and was very highly applauded by a numerous and respectable auditory, and bids fair to repay the industry of the performer, who has got this Lecture up for the entertainment of the Public. The present extreme length of it, however, is not a circumstance much in its favour."[3]

"The LECTURE ON HEADS, a singular and original species of entertainment, invented by G. A. Stevens, and exhibited by him at several different periods with a high degree of encouragement and applause, was last night revived at Covent-garden theatre by Mr. Lee Lewes, who has purchased the apparatus of Mr. Stevens.

"The recital of this Lecture received great advantages from the very superior powers, as speaker and actor, which Mr. Lee Lewes possesses, in the easy, spirited volubility with which the whole was recited, and the strong and varied powers of imitation with which those characters were given that were intended to be personated.

"The Lecture was introduced by a Prologue, written by Mr. Pilon, which abounded with temporary allusions to the late riots, and contained a warm eulogy on the character of Lord Mansfield. The principal additions were, the head of Mr. Stevens, who was complimented in very warm and friendly strains, on the qualities of his head and heart, and on the singular turn for keen wit, shrewd humour, and sarcastic observation, which he certainly possessed.

"The head of a male and a female moderator of the debating societies, a fashionable foreigner and projector of a celebrated Feté, which failed in giving *universal* satisfaction; and the head of an English sailor, a Frenchman, a Spaniard, and a Dutch merchant. These heads are given perfectly in Mr. Steven's manner, and in a higher stile of composition: the last group introduces a sarcastic review of the conduct of different powers in their interference with our dispute with America, in which there are several good hits, and a great variety of temporary allusions are interspersed throughout the whole.

"The Lecture, however, as it now stands, is most palpably too long; and the pruning, which would reduce it to a proper length, would also introduce other material improvements; many of the characters appear duplicates of each other, particularly the female heads—satire in every variety of form has been exhausted on the subject, and fashion seems to gather obstinacy from the reproof. Many of the serious observations may also be spared, and a greater appearance of good humour suffered to pervade the whole. To laugh at folly rather than to scourge vice, ought to be the most ostensible object of an exhibition of this kind, from which the audience expect entertainment rather than instruction."[4]

"Yesterday evening Mr. Lee Lewes, delivered to a very respectable audience assembled in this Theatre, the LECTURE upon HEADS of George Alexander Stevens, which, (as he had advertized) had been revived and adapted to the Times, and in which were introduced several new characters.

"The Lecture, as originally written, our readers will recollect, was a plain, pleasant, and powerful satire, more remarkable for broad humour than chaste wit, and pretty plentifully interspersed with puns, some of them passable, and some of them but very middling. The additions to it are the Head of G. A. Stevens; the Debating Societies dissected, with the Heads of a Male and Female Moderator, a Fashionable Foreigner, Four National Characters, with the Heads of an English Sailor, a Frenchman, a Spaniard, and a Dutch Merchant, which in regard to stile are not equal to the original Lecture. They contain some tolerably good points, and are rather chargeable with favouring of low wit, than of sinking into downright dullness and insipidity. In the revision of Mr. Stevens's lecture, the adapter, who performed the undertaking, has been somewhat careless, retaining, in more than one place, parts of the satire which are now so far obsolete, that they do not accord with modern manners.

"Mr. Lee Lewes did great justice to many parts of the Lecture, particularly where the talents, of what in the Green-room phrase is called, a low comedian, were necessary for heightening the caricature, but where the matter depended on a nice and marking mode of expression, or where the language was serious and declamatory, he was not equally successful; in the latter case, he suffered himself to fall into a most ear-fatiguing monotony, and in the former he did not appear to feel which was the pressing and pointed portion of the satire. Mr. Lee Lewes should get some critical friend to hear him rehearse, and correct his pronunciation. The character of a Publick Lecturer is not that of an *ignoramus* in the learned languages, and even if it were defensible in a professed general censor to be unacquainted with the Latin and French tongues, it is surely unpardonable for him not to know how to speak English correctly. Mr. Lee Lewe's classical friends will inform him, that 'simplex mundi*tius*,' and 'camera necessar*a*,' are not Latin, and he ought to know himself, that we have no such words in the language as '*Des*sertation,' and '*Grem*marians."

"Previous to the Lecture Mr. Lee Lewes spoke a Prologue, which we were not in time to hear, but it was generally said, that it was a very witty performance. We understand, it turned upon the late riots, and gave proof of a happy imagination in the writer.

"When the Lecture was over, Mr. Lee Lewes walked forward, and informed the Audience, that Mr. Harris had confined his grant of the use of the Theatre, to one night only, but, if his endeavours to please, were honored with the public approbation, he meant to apply to Mr. Harris, for an indulgence for two more Evenings. The Lecture having been very loudly applauded, we have no manner of doubt, but Mr. Harris, from motives of benevolence, will grant Mr. Lee Lewes's request."[5]

Lewes inserted the following notice in three newspapers: "The Lecture upon Heads was exhibited last night, at this Theatre, [CG] and received by a crouded audience with uncommon approbation, and as Mr. Lee Lewes has obtained a further indulgence of two more at this Theatre. Ladies and Gentlemen are requested to take notice, that it will be performed tomorrow and the Monday following.—As many Ladies and gentlemen were disappointed of hearing the *Prologue*, which is so generally admired, they are particularly requested to take notice that Mr. Lee Lewes will begin *exactly* at seven o'clock."[6]

This comment appeared in the same issue: "Mr. Lee Lewes, in his Lecture last Monday evening, took occasion to mention our female geniuses in the following manner:—'In history have we not a Macauly? In moral entertainment have we not a Griffith? and in the last new comedy of the Belle's Stratagem, have we not an author, who rivals the genius of Drury?' It is wonderful, says a correspondent, that to this groupe was not added a Montague, who in purity of stile, improved observation, and elegance of taste, does not rank second to any star in the female constellation which has adorned the age."[7]

June 29. The Head of a Libeller was omitted from this performance, perhaps a concession to the criticism that the work was too long.

July 3. "For the last time."[8] There was a good house, however, and the *Lecture* continued. Lewes was very irritated by the placement of his newspaper advertisement, expecting it to be printed in the first instead of the second column of the first page. He wrote the editor, Mr. Woodfall, expressing his concern as well as his displeasure with Woodfall's June 27 criticism of the *Lecture*. That same day Woodfall indicated that the advertisement would be moved and promised to print Lewes's letter in full: "The printer has complied with Mr. LEE LEWES's requisition, as to the mode of inserting his Advertisement, and will, if he conveniently can, *treat* his readers with an exact copy of the Lecturer's *curious* Epistle in to-morrow's paper. The insertion of it today, might possibly have been construed into an unfair attempt to prejudice the receipt of Mr. LEE LEWES this Evening.—God send him a large one!"[9]

True to his promise, Woodfall published the correspondence the next day and included his own defense of the prerogatives of the critic.

"Literal Copy of a Letter Received by the Printer on Sunday Evening. SIR, 'I have repeatedly requested to have my Advertisement inserted in your paper

According to the enclosed Copy—And under the Haymarket Announcement—if you are determined it shall not be so, your *Will* must be my Law, in this Matter, but, Sir, your *Verbal* Criticisms (which Among the Literati are held in most Sovereign Contempt) shall never have a dictatorial Authourity over me, and you may depend upon it, Sir, I *will* hold up the OFFENDER in *Propriis Coloribus* (that is good Latin I presume Mr. Woodfal,) I think I have as good a Vehicle to Convey the reply Churlish in, as you have to give the reproof Villanous in—Now Sir, you are possessed of MY MIND—to be sure you have this advantage, you have given the first *Blow*, but I have known as Renowned Champions as yourself fall a Sacrifice to their own Art—if you triumph— (which at Most can be but temporary) I shall Not be the first Man you have attempted to sacrifice to what you may call friendship, and what I term Servility—I mean your Conduct to Mr. Henderson this Sir, with many other Anecdotes in your public Sphere—may (to make use of your own Words) serve to furnish the town with a (Good *Copy* of the inimitable) Critic—I *will* gratify my resentment in *this* Manner, and Justify it in *Any* Manner. CHARLES LEE LEWES' "

This was followed immediately in the paper by:

"Bow-street, July 2, 1780. The cause of the Printer's having been honoured with the above *curious, civil,* and *witty* epistle was this: On Tuesday the 27th ult. in exercise of that right of passing a free opinion on the merits or demerits of a public spectacle or entertainment, which every man enjoys, some remarks were printed in this paper on the mode in which Mr. Lee Lewes delivered George Alexander Steven's Lecture upon Heads at Covent-Garden Theatre the preceding evening. The publick have had those observations before them; they are now in possession of the letter they gave rise to, and both together the Printer conceives will be full as much as they may desire to see upon the subject, he therefore forbears to add a single comment."[10]

July 6. "By particular DESIRE, and positively for the LAST time."[11] The *Lecture* was drawing good crowds, but Covent Garden was no longer available. Lewes moved to another house and continued for eight additional performances. The price scale remained the same, except for the upper gallery which did not exist. The Head of a Libeller was still deleted.

July 12. "AT GREENWOOD'S GREAT ROOM, in the Hay-Market, THIS DAY the 12th inst."[12] The remainder of the advertisement was essentially the same as that of the June 29 performance.

July 17. "For the first time, the Head of a HYDRA CRITIC."[13] Probably Lewes's continuation of the spat with Woodfall.

July 24. "POSITIVELY the LAST NIGHT."[14]

Several months after Lewes's engagement there was printed anonymously "A

Parody on the Rosciad of Churchill," which contained the following scurrilous verses.

"VERSES *addressed to Mr. L. L——s, collected from different News-papers, published during his Exhibition of Mr. Alexander Stevens's Lectures upon Heads.*"

To Mr. L. L——s.

Great Orator, whose Lectures show,
The import of plain Aye and Noe;
Whose native humour claims the praise,
And tribute of superior lays;
How pleas'd would Alexander be,
Was L——s mum as well as thee;
For when the horse-t——d, pert and prim,
Exclaim'd—how well we apples swim!
The golden pippen surely thought,
The compliment was dearly bought.

To the same.

'Tis strange, that of all the strange heads you have shown,
The strangest, all strangers observe, is your own;
This strangest, to me, sir, the stranger appears,
'Cause, strange to relate, it has still got its ears.

To Ditto.

A sapient sage, long dead and gone,
Swore many heads exceeded one;
But could old slyboots rise to view
Your heads, your apish tricks, and you.
His observation now would be,
The fewer heads the better, L——.

On the same.

Great sir, your most obsequious slave,
One boon with due respect I crave;
Foe, like yourself, to impudence,
And loth to give the least offence;
I tremble whilst I thus accost
An hero, who's himself an host;
But trusting to the voice of fame,
Which adds such lustre to your name;
And well convinc'd the good and wise,
To ease the anxious heart rejoice;
Submissively I beg to know,
The cause of what's observ'd below.

Since asses bray, and magpies chatter,
Apes grin, and scavengers bespatter;
Why should we waste our time, to see
Such feats exhibited by thee?

On the same.

Hic stolidus sedet ipse loquax—mirabile visu;
Quae dicit? vel quae dicere vult?—stolida.

Translation.

Here, sitting on a three-legg'd stool,
Behold this brazen, brainless fool;
What does the noisy blockhead utter?
He roars—O bravo, bread and butter.

On Ditto.

If Lee by his feats,
Whatever he eats
Must merit, or otherwise fast;
No wonder a slice,
Of butter'd bread nice,
Is deem'd such a noble repast.

On the same.

Pure as Fleet stream a-down its channel goes,
Thine eloquence benevolently flows;
Hard as the bricks that form that current's bed,
And eke as much a vent for filth—thine head.

On the same.

Last night, a certain senseless cub,
Whose back my fingers itch'd to drub;
A prating, self-conceited fool,
Declar'd he thought your lectures dull:
Your observations trite, or stole,
And nothing good throughout the whole;
Then swore your matchless eloquence,
(Detractive knave) was impudence.
Scoundrel, quoth I, you little know
The merit of my friend, I trow;
His noble soul I need not mention,
That's evident beyond contention;
And bless'd the Wight that owns a scull
Of wit and wisdom half so full;

I grant indeed 'tis cas'd with brass,
So thick that not a jot can pass;
But calculation plainly shews,
That most remains when least we use.

On Ditto, upon his late Expedition to Newbury.

Friend Lee of late,
(Of pasteboard pate,
A knight of high renown)
Oppress'd with curse
Of empty purse,
One morn forsook the town.

His scheme was this;
Not much amiss
By all it will be granted;
For all must know,
What long ago,
The Hydra Critic wanted.

Since Cr——v——n's heart,
Has found the art,
To quit her snowy breast;
Her head, perchance,
Might take a dance,
And then—you guess the rest.

That seat of sense, and wit refin'd,
By BREAD-AND-BUTTER-NICE purloin'd;
And snug betwixt his shoulders plac'd,
Instead of Noddle copper-fac'd;
His Lectures then of course must please,
And *happy bravo* live *at ease.*[15]

1. *Morning Chronicle*, June 26, 1780.
2. From the 1808 edition of the *Lecture*, pp. viii–ix. The "Surrey riots" were very severe disturbances in Bow Street. There were numerous robberies, shopliftings, and injuries. The house of Sir John Fielding was demolished, and over one hundred persons were tried at Sessions. A number of those convicted eventually were executed. "There were more Counsel, and a greater number of gentlemen of rank in court yesterday, than were ever known upon any former occasion." *Morning Chronicle*, June 29, 1780.
3. *London Chronicle*, June 24–27, 1780.
4. *Gazetteer and New Daily Advertiser*, June 27, 1780.
5. *Morning Chronicle*, June 27, 1780.
6. Ibid., June 28, 1780.
7. Ibid.

8. Ibid., July 3, 1780.
9. Ibid.
10. Ibid., July 4, 1780.
11. Ibid., July 6, 1780.
12. Ibid., July 12, 1780.
13. Ibid., July 17, 1780.
14. *Gazetteer and New Daily Advertiser*, July 24, 1780.
15. From *A Parody on the Rosciad of Churchill*, pp. 34–40. (London, 1780). The work is
    anonymous. The preface, dated September 22, 1780, is signed Grubstreticus.

NEWBURY.

September ? 1780 (1? perf.).

Evidence for a performance of the *Lecture* by Lewes in Newbury comes from
the prologue (see below) published in most of the "authorized" editions as well
as the satirical poem included in *A Parody on the Rosciad of Churchill* (q.v.). The
preface to the *Parody* is dated September 22, 1780; Lewes had completed the
London engagement in late July. He apparently took to the road for a brief
period since we also have a record of a provincial performance in Bath on
September 11. The Newbury performance was probably also given in September and seems to have been a one-night stand commissioned by Lady Craven.

ADDITIONAL LINES TO THE PROLOGUE
SPOKEN AT NEWBURY

In consequence of Lady Craven bespeaking the Lecture, who
had published some Lines on dreaming she saw
her Heart at her Feet.

WRITTEN BY MR. PRATT.

'MIDST scenes like these, for so her lines impart,
The QUEEN OF BENHAM lost that gem her heart;
Scar'd by the din, her bosom treasure flew,
And with it every grace and muse withdrew.
But far, or long, the wanderer could not roam,
For wit and taste soon brought the truant home;
One tuneful sonnet at her feet it sung,
Then to her breast, its snowy mansion, sprung;
Thither it went, the virtues in its train,
To hail the panting blessing back again.
On its fair throne it now appears as Queen,
And sheds its lustre o'er this humble scene;

Its radiant scepter deigns o'er me to spread
The genial beams which fancy feign'd were fled.
Ah, no! her gentle heart this night is here;
Where'er 'tis wanted—you will find it there:
In vain the Muse shall fix it on the floor,
It knocks this ev'ning at the Lecturer's door,
And smiles, with him, that riot is no more.[1]

1. From the 1808 edition of the *Lecture*, p. x.

BATH.

September 11, 1780 (1 perf.).

Almost certainly by Lewes after the London run. The prologue below appears in several of the "authorized" editions.

> N.B. At Bath the following lines
> were spoken 11th September, 1780.
> Written by Mr. Pratt.

Nor Thames the limit of the raving throng,
Which, like some lawless comet, swept along,
Spreading, like putrid air, from man to man,
The empoison'd pestilence still catching ran;
And here, even *here*, where pleasure keeps her seat,
Health gushes round, and sickness seeks retreat;
E'en Bath, fair Bath, confess'd her growing fright,
When tracks of fire fierce burnt the breast of night,
When fury's glare, *unholy*, struck the eye,
And forc'd awhile each gentler guest to fly.
But *now*, that peace *here too* resumes her reign,
And brings to Bath her graces back again,
I venture forth to greet the happy land,
And bring well-tim'd *amusement* in my hand;
Some gentle harmless block heads too, I bear,
Come down to pass a week in this gay air;
Some of the worthies have been here before,
And humour brought them on this very floor,
And some are new, but will escape all dangers,
Bath's too well bred to turn her back on strangers.[1]

1. From the 1785 (London) edition of the *Lecture*, pp. v–vi.

LONDON: ASSEMBLY ROOM, KING'S ARMS TAVERN.

January 26? to April 2, 1781 (21 perfs.).

"By Permission of the Right Hon. the LORD MAYOR. IN the Assembly Room, at the late King's Arms Tavern, Cornhill, THIS EVENING, Feb. 2, a YOUNG LADY will deliver A LECTURE ON HEADS, With THEATRICAL IMITATIONS. Having had the honour privately to perform before their Majesties, the Royal Family, and principal Nobility in England, with that applause due to her inimitable abilities and most astonishing memory. Will be continued every Monday and Friday during the Limitation. The Room (which is large) will be kept agreeably warm. The doors to be opened at seven o'clock, and the performance commence at eight precisely. Admittance One Shilling."[1] The performance appears to have alternated with a Female Debating Society, which addressed such questions as "Which is the greatest enemy to society, the crafty hypocrite, or the open debauchee?"

1. *Gazetteer and New Daily Advertiser*, February 2, 1781. This performance was for the "Third Night." This advertisement sounds very much like Miss Rose again.

LONDON: HAYMARKET THEATRE.

February–April 2, 1781 (21 perfs.?).

March 16. "Haymarket Theatre. Mr. Lee Lewes most respectfully informs the public that he shall on Friday next lay before them the Original Lecture upon Heads, at the above Theatre, the receipt of that night will be added to the subscription for the relief of the distressed in the West India Islands. He proposes to deliver his Lecture Twelve Nights during Lent and on each Night to produce a New Character. The First will be A DORMOUSE CRITIC. The Second a BAILIFF.—The Third a PAWN BROKER.—the Fourth a VESTRIAN ADONIS.—The other characters are in Contemplation."[1]

1. Unidentified newspaper clipping, March 9, 1781.

ANNAPOLIS AND BALTIMORE, MD.

June 14, 22, 28, July 3, 5, August 17, 25, September 14, 15, 18, October 1, 1781 (11 perfs.).

Mr. Wall does Heads and Noses.

June 14. [Annapolis. The Theatre. Mr. Wall.] "A Medley of THEATRICAL TRIFLES, viz. A CRITICAL DISSERTATION [ON] NOSES . . . THEN THE OLD LECTURE ON

HEADS, Not Performed these Eight Years; with a Prologue on JEALOUSY. The whole to conclude with an EPILOGUE, never spoken here before, by Miss WALL. To begin at Seven o'Clock. BOXES Two State Dollars. PIT One. No persons to be admitted without Tickets, which may be had of Mr. Mann at the Dock, at the Coffee-House, and of Mr. Wall near the Town Gate."[1] The program also included songs by Miss Wall.

June 22. [Baltimore. Mr. L'Argeau's Dancing Room.] "Mr. WALL, From Annapolis, will present . . . A new LECTURE on HEADS, with Entertainments, viz. AN EPILOGUE, by Miss Wall, a Child of seven Years. After the first Part of the LECTURE, she will sing an AIR, accompanied by Mr. WALL on the Mandolin. An EPILOGUE on JEALOUSY. . . . The whole to conclude with an EPILOGUE, addressed to EVERYBODY, not aim'd at ANYBODY, will be spoken by SOMEBODY, in the Character of NOBODY. TICKETS at Three State Dollars each."[2]

June 28. [Baltimore. Mr. L'Argeau's Dancing Room. Mr. Wall.] "THE OLD LECTURE on HEADS, not performed here these Eight Years . . . To which will be added, a critical *Dissertation* on NOSES, wherein will be introduced *Hippisley's* Drunken Man. After the *Dissertation*, the Prologue of the Picture of a *Play-House*, or Bucks have at ye all. The whole to be concluded with an EPILOGUE, never spoken here before; by Miss Wall."[3]

July 3. The same as above.[4]

July 5. [Baltimore. Mr. Johnson's Sail-Warehouse, on Fell's Point. Mr. Wall.] "A new LECTURE on HEADS, with Entertainments . . . An EPILOGUE on JEALOUSY . . . To which will be added, a critical DISSERTATION on NOSES: In which will be exhibited a *Roman-Nose*—a *Turning-up-Nose*—a *Ruby-Nose*—A *Blunt-Nose*—and Mother Gubbin's *Hook'd Nose,* and *Chin.* The whole to conclude with an EPILOGUE, addressed to *Everybody,* not aim'd at *Anybody,* will be spoken by *Somebody,* in the Character of *Nobody.*"[5]

August 17. [Annapolis. The Theatre. Mr. Wall.] "A MEDLEY of THEATRICAL TRIFLES, viz. The NEW LECTURE on HEADS, Being the last Time of performing it in Annapolis . . . [followed by six additional entertainments/Boxes Half a Dollar, Pit Two Shillings and Six-pence, new Emission."[6]

August 25. [Annapolis. The Theatre. Mr. Wall.] "A FARRAGO OF THEATRICAL AMUSEMENTS . . . Then, a Critical Dissertation on NOSES, in which will be exhibited a Roman Nose, a Turning-up Nose, a Ruby Nose, a Blunt Nose, and an hooked or Parrot's Beak Nose and Chin . . . Boxes Five Shillings, Pit Three."[7]

September 14. [Annapolis. The Theatre. Mr. Wall.] ". . . Then the NEW LECTURE on HEADS . . . Boxes Half a Dollar, Pit Two Shillings and Six-Pence."⁸ The "New Lecture" is repeated despite the August 17 announcement.

September 15. [Annapolis. The Theatre. Mr. Wall.] "A PROLOGUE by Mr. Wall, in the Character of a Master Mason . . . A Critical Dissertation on NOSES . . . [The same Noses as July 5.]"⁹

September 18. [Annapolis. The Theatre. Mr. Wall.] "The NEW LECTURE on HEADS . . ."¹⁰ The following holograph note has been added at the bottom of the broadside: "A Band of Music will be provided. N.B. This Band belong'd to the French Army who were on their way down to Virginia, to attack Lord Cornwallis."

October 1. [Baltimore. Mr. Lindsay's Coffee House on Fell's Point. Mr. Wall.] ". . . A CRITICAL DISSERTATION ON NOSES [as earlier] . . ."¹¹

The above entries were verified by examining the broadsides housed at the Museum and Library of Maryland History in Baltimore. The identifications below are coded as follows: (Randall) The Blanchard Randall Theatre Collection at the Museum; (Wheeler) Joseph T. Wheeler, *The Maryland Press, 1777–1790* (Baltimore; 1938); (Evans) Roger P. Bristol, *Supplement to Charles Evans' American Bibliography* (Charlottesville, 1970). The series of numbers in the following notes refer to Randall, Wheeler, and Evans respectively.

1. 1; 106; not in Evans.
2. 2; 116; 43936.
3. 3; 117; 43938.
4. 4; 118; 43939.
5. 5; 119; 43937.
6. 6; 107; 43925.
7. 7; 108; 43927.
8. 8; 109; not in Evans (?).
9. 9; 110; 43930.
10. 10; 111; not in Evans.
11. 13; 121; 43935.

MONTEGO BAY, JAMAICA: MR. BOOTH'S LONG ROOM.

November 6, 1781 (1 perf.).

"The *Cornwall Chronicle* prints in its issue of October 13th a news item . . . to this effect: 'We hear Mr. [William] Moore, who has been delivering the Lecture on Heads and other entertainments, with universal applause, in Kingston and Spanish Town, is on his passage for this quarter, where he intends repeating

the same; and, from the general approbation he has met with, we may expect
both pleasure and amusement'. . . .

". . . on November 6th, 'by Particular Desire,' [he] delivers the *Lecture on Heads*
at Mr. Booth's Long Room and follows it with other entertainments. [Audi-
ences were large and enthusiastic and] on the 10th he pays his respects to them
and 'begs leave to assure them language is too weak to express his Gratitude for
the generous support and universal approbation he has met with. . . .'"[1]

Although the records are scanty, it appears that Mr. Moore presented the
Lecture in Jamaica both before and after the above date.

1. Richardson Wright, *Revels in Jamaica* (New York, 1937), pp. 161–62.

BALTIMORE, MD.: THE THEATRE.

January 19, 1782 (1 perf.).

A permanent theatre was built in Baltimore and opened on January 15, 1782.
Four days later John Henry presented the *Lecture* in Spanish and charged two
pesos for admission. The playbill (and translation) is given below. The syllabus
is very similar to other *Lectures* by Henry, but this is the only non-English
version I have encountered. The various histories of the city that have been
examined give no clues to explain a Spanish *Lecture*. It may have been done in
connection with an ethnic occasion or to honor a visiting dignitary. This is also
the first indication I have found that Henry was proficient in the language.
There is, of course, the possibility that the *Lecture* was given in English but
advertised for a Spanish or Latin American audience.

"VIERNES 19 DE ENERO DE 82 EN LA CASA de Comedias. El Sr. Henrique de la
Compañia Americana de Comediantes ofrece un Solilquio compendioso sobre
las materias siguientes. Primera parte. La introducion: Alexandro; Cherokee;
Charlatan; Las armas del dicho; Oracion en alabanza de las Leyes; El Majo
peinado con plumas; La utilidad de los Plumages á la moda; El Petimetre
enpolvado; El Apasionado de las diversiones; Su criado; Las Armas de alguno;
Ninguno; Qualquiera; y cada uno; El destino del carino; Generosidad; Amis-
tad Patriotismo, y Capacidad; Flor del merito; Su contraste; Honrades; Adula-
cion, y Reprehension. Segunda. Cabeza de las Señora; Trage antiguo de
montar; Idem de moda; Vendedora de pescado; Risueño y lloroso Filosofo;
Singulo de Venus; Bata de Cleopatra; Gorro Frances; La Casada; Criada Vieja;
Cortejo avejentado. Tercera. El Majo Casado; Muger escandalosa; Maestro de
las Damas; Estafador; Politico de lastertulias; Jugador; su Entierro y Monu-
mento; Cabeza del Fanatico. Quarta. Oracion funebre del famoso Comediante
Ingles Garrick comunmente intitulada *Sombras de ShakeSpear*. ENTRADA DOS
PESOS A la hora acostumbrada despues de la Oracion."[1]

Friday, January 19, 1782. At the Play House. Mr. Henry of the American Company of Comedians presents a compendious Monologue on the following subjects. Part one. Introduction: Alexander the Great; Cherokee Chief; Quack Doctor; His Arms; Oration in Praise of Law; Macaroni; Fashionable Head-dresses[?]; Face painting; Life of a Blood; His Servant; The Coat of Arms of Somebody, Nobody, Anybody, and Everybody; Vanity [?], Generosity; Friend-ship; Patriotism; and Genius; Flower of Merit; its Contrast; Honesty Flattery, and Reproach. Part two. Ladies' Heads; Riding Hood; Ranelagh Hood; Bil-lingsgate; Laughing and Crying Philosophers; Venus's Girdle; Morning Head-dress of Cleopatra; French Night Cap; Married Lady; Servant Maid; Old Maid. Part three. Head of a Married Blood; Woman of the Town; Master Among the Maids; Swindler; City Politician; Gambler; His Funeral and Monument; Head of a Fanatic. Part four. Monody to the Famous English Actor, Garrick com-monly entitled 'The Shadows of Shakespeare.' Admission two pesos. At the usual hour after prayers [?].[2]

1. This broadside is not listed in Wheeler or Evans but is in the Randall Collection, no. 81. See also, Lynn Haims, "First American Theatre Contracts," *Theatre Survey*, vol. 17, no. 2, November 1976, p. 191, n. 5.
2. The translation is a combination of the literal and the conjectural. The intent is to provide English rubrics which most closely correspond to versions of the *Lecture* given during the period.

MANCHESTER: THEATRE ROYAL.

February 11, 1782.

"Munden's benefit on February 11 gave him his first opportunity of playing Dogberry in *Much Ado About Nothing*; he also sang a comic song 'in the character of Punch', gave a 'A Lecture upon Lectures', which introduced 'a Lick at his Own Head', and brought the evening to a close by appearing as Robin in *The Waterman*."[1]

1. J. L. Hodgkinson and Rex Pogson, *The Early Manchester Theatre* (London, 1960), p. 101. The performer was J. S. Munden, the comedian.

LONDON: ALTERNATELY AT A ROOM IN PANTON STREET AND IN CORNHILL.

February 15, 16, 19, 20, 27, 28, March 4, 5, 1782 (also probably 19 additional performances between March 6 and 27; approx. 27 perfs.).

The lecture continued to be performed at the most unlikely places. It was included as one part of an entertainment by the popular magician Philip

Breslaw. Three other parts consisted mostly of deceptions. It would be interesting to know whether the satirical sketch on Jonas, the conjuring Jew, was included. Breslaw probably would have enjoyed this bit of fun at the expense of one of his colleagues despite the fact that Jonas had since retired from the stage and had become a money lender: "BRESLAW's Variety of NEW ENTERTAINMENTS in the CITIES of LONDON and WESTMINISTER. AT the GREAT ROOM, PANTON-STREET, HAYMARKET, This Day. And likewise at Mr. LOFT's GREAT ROOM, late KING's ARMS TAVERN, CORNHILL, Tomorrow . . . Part III The celebrated Miss ROSEMOND, a Child about eleven Years of Age, will deliver a SATIRICAL LECTURE on HEADS; the Particulars of which will be expressed in the Bills . . . The Rooms will be kept warm, and elegantly illuminated. Admittance, Two Shillings each Person . . . Any Person inclinable to learn some Deceptions on reasonable Terms, may, by applying to Mr. Breslaw, No. 57, Hay-market."[1]

March 8. [In Panton Street on Mondays, Wednesdays, Fridays and Saturdays] "and at Loft's on Tuesdays and Thursdays."[2]

March 14. Above advertisement repeated.[3]

March 24. "This and every Evening" [at Panton Street].[4]

March 26. "This and Tomorrow Evening" [at Panton Street. Last advertisement].[5]

1. *Public Advertiser*, February 15, 1782. See also, Thomas Frost, *The Lives of the Conjurers* (London, 1881), p. 132.
2. *Public Advertiser*, March 8, 1782.
3. Ibid., March 14, 1782.
4. Ibid., March 24, 1782.
5. Ibid., March 26, 1782.

NEW YORK, N.Y.: JOHN STREET THEATRE.

May 8, 1782 (1 perf.).

Odell refers to 1782 as the "last season of the military actors" in New York. "The performance of April 29th—[was] advertised as the last for this season. . . . But the theatre was again opened on May 8th, for the benefit of four actresses (I suppose), who must have assisted during the winter's playing."[1]

"(By particular DESIRE) This Evening will be performed, The COMEDY of the BUSY BODY, To which will be added The Farce of the IRISH WIDOW, Being for the benefit of Mrs. Hyde, Mrs. Batten, Mrs. Fitzgerald, and Mrs. Smith. Between the Play and Farce a part of the celebrated *Lecture on Heads* Will be attempted by a Gentleman. *Also a* SONG, By Mrs. HYDE. Places for the Boxes to be taken at Mrs. Petit's, from Eleven till Two o'Clock, every day Sunday excepted. Tickets to be had at the usual places. *Vivant Rex & Regina*."[2]

1. George C. D. Odell, *Annals of the New York Stage* (New York, 1927), vol. 1, pp. 218–220.
2. *Royal Gazette*, May 8, 1782.

BATH: THEATRE ROYAL (?).

May 22, 1782 (1 perf.).

"For Haughton's benefit on 22 May at Bath, he [Creswick] delivered a 'Lecture upon Hearts' at the end of the mainpiece."[1]

1. Philip Highfill, Jr., K. Burnim, and E. Langhans, *A Biographical Dictionary of Actors, Actresses, Musicians . . . in London, 1660–1800* (Carbondale and Edwardsville, 1973– 78), vol. 4, p. 44.

PHILADELPHIA, PA.

July 1782.

And here's one that didn't quite make it! On July 1, 1782, John Henry applied to the City Council for permission to perform stating: "I find our Theatre here entirely out of repair, and a debt for Ground rent and taxes incurred to the amount of 174 pounds. I learn also that it has been used for some time by permission for the exhibition of a Wire Dancer, on this account I presume to address your Excellency [President Moore] for Permission, for one Night only, to deliver a Lecture on Heads, for the purpose of paying the above debt, incurred since our Banishment."[1]

"On July 2, 1782, the Council 'ordered, that said request be not granted' because this lecture on heads, . . . was merely one of the various subterfuges so often employed to circumvent the laws against the theatre."[2]

1. *Pennsylvania Archives*, ed. Samuel Hazard (Philadelphia, 1852), first series, vol. 9, p. 573.
2. William S. Dye, Jr., "Pennsylvania *versus* the Theatre," *Pennsylvania Magazine*, vol. 55, no. 4, 1931, p. 361.

NEW YORK, N.Y.: JOHN STREET THEATRE.

August 1, 8, 16, September 11, 1782 (4 perfs.).

August 1. "*By Permission.* On THURSDAY, *August 1st*, Mr. HENRY, Will deliver, in TWO PARTS, *A Lecture on Heads.* (*Syllabus*, as Follows.) PART I. ALEXANDER—

Cherokee—Quack-Doctor—his Arms—Cuckold—Lawyer—Oration in praise
of Law—Maccaronies—Son of the Turf—Jockey—Arms of No-body—Somebody—Any-body—and Every-body—Sciences—Flower of Merit—its Contrast—Honesty—Flattery—and Reproach. PART II. Riding-Hood—Ranelagh-
Hood—Fish-Woman—Laughing and Crying Philosophers—Venus's Girdle—
Morning Head-Dress of Cleopatra—French Night-Cap—Married Lady—Old
Maid—Old Batchelor—Married Buck—Master among the Maids—Gambler—
his Funeral—A City Politician. . . . [The Lecture was followed by the Monody
'Shadows of Shakespeare'] To begin at half past Seven o'Clock. Tickets, Prices,
and Places as usual."[1]

August 5. The same program, with some additions, was advertised for August
5 but was not presented.

August 8. The August 1 performance was repeated. "(SECOND NIGHT.) Positively TO-MORROW Evening." Hippesley's "Drunken Man" and "A Picture of a
Play-House, Or, Bucks have at ye all!" were added.[2]

August 16. "The Third, and positively the last Night. ON FRIDAY Mr. HENRY,
Will deliver, with Alterations, *A Lecture on Heads* In which will be introduced
The Heart of a British Sailor, AND The Head of a Fanatic. . . . The doors to be
opened at seven, and to begin precisely at eight o'Clock."[3]

September 11. "THIS EVENING, Mr. HENRY, Proposes Exhibiting a *Rational Eve-
ning's Entertainment*, in Four Parts: PART I. Selections from G. A. Stephens's
Lecture on Heads . . . PART III. Ladies and Gentlemen's HEADS: And the
Dissection of the Heart of a *British Sailor* . . . * * *To please his Friends in the
upper Regions, he will conclude the whole with their favourite Interlude of
Hippesley's Drunken Man."[4]

1. *New York Gazette*, July 31, 1782.
2. Ibid., August 7, 1782.
3. Ibid., August 14, 1782.
4. Ibid., September 11, 1782.

KINGSTON, JAMAICA: THE THEATRE.

November 16, 1782 (1 perf.).

On this date a benefit performance for the American Company was given by
the army. Farquhar's *The Recruiting Officer* and Macklin's *Love à la Mode* were
given with parts of the "Lecture on Heads" between the two plays "attempted
by an officer."[1]

1. Richardson Wright, *Revels in Jamaica* (New York, 1937), p. 187.

DUBLIN AND LIVERPOOL.

March, October 1783.

"In March 1783, when she could get no money from the Crow Street managers, Mrs. Gardner delivered at the Capel Street theatre a 'Course of humorous, entertaining, polital and satyrical Lectures, never before exhibited'; *Freeman's Journal* reports the audience as numerous and polite, and as testifying their high esteem of her extraordinary merit."[1]

"*Mrs. Gardner* is at this Time giving Lectures on Heads, &c. at Liverpool—and she is said to pick up a good many Half Crowns."[2]

1. Godfrey Greene, "Mrs. Sarah Gardner: A Further Note," *Theatre Notebook*, vol. 8, no. 1, October–December 1953, p. 10.
2. *Public Advertiser*, October 30, 1783.

BARBADOS, WEST INDIES: FREE MASON HALL.

July 19, 1783 (1 perf.).

"A Lecture on Heads by Mr. Perch at Free Mason Hall as delivered 15 years ago in Theatre Royal, Haymarket, for $1.00. Means to pursue the same line as the learned Mr. Singleton who delivered the above lecture some years ago in this island at one dollar a ticket. He cannot therefore impose upon the generous public by presuming to ask *Two* . . ."[1] N.B. In the same paper Chadwick advertises at $2.00 for July 22, 1783.

1. *Barbados Mercury*, July 19, 1783.

BARBADOS, WEST INDIES: FREE MASONS ROOM.

July 22, 1783 (1 perf.).

"Mr. Chadwick presents George Alexander Stevens lecture on Heads, lately exhibited in London, at Free Masons Room (Gallery) on July 22. $2.00 each. Dancing after."[1]

1. *Barbados Mercury*, June 28, 1783.

PHILADELPHIA, PA.: SOUTHWARK THEATRE.

April 1, 12, 19, 26, May 11, 14, June 9, 1784 (7 perfs.).

With the antitheatre statutes still in effect, Hallam spent the better part of this ten-week period presenting the *Lecture* and, perhaps, some other entertainments. George Washington, who was in Philadelphia at the time, "purchased four Play Tickets"[1] on May 22. I have been unable to locate any information regarding the nature of the performance since nothing was advertised in the *Pennsylvania Packet* for that day. The *Packet* carried nine notices for seven different performances. Pollock says, "Our record is probably incomplete."[2] I am sure mine is as well.

April 1. "THEATRE. This EVENING will be delivered, A Lecture on Heads, and Strictures upon the most eminent Dramatic Authors—serious, comic and satire. A Poetical Address to the Public will open the Evening's Entertainment; and the whole will be properly diversified with Music, Scenery, and other Decorations. Tickets to be purchased at Mr. *Bradford*'s Book-store, in Frontstreet near the Coffee house; and places for the Boxes to be taken at the *Theatre*, from nine to one o'clock on Monday, and the following Mornings. Boxes 7s6—Pit 5s—Gallery 3s. *Vivat Respublica.*"[3]

April 12. "On MONDAY next, the Twelfth of April . . . The doors will be open at 6, and the *Lecture* begin at 7 'o'clock . . . No money to be received at the door."[4]

April 19. "On MONDAY next, the 19th of April . . ."[5]

April 26. "On MONDAY next, the 26th of April. . . . Mr. Hallam being obliged to postpone the new exhibition announced to the public, respectfully informs those who have not yet visited the theatre, that on Monday next he purposes, for the last time, to repeat the original entertainment; at the close of which, he hopes he shall be able to fix the time for delivering his second course of lectures."[6] The earliest located record of the "new exhibition" is for May 11.

May 11. "On TUESDAY next, the 11th of May, 1784, will be delivered, a *New* Course of Lectures upon Heads, Serious, Comic and Satiric. The first part will chiefly consist of a Poetical Address to the audience, and a Dissertation upon the Passions, with Examples selected from the most eminent dramatic writers. The second part will exhibit a Groupe of Female Portraits, faithfully drawn and characteristically represented; and The Third part will consist of various Male Caracatures, with a concluding Address to the audience."[7]

May 14. The last Night of Performance . . . TO-MORROW EVENING, being the 14th of May, 1784, . . . At the close of the first part of the Lecture will be recited a

MONODY, In honor of the CHIEFS who have fallen in the Cause of *America*, accompanied with suitable Decorations."[8]

June 9. "On WEDNESDAY EVENING next, being the 9th Instant, June—. . . . Previous to the first part of the Lecture will be recited, a MONODY . . ."[9]

1. Paul Leicester Ford, *Washington and the Theatre* (New York, 1899), p. 28.
2. Thomas Clark Pollock, *The Philadelphia Theatre in the Eighteenth Century* (Philadelphia, 1933), p. 135.
3. *Pennsylvania Packet*, April 1, 1784.
4. Ibid., April 10, 1784.
5. Ibid., April 17, 1784.
6. Ibid., April 22, 1784.
7. Ibid., May 8, 1784.
8. Ibid., May 13, 1784.
9. Ibid., June 8, 1784.

BARBADOS, WEST INDIES: THE THEATRE.

August 7, 1784 (1 perf.).

"This evening at the Theatre, by the particular desire of several gentlemen in order to assist Mr. Chadwick he will for the third time deliver the celebrated George Alexander Stevens much admired LECTURE ON HEADS. After the lecture will be introduced a celebrated interlude taken from Mr. Foote's comedy of THE MINOR. . . . Prices: Boxes and Pit one dollar; gallery half dollar."[1]

1. *Barbados Mercury*, August 7, 1784.

JAMAICA: MONTEGO BAY, ETC.

August 21+, 28, September 8, 25, October 9+, 1784 (5+ perfs.).

After a brief stay the American Company left Jamaica to return to America. "Thomas Wignell, however, seems to have lingered behind. . . . We find him offering, on August 21st, 'A Dramatic Fête in three parts, consisting of a variety of Entertainments Serious, Comic and Satirical, taken from the celebrated Lecture on Heads and Hearts, with suitable Decorations.' The scenery gone, he must have been put to some expense to scrape together these decorations. The bill concluded with that hardy favorite, *Bucks Have at Ye All*. This will be played for three nights, 'the liberty of renting the theatre being restricted to three exhibitions, T. Wignell respectfully solicits the patronage of his friends to an humble attempt to entertain them.' "

August 28. "August 28th finds the 'Dramatic Fête' repeated, being followed this time by a 'poetic Vision called the Court of Momus, in which will be exhibited a variety of well-known Dramatic Characters. . . .' The performance brings forth a puff in the *Chronicle* of September 4th, in which Mr. Wignell is lauded for his spirited presentation of the fête which has been 'for such a number of years a standing dish with the lovers of true humour and elegant satire.' The audience seems to have been numerous and genteel. He is forced to postpone his third and last performance till some time later."

September 8. "Meanwhile he rides around the coast road, twenty-five miles westward, to Lucea, where, in the court house on September 8th, he exhibits his 'Dramatic Fête.' "

September 25, October 9. "September 25th sees him back in Montego Bay with his fête, and on October 9th he repeats it. . . ."

"Mr. Wignell . . . moves to another town: he is amusing the genteel of Trelawny Parish, to the eastward of St. James's. At the court house in Martha-Brae he presents the 'Dramatic Fête.' First a prologue from the *Lecture on Hearts*, then *Bucks Have at Ye All*, and finally 'A Poetic Address to the Ladies in the character of a Mason, in which will be discovered the Grand Secret of Masonry.' After the performance came a ball. For all this he charged 14s 4d. However, he warns the populace that he intends leaving Martha-Brae the next Monday noon. The following Saturday in the *Chronicle* he publishes his 'sincere acknowledgements to the Ladies and Gentlemen of the parishes of St. Ann, Trelawny, St. James and Hanover for their distinguished patronage of his humble attempts to entertain them.' "[1]

1. Richardson Wright, *Revels in Jamaica* (New York, 1937), pp. 204–5, 7.

ANNAPOLIS, MD.: THE THEATRE.

September 30, October 12, 14, 1784 (3 perfs.).

"By Permission. THEATRE. For Two Nights Only. The public are respectfully informed, that Mr. HALLAM will, this evening, being the 30th of September, Exhibit A COURSE OF LECTURES, Serious, Comic, and Satiric, As are expressed in the Bills for the Day."[1]

1. *Maryland Gazette*, Annapolis, September 30, 1784. Although not specifically stated, it is reasonable to assume that the performance was the *Lecture on Heads* since it was Hallam's forte.

HULL: THEATRE ROYAL.

November 19, December 31, 1784 (2 perfs.).

The lecture was given by Miss Wilkinson (no relation to Tate, and later to be known professionally at Covent Garden as Mrs. Mountain) as part of a benefit for Mr. Buck. She was engaged to play in *The Maid of the Mill* "for that night and after that to repeat George Alexander Stevens's Lecture on Heads, and in point of speaking, deportment, singing, humour not void of discrimination, I do honestly confess and profess, that I have seldom witnessed such a performance at so early an age; for I do not believe she was more than fifteen, and in every part of the difficult task she had to sustain, I do not think but a London audience would have joined in my humble opinion, that her merit was undoubted, and not only gave promise for a little but a great deal; which makes me think that not only from what she performed that night, as a novice, I was convinced she could have done a great deal more had she only been put to the trial."[1]

December 31. On the last day of the year Miss Wilkinson again gave the *Lecture on Heads* and also performed in *Lionel and Clarissa*, both for her own benefit. In the latter play Tate Wilkinson played Oldboy, Mrs. Jordan played Lionel, and Miss Wilkinson played Clarissa. "Miss Wilkinson had a fine crowded house, and she added the Lecture on Heads, and obtained repeated and additional sanction and applause to her performances."[2]

1. Tate Wilkinson *The Wandering Patentee* (York, 1795), pp. 175–76.
2. Ibid., p. 178.

PHILADELPHIA: SOUTHWARK THEATRE.

December 7, 14, 23, 1784; January 17, 24, 31, March 1, 8, 15, 17, 29, April 2, 5, 9, 20, 21, May 9, 11, 16, 19, 26, June 6, 8, 13, 29, July 11, 1785 (26 perfs.).

The company, which had left Philadelphia in June 1784, returned in December for a new season. With the antitheatrical laws still in effect, they resorted to "Lectures," "Pantomimes," "Entertainments," and a variety of other diversions. None of the advertisements between December 1784 and July 1785 makes specific reference to Stevens or the *Lecture on Heads*. It may be assumed on the basis of some tenuous evidence, however, that Stevens's material appeared on the stage in some form. First, variations of the *Lecture* were a staple for Hallam and other members of the company. They were the basis of the run during the spring of 1784, and there is little reason to suppose that substantive changes had been made. It may also be significant that Thomas Wignell, who stayed on in Jamaica in August 1784 after the American Company had returned to America, was offering a program of "Entertainments Serious, Comical and Satirical, taken from the celebrated Lecture on Heads and Hearts [q.v.] . . ."[1] The terminology is used with great frequency although Stevens is not always credited as the author. Second, we have John Durang's word that "at this time, 1785, Lewis Hallam, Mr. Allen and wife, and Mr. Moore, where [*sic*] performing in the old Theatre, South St., under the head of 'Lectures on Heads.' Mrs. Allen sung; they gave scenes of plays and scraps of pantomimes."[2] This statement, except for the reference to "Lectures on Heads," is almost totally substantiated by the newspaper notices of the period. Durang was seventeen years old at the time and a member of Hallam's company when it opened its New York season later in 1785. He was about forty-eight when he wrote his memoirs. Alan Downer is careful to note that Durang's "memory may play him tricks when it comes to chronology,"[3] and we have learned from William Dunlap's inaccuracies to be careful about what we accept as fact. Nevertheless, the information cannot totally be ignored.

December 7. "LECTURES (Being a mixed Entertainment of Representation and Harmony) will be opened, on Tuesday the 7th instant, by a MONODY, . . . The Entertainment consisting of three Parts will present: First. A *serious* investigation of Shakespear's morality, illustrated by his most striking characters [most probably consisting of scenes from the plays] . . . Second. A poetical introduction to a display of characters, *comic* and *satyric*; in which those light follies and foibles that escape more serious animadversion, will be exposed to the lash of ridicule, and a scene of innocent mirth opened to the heart, without sacrificing sense to laughter or decency to wit. The impertinence of the fine gentleman, the profligacy of the rake, the humours of the low, and the vanity of the high will be ludicrously portrayed in a variety of shapes, and the force of satyr happily directed to the nobler purposes of admonition. Third. A dissertation on the passions, shewing the different complexions they assume, and their various modes of expression, according to the circumstances of character and situation.—Love and jealousy.—Humanity and libertinism.—Pride and poverty—often uniting in the same breast, but rarely appearing in the same garb. . . . Boxes 7s6. Pitt 5s. Gallery 3s9. . . . The doors will be open at Five o'clock, and the performance begin at Seven."[4]

December 14. "On Tuesday the 14th instant . . . [the same program] With Alterations and Additions . . . The doors will be open at half past Five o'clock . . ."[5]

December 23. "On Thursday, the 23d instant . . . [the same basic program with additions including 'Bucks Have at Ye All'] . . ."[6]

January 17, 24. The newspapers now seem bent on a vindictive campaign to confuse future generations of theatre historians thoroughly. On January 9 we learn that "AN ENTIRE NEW LECTURE . . . Will be Exhibited on *Monday the 24th of January*".[7] On January 12 the same newspaper advises us, in an identical notice, that the program "will be given on *Friday the 14th of January*."[8] The following day another newspaper repeats a version of the previous notices, again announcing the fourteenth. At the bottom of the advertisement, however, we learn that "The public are respectfully informed, that the intended Exhibition for Friday next, [the 14th?] is unavoidably postponed till Monday evening, [presumably the 17th] as a principal part of the machinery (not withstanding every exertion has been made to bring it forward) will not be ready for representation till that time."[9] The advertisement is repeated on the fourteenth, and the same issue carried a quatrain commemorating Stevens's death.[10]

January 31. "Will be exhibited on Monday the 31st of January."[11] This "ENTIRE NEW LECTURE" advertised through January contained, in addition to "a variety of New and entertaining Characters, Comic and Satiric," such attractions as Garrick's ode on dedicating a building to Shakespeare, a statue of Shakespeare with moving festoons, two scenes from "Loutherberg's *Eidiphusicon*," another Garrick address, and an assortment of songs.

Pollock[12] lists a performance for February 21 for which I can find no corroborating evidence. He does not list the advertisement for a February 28 performance "*for the Benefit of the* POOR . . . LECTURES, MORAL and ENTERTAINING . . . The Whole to conclude with a Grand PANTOMINICAL [*sic*] FINALE. With MUSIC, SCENERY, MACHINERY and DECORATIONS entirely NEW." The performance, however, was not given and the advertisement concluded with the following: "The Public are most respectfully informed, that though the greatest attention and industry has been made use of to finish the machinery necessary for an exhibition on Monday next, the directors find it impossible to have it in readiness by that time; they have therefore postponed it to the Monday following, that every part may be as compleat as possible, in hopes of meriting the approbation of the Public."[13]

A letter to Mr. Carey, publisher of the *Pennsylvania Evening Herald*, was published in that paper also on February 19. The letter was dated the eighteenth and the writer obviously was unaware of the cancellation. The appearance of the letter is particularly interesting since the *Herald* did not advertise these lectures until July. It is unlikely that the letter was a piece of paid puffery: "Mr. Carey. Through the medium of your paper, I beg leave to recommend to my fellow citizens, the generous benevolence of Mr. Hallam and Mr. Allen, in their liberal endeavours to stop the cries of want, by a well-timed benevolence, arising from the sources of sentimental amusement. I think it will redound to the honour of our citizens should the newspapers inform us, that, 'on the 28th Inst. there was a splendid entertainment at our theatre: the benefit arising therefrom, *for the use of the poor*, amounted to upwards of one hundred and fifty pounds, for which the corporation return their most sincere thanks.' 'Once see the LECTURE, and I'm sure you'll own, No scene to hurt your feelings has been shewn.' DRAMATICUS." [14]

March 1. The benefit was finally presented "on TUESDAY the FIRST of MARCH . . . In order to make this Night's Entertainment as advantageous to the POOR, as the very great Expence attending the PANTOMIMICAL FINALE will permit, the Directors hope the Public will not be offended, if the Price of Admittance to the GALLERY is raised to FIVE SHILLINGS each . . ."[15]

March 8. "On TUESDAY the 8th of March . . ."[16] The same program.

March 15. "On TUESDAY the 15th of March . . ."[17] The same program.

March 17. "On THURSDAY the 17th Instant . . ." A similar program with the addition of "LES GRAND OMBER CHINOIES" [*sic*].[18]

"The EXHIBITION intended for *Thursday Evening* [March 24th], is postponed on account of its being HOLY THURSDAY, until the following week. The particulars will be expressed in the bill for the day."[19]

March 29. "On TUESDAY, 29th Inst . . . a mixed entertainment," which may not have included the *Lecture*.[20]

April 2. "The 2nd of April, Will be delivered an entire new LECTURE, Moral and Entertaining; preceding the Lecture a new Prologue, in the Character of an OLD WOMAN, After which will be presented a variety of Characters and Caricatures, Comic, Satiric and Entertaining . . ."[21]

April 5. "THIS EVENING, the 5th of April . . ."[22] The same program.

April 9. "On SATURDAY, the 9th instant . . ."[23] A similar program with variations.

April 20. "On Wednesday Evening, the 20th instant . . ."[24] Similar to the January 31 performance. Pollock does not list this.

April 21. "On Thursday Evening, the 21st instant . . ."[25] With an additional scene.

May 9. "On Monday Evening, the 9th of May . . ."[26] The *Lecture* with a combination of earlier entertainments and "Les Petites Ombres Italienes."

May 11. "On Wednesday Evening, the 11th of May . . ."[27] The same.

May 16. "On Monday Evening, the 16th of May . . ."[28] The same.

May 19. "THIS EVENING, the 19th of May . . ."[29] The same.

May 26. "THIS EVENING, the 26th of May . . ."[30] The same with additions.

June 6. "On *Monday* the 6th Instant . . . An entire New Lecture: Consisting of—A Variety of Characters; Never before attempted . . ."[31]

June 8. "*This evening*, the 8th Instant . . ."[32] The same.

June 13. "On MONDAY the 13th Instant . . ."[33] The same.

June 29. "On THIS EVENING . . ."[34] With variations.

The *Packet* printed three advertisements for a performance on July 6,[35] but it is cancelled in the *Journal*: "The PUBLIC are most respectfully informed that the EXHIBITION at the THEATRE, INTENDED FOR This EVENING, Is unavoidably postponed to some future time, on account of the INDISPOSITION of Mrs. Allen."[36]

July 11. "*Positively the Last Time* . . . THIS EVENING . . ."[37] With variations.

1. Richardson Wright, *Revels in Jamaica* (New York, 1937), p. 204.
2. Alan S. Downer, ed., *The Memoir of John Durang* (Pittsburgh, 1966), p. 16. A footnote to this entry (no. 15, p. 144) states: "The comic 'Lecture upon Heads' had been originally devised and performed by George Alexander Stevens at the Haymarket in London, January 8, 1755. It was freely plagiarized by Stevens' contemporaries and successors." Downer, of course, is referring to a completely different lecture. See *supra.*
3. Ibid., p. xiv.
4. *Pennsylvania Packet*, December 6, 1784. Pollock (p. 43) reproduces the substance of this announcement indicating that it "repays reading as a literary puzzle."
5. *Pennsylania Packet*, December 14, 1784.
6. Ibid., December 22, 1784.
7. *Pennsylvania Journal*, January 9, 1785.
8. Ibid., January 12, 1785.
9. *Pennsylvania Packet*, January 13, 1785.
10. Ibid., January 14, 1785.
11. *Pennsylvania Journal*, January 26, 1785.
12. Pollock, p. 135.
13. *Pennsylvania Journal*, February 19, 1785.
14. *Pennsylvania Evening Herald*, February 19, 1785.
15. *Pennsylvania Journal*, February 26, 1785.
16. Ibid., March 5, 1785.
17. Ibid., March 12, 1785.
18. Ibid., March 16, 1785.
19. Ibid., March 23, 1785.
20. Ibid., March 26, 1785.
21. *Pennsylvania Packet*, April 2, 1785.
22. Ibid., April 5, 1785.
23. Ibid., April 8, 1785.
24. Ibid., April 18, 1785.
25. Ibid., April 20, 1785.
26. Ibid., May 7, 1785.
27. Ibid., May 11, 1785.
28. Ibid., May 14, 1785.
29. Ibid., May 19, 1785.
30. Ibid., May 26, 1785.

31. Ibid., June 4, 1785.
32. Ibid., June 8, 1785.
33. Ibid., June 11, 1785.
34. Ibid., June 29, 1785.
35. Ibid., July 2, 4, 6, 1785.
36. *Pennsylvania Journal*, July 6, 1785.
37. *Pennsylvania Packet*, July 11, 1785. Pollock (p. 136) lists this performance for July 9.

HALIFAX, NOVA SCOTIA: PONTAC ASSEMBLY ROOM.

May 31, June 8, 15, 1785 (3 perfs.).

May 31. "By permission of *His Excellency* the Governor In the ASSEMBLY-ROOM at PONTAC. This present EVENING, May 31st, 1785. WILL BE PRESENTED, A Comic, Sentimental, Dramatic *Entertainment*, called Fashionable Raillery, Selected from the LECTURE on HEADS and HEARTS, from the Productions of Garrick, Otway, and Dramatic Poets: WITH PROPER SCENERY AND APPARATUS, Regularly arranged in fours Parts, By WILLIAM MOORE, COMEDIAN. *** Mr. MOORE presents his best Respects to the Ladies and Gentlemen of this District, and in Order to prevent Confusion, informs them no Person can be admitted without a Ticket, which may be had at the *Bar*, or at Mr. *Howe's Printing Office*, as the *Doorkeeper* is ordered not to take Money. N.B. *To prevent Disputes*, Mr. Moore *humbly entreats the Ladies and Gentlemen who intend honouring his Endeavours to give them Entertainment, will be kind enough to take places, the Hours for which will be from Ten to Twelve the Day of Performance, and at the same Time request they will send their Servants to keep said Places, by Seven o'Clock in the Evening.* TICKETS ONE DOLLAR each. The Time of Beginning will be exactly at Half past Seven o'Clock."[1]

June 8. "THE LAST NIGHT BUT ONE . . . From the Theatre Royal in England and last from Jamaica where he has performed the above mentioned Entertainment with universal Applause To be preceded with a new Poetical Address written by the Performer. The Evening's Entertainment will conclude with POETICAL VISION, called THE COURT OF MOMUS . . . N.B. Mr. Moore entreats those Ladies and Gentlemen who intend honoring him with their Patronage to attend this and the ensuing Night of Performance as he embarks for Quebec, the latter end of next Week, and that the Performance will be considerably varied each Night. The Time of Beginning will be at *Eight* o'Clock precisely."[2]

June 15. ". . . After the Lecture, AN EULOGY ON FREE MASONRY In the Character of MASTER MASON. . ."[3]

1. *Nova Scotia Gazette and Weekly Chronicle*, May 31, 1785.
2. Ibid., June 7, 1785.
3. Ibid., June 14, 1785.

LONDON: HAYMARKET (THEATRE ROYAL), SADLER'S WELLS.

August 2, September 12, 13, 15, 16, 19, 20, 23, 26, 1785 (9 perfs.).

". . . End of Rosina, a new Lecture on Heads, by the two Miss Vernell's being their first Appearance on any Stage. . . . Boxes 5s. Pit 3s. First Gal. 2s Second Gal. 1s. Places for the Boxes to be taken of Mr. Rice, at the Theatre. The doors to be opened at Six o'clock, and to begin precisely at Seven. Vivant Rex & Regina."[1] More than a month later the Vernells moved to Sadler's Wells, where they continued the *Lecture* as part of an extensive bill which included dancing, dog tricks, a learned pig, an 8' 4" Irish giant, catches, and glees.

September 12. "For the Benefit of Mr. Williamson and Mrs. Baker . . . By particular Desire, for that [this] Night only, will be delivered A New COMIC LECTURE ON HEADS; As performed (with the greatest Applause) at the Theatre Royal, Hay-market by the Two Miss VERNELLS. In the First Part of the Lecture will be introduced the Cockney, Scotchman, Irishman, Welshman, Modern Beau, and Female Italian Singer; with the so much admired Air called ARNO's STREAMS. In the Second Part, the Jew, Quack Doctor, Lawyer, Termagant, and Typsy Lady . . ."[2]

September 13. "Benefit for Mr. Doyle and Mr. Whittow."[3]

September 15. "Benefit for Mr. Lowe and Mr. Boyce."[4]

September 16. "Benefit for Mr. Burrell."[5]

September 19. "Benefit for Mr. Bruguier and Mr. Huntley."[6]

September 20. "Benefit for Mr. Rayner and Miss Webb."[7]

September 23. "By Particular desire."[8]

September 26. "Last Night."[9]

1. *Public Advertiser*, August 2, 1785.
2. Ibid., September 12, 1785.
3. Ibid., September 13, 1785.
4. Ibid., September 15, 1785.
5. Ibid., September 16, 1785.
6. Ibid., September 19, 1785.
7. Ibid., September 20, 1785.
8. Ibid., September 23, 1785.
9. Ibid., September 26, 1785.

NEW YORK, N.Y.: JOHN STREET THEATRE.

August 11, 20, 26, September 1, 1785 (4? perfs.).

A month after the Philadelphia engagement Hallam and his colleagues came to New York and resumed their performances at the John Street Theatre. On August 11 the unspecified *Lectures* were repeated. The notice is similar to those printed earlier that year.

August 11. "The Lecture will be delivered in two parts, each part preceded by a Poetical Introduction so a display of characters, *comic* and *satiric* . . . will be exposed to the lash of ridicule, judiciously portrayed in a variety of shapes, and the force of satire, happily directed to the nobler purposes of admonition. . . . Doors will be opened at half past six o'clock and the performance to begin at half after seven . . . TICKETS (without which no person can be admitted) to be had at Mr. GAINE's Book-store, in Hanover-square. Box 8s. Pit and Gallery 5s. *Vivat Respublica*."[1]

August 20, 26. Additional lectures.[2]

September 1. "THIS EVENING WILL BE DELIVERED NEW LECTURES, *Serious, Comic and Satiric*, . . . BOX 8s. PIT 6s. GALLERY 4s. No person to be admitted behind the Scenes, on any account whatever."[3]

1. *New York Packet*, August 11, 1785.
2. George C. D. Odell, *Annals of the New York Stage* (New York, 1927), vol. 1, pp. 232–33.
3. *New York Packet*, September 1, 1785.

SAVANNAH, GA.: THEATRE IN BROUGHTON STREET.

January 26, 27, February 2, 14, 21, 24, 1786 (6 perfs.).

"MR. GODWIN respectfully informs the Publick, that, having procured a Book of Stevens's Lecture on Heads, and the Paintings and Apparatus being nearly compleated, on THURSDAY EVENING next, 26th instant will be performed, LIFE's MIRROR; Or, All the World's a Stage. PART I. Prologue. Introduction. Alexander the Great. Cherokee Chief. Quack Doctor. Quack Doctor's Coat of Arms. Cuckold. Snip Cabbage, (a Tailor) and Mynheer Jan Vantimtamtiraletaheer Van Cowhorn (a Butcher;) Humorous Dialogue between them, Plain Simple Head. Lawyer. Humorous Dissertation in Praise of the Law. End of the First Part, Garrick's Country Clown. PART II. A Monument with a Bust of General Richard Montgomery, who fell in storming Quebeck, 31st December, 1775: The Descriptive Ode was written by Mr. Sheridan. Head of the celebrated Doctor Benjamin Franklin, with a Motto. Sir Full-Fed Domine Double Chin. The Politician: 'A Tale.' The Zone, or Girdle of Venus. Great Virtue ascribed to it, 'Whatever Lady wears Venus's Girdle will infallibly possess the Beauties of Venus.' Head of an Old Maid, with a Soliloquy. A Monument with a Bust of David Garrick. An Ode to him on quitting the Stage. Testimonies to the Memory of Garrick, from the Works of SHAKESPEARE. Mrs. Godwin in Character of the Tragic Muse at the Monument of Garrick. Honesty. On the Term Nothing. A Methodist, with a Tabernacle Harangue . . . The Door will be opened at Half past Five, the Exhibition begin at Half after Six, and terminate by Ten o'Clock. *Vivat Respublica!*"

January 27. For the January 27 performance "Select Pieces of MUSICK between the Parts."[2]

February 2. Mrs. Godwin's benefit. "To the Lecture on Heads exhibited the first Night will be added the following *New* Heads: Nobody. Four Court Knaves. Nobody's Arms. Everybody's Arms. The Lady of Ostentation's Manor. Architecture, Painting, Poetry, Astronomy, and Music. Statue of Flattery. Spanish Lady. Jealous Husband. Epilogue to the same, representing a Spaniard, an Italian, a Dutchman, and John Bull. PART II. A Dialogue by Mr. and Mrs. Godwin, with an Address to the Audience . . . *The former heads will be introduced in the different Parts of the Lecture.*"[3]

February 14. "For the BENEFIT of the MUSICIANS, . . . will be exhibited, the following Addition to the LECTURE ON HEADS, Selected from Tragedy, Comedy, and Farce: A new Prologue, in Character of Somebody, with a malicious Design against Nobody. Head of a Gamester. Scene from the Tragedy of that Name, in the Character of Beverley. A Sharper. His Monument. Head of Major O'Flaherty. Lady Rusport. Old Varland. Two principal Scenes from the Comedy called, The WEST-INDIAN. Old Batchelor. New Married Lady. Laughing and Crying Philosophers. New Ladies Heads . . . Head of Isaac Mendoza and the Duenna, from the celebrated Opera of that Name . . . * * *Mr. Godwin respectfully assures the Public that every Effort shall be exerted to render the Exhibitions pleasing and new. The above Additions to the Lecture on Heads are for the Benefit of the Musicians, as a Reward for their Attention, and to induce them to settle in this State."[4]

February 21. Essentially the same as the February 14 performance with some minor variations. Also a benefit for the musicians. ". . . the Characters of Beverley and Jarvis . . . Ensign Dudley . . . Lady Rusport, and Miss Rusport will be personated by Performers. Six New Heads . . . N.B. Four new Boxes are added to accomodate nine Persons each; and, in order to obviate Mistakes and Disputes, a proper Distinction is made in the Price of Tickets for Boxes and back Seats. Ladies and Gentlemen who take Boxes are requested to send Servants at Half past Four to keep them."[5]

February 24. "The whole of George Alexander Stevens's celebrated LECTURE ON HEADS, Which has been performed upwards of One Hundred successive

Nights to crowded Audiences in London, and met with the most universal Applause. Prologue. Introduction. Alexander the Great. Cherokee Chief. Quack Doctor. Cuckold. Dutchman. Plain Simple Head. Lawyer. Humorous Oration in Praise of the Law . . . An Interlude . . . Heads of Honesty and Flattery. Cleopatra. French Nightcap. Face Painting. Old Batchelor. Lass of the Spirit. Quaker. Frenchman and Englishman. City Politician . . . Horse Jockies. Nobody. Lottery of Life. Physical Wig. Dissertation on Sneezing and Snuff-taking. Tea-Table Critic. Learned Critic. Life and Death of a Wit. Head of a Methodist Field Preacher with a Tabernacle Harangue . . . *Mr. Godwin will not exhibit the Lecture on Heads after the above Night, unless by Desire of a select Party of Ladies and Gentlemen, who may engage the Theatre, making a Party not less than Forty-five.*"[6]

Several weeks later Godwin announced his retirement from the stage. It was to be a short-lived farewell: "Mr. Godwin having entirely relinquished the STAGE, respectfully gives notice that he continues Tuition in DANCING, at Mrs. Aikin's Boarding School, and at his present Dwelling near the Market."[7]

1. *Georgia Gazette*, January 19, 1786.
2. Ibid., January 26, 1786.
3. Ibid., February 2, 1786.
4. Ibid., February 9, 1786.
5. Ibid., February 16, 1786.
6. Ibid., February 23, 1786.
7. Ibid., March 16, 1786.

CHARLESTON, S.C.: HARMONY HALL.

July 11, 1786 (1 perf.).

The lecture presented by Mr. Godwin for the opening of Harmony Hall:

"Harmony Hall at Louisburg, without the city. On Tuesday Evening, 11th July, (By Desire) will be performed a grand concert of Music in three Acts, selected from the most celebrated composers. Between the Acts will be exhibited, a variety of paintings, consisting of ancient and Modern Heads, with a Lecture, by Mr. Godwin. Syllabus of the Lecture: Prologue—Tragic and Comic Muse—the celebrated Dr. B. Franklin, with the Motto affixed to his bust at Paris—Alexander the Great—Cherokee Chief—Quack Doctor—his coat of arms—Snip Cabbage and Mynheer Janvantimtamteeraleeraletta heer van Cowhorn—Plain Simple Head—Lawyer—Oration in Praise of the Law—Nobody's Head—or the Term Nothing—Lottery of Life—Statues of Honesty and Flattery. After the Second Act of the Concert, a Monument, with Transparencies, and a Bust of General Richard Montgomery; who fell in storming Quebec, December 31st, 1775. An Ode, by Mr. Godwin The Family of Nobody—

Architecture, Painting, Poetry, Astronomy and Music—Ladies Heads—
Ancient Riding Hood—Modern Ranelagh Hood—Billingsgate—Laughing
and Crying Philosophers—the Zone, or Girdle of Venus—Great Virtue
ascribed to it—'Whatever Lady wears Venus's Girdle, will infallibly possess the
Beauties of Venus'—Don Lewis Choleric de Testy de Halfwitto and Spanish
Wife—Characteristics of a Spaniard, Italian, Dutchman, Frenchman, and Englishman—on Face Painting—Young Married Lady—Old Maid—Old Bache-
lor—Woman of the *Ton*—Man of the *Ton*, or a Blood, with *Bucks, Have at Ye all!*
. . . A Person will attend at the Office of Harmony Hall, every Day, to let Boxes.
Front Boxes are for Parties of Ten, and Side Boxes for Parties of Six. Each Box
has a Key, to be given to the person who takes it. The Gate fronting Boundary
Street will be opened at Half past Five, and the concert commence at Seven
o'Clock. Tickets for the Pit, at Five Shillings each, to be had at Mr. Waller's
Store, on Beal's Wharf, at Bowen and Markland's No. 11, Elliot-street, and at
the Office above mentioned. No admittance to the Boxes but by Parties—No
more Tickets for the Pit are issued than to the Number of Persons it will
accomodate; therefore Ladies and Gentlemen are desired to apply for Tickets
early, as the Door-keeper is under a binding engagement to reject Money at the
Door. New Heads, with Singing and Dancing, each Night of the Concert."[1]

The evening was a success as evidenced by the following comments which
appeared in the local newspapers during the three days following the opening.
Such critical reviews are indeed uncommon during this period, most information being limited to announcements, broadsides, and advertisements.

"The audience received the lecture with great satisfaction and rewarded the
lecturer with unbounded applause; however it will be an improvement if the
future lectures are calculated to take up less time, it being impossible for a
single person to entertain his auditors for three hours, without their falling into
a condition of indifference and lassitude; the truth of this observation was
evident last night, although Mr. Godwin was equally if not more successful than
George Alexander Stevens, who performed the material parts of the lecture
eighty nights running at the Haymarket theatre to crowded audiences."[2] The
next entry was in the same paper: "A demi-rep sported her person in the first
row of the Pit, Tuesday Evening at the Lecture, and in this conspicuous
situation was thrown into much confusion when the lecturer held the mirror
up to nature; showing to virtue its endearing graces and loveliness, to vice, its
odiousness and deformity."[3]
"The beauty and airiness of this elegant little theatre, the brilliancy with which
it was lighted, the masterly execution of the paintings, the spirit and humour
with which Mr. Godwin delivered the lectures, the excellence of the music, in
short, the *tout ensemble* of the one whole entertainment were so highly pleasing
that the audience testified their satisfaction by repeated bursts of applause; and
notwithstanding the length of the entertainment, which lasted nearly three
hours, there was not a symptom of indifference or lassitude. [An obvious retort
to the previous review.] During the whole entertainment there was not the

smallest disturbance or interruption. The whole was conducted with the utmost regularity and decorum, and the audience retired pleased, instructed and delighted."[4]

And to conclude the relevant observations of the opening night: "As no part of Mr. Godwin's much admired lecture was received with a higher relish than the Law-case, the following is offered to the consideration of the Manager of Harmony Hall."[5] The following consisted of a recital of the popular story of the farmer, the bull, the goat, and the ferry boat. Godwin was to have repeated the program on July 20 but was forced to cancel it due to an "indisposition" which later turned into a "dangerous illness." He was sufficiently recovered by September to perform again.

1. *Columbian Herald and Independent Courier*, July 6, 1786.
2. *Charleston Morning Post and Daily Advertiser*, July 12, 1786.
3. Ibid.
4. *Columbian Herald and Independent Courier*, July 13, 1786.
5. *Charleston Morning Post and Daily Advertiser*, July 14, 1786.

CHARLESTON, S.C.: HARMONY HALL.

September 12, 1786 (1 perf.).

Having recovered from his earlier illness, Godwin repeated the *Lecture on Heads* at Harmony Hall: "Harmony Hall, at Louisburg, without the city, On Tuesday Evening, September 12th, Will be Performed, A Grand Concert of Music. Between the Acts will be exhibited A Variety of Heads Selected from Stevens's Lecture. A Prologue by Mr. Godwin, On his first appearance after his late dangerous Illness. Previous to the Lecture Garrick's Country Clown by Mr. Godwin. After the Lecture an Interlude called 'The Broken Bridge Or the Maccaroni Traveller and Indolent Carpenter,' By Messrs. Godwin and Kidd To which will be added A Comedy in Two Acts, called 'The Old Maid' . . . Tickets to be had at Harmony Hall only, where boxes may be taken. Box 7s. Pit 5s . . ."[1] The performance was noted the following day: "Mr. Godwin being recovered from his late indisposition, delivered a part of Stevens's Lecture last night at Harmony Hall, with great applause."[2]

1. *Columbian Herald and Independent Courier*, September 4, 1786.
2. *Charleston Morning Post and Daily Advertiser*, September 13, 1786.

PHILADELPHIA, PA.: CITY TAVERN.

February 7, 9, 1787 (2 perfs.).

Hearts again: ". . . At the City Tavern, Will be delivered by Mrs. Kenna, A Lecture on Hearts. The paintings are done by an eminent artist, and will be exhibited in the course of the Lecture. PART FIRST. The Heart of an Honest Sailor,—The Heart of a Bad Agent,—The Heart of a Bully,—The Heart of an Officer,—The Heart of an Usurer,—A sound upright Heart. The end of Part First to conclude with a comparative View of QUEEN ELIZABETH'S HATS, and the MODES and FASHIONS of the Present TIMES. PART SECOND. FEMALE HEARTS,—The Heart of a Millener [sic],—The Heart of an Old Maid,—The Heart of an Amiable Woman, The whole to conclude with *Satan's Address to the Sun, from Milton.* Admittance, Six Shillings. To begin precisely at seven o'clock."[1]

1. *Pennsylvania Mercury and Universal Advertiser,* February 9, 1787.

CHARLESTON, S.C.: HARMONY HALL.

May 1? June 19, 21, 1787 (3? perfs.).

Godwin continued to perform after his recovery but soon faced new problems. "On March 28 the South Carolina Legislature enacted a Vagrancy Law which classified actors with beggars, unlicensed pedlars, and fortune tellers."[1] Godwin, as did so many other performers, turned to various subterfuges for his livelihood. Early in May he started a series of patriotic lectures based on thirteen famous Americans embellished with portraits in the form of transparent paintings. Late in June he was again doing the Stevens lecture.[2] "For the Benefit of Mr. Godwin at Harmony Hall Tuesday Evening, June 19 Will be exhibited A Moral, Serious, Comic and Satirical 'Lecture on Heads' In Three Parts To Conclude with a Splendid Set of Thirteen Portraits."[3]

1. Mary Julia Curtis, "The Early Charleston Stage, 1703–1798" (Ph.D. diss., Indiana University, 1968), p. 160.
2. Ibid., p. 437.
3. Eola Willis, *The Charleston Stage in the Eighteenth Century.* (Columbia, S.C., 1924), p. 144.

EDINBURGH: THEATRE ROYAL, SHAKESPEARE SQUARE.

May 19, 1787 (1 perf.).

"From May 10th to 19th the Theatre was closed. On the latter date, however, it opened, with Lee Lewes as an especial attraction. After acting in several pieces, Lee Lewes gave his 'Lecture on Heads.'"[1]

1. James C. Dibdin, *The Annals of the Edinburgh Stage* (Edinburgh, 1888), p. 200.

NEW YORK, N.Y.: THE THEATRE.

June 6, 1787 (1 perf.).

". . . Between the Play and the Entertainment [Cumberland's *The Fashionable Lover* and Foote's *The Author*] will be delivered a Whimsical, Rhapsodical, Epilogue Address, by Mr. Wignell, in the character of Nobody, being intended as a Satire upon Every Body, without offense to Any Body."[1] This was a benefit for Mrs. Morris.

1. *New York Packet*, June 5, 1787.

BARBADOS, WEST INDIES: MRS. BENNET'S LONG ROOM.

July 18?, 1787 (several perfs.).

"At Mrs. Bennet's Long Room, George Alexander Stephens's Lecture on Heads; 3 parts—51 items not including 2 songs. Two Negro Heads will be introduced with a curious dialogue between them. To conclude with the much admired Negro Song of Sabina, accompanied with the Banger. Tickets 6/—and 3d. Commencing at 7 p.m."[1] The advertisement was repeated fifteen times between July 25 and October 13. A newspaper review tells us that the few present were not adequate to expenses. The exhibitor requested the gentlemen present to undeceive the ladies of the idea that the performance was indecent.[2]

1. *Barbados Gazette and General Intelligence*, July 18–21, 1787.
2. Ibid., July 25–28, 1787.

LONDON: ROYALTY THEATRE.

July 23–25, 27, 28, 30, 31, August 3, 4, 6–11, 16, 18, 22–25, 27–31, September 1, 3, 15, 19, 22, 24–29, October 1–5, 8, 11-13, 17–20, 22, 24, 26, 27, 29–30, November, 2, 3, 5–10, 21, 28, 29, December 10, 15, 17, 18, 20, 21, 1787; August 1, 6, 8, 18, September 10, 15, 1788 (80 perfs.).

In 1787 all of the *Lectures* were done by Lee Lewes with the following exceptions: August 6, 7, 27, 29, December 15, 17, 18, 21 by Palmer; August 9 and September 3 by Lewes and Palmer. In 1788 all of the *Lectures* were done by Palmer except for September 10 when it was done by Arrowsmith during his own benefit: "Several Comic Subjects from the LECTURE ON HEADS by Mr. LEE LEWES. . . . George Alexander Stevens; Sir Whiskey Whiffle, Master Jackey, a Female Nimrod; a comical Fellow; a specimen of Bar Elocution and Oratory; a generous Fellow; an honest Fellow; a devilish clever Fellow; and a Drunken Fellow."[1]

July 25. "George Alexander Stevens, an Over-dressed Lady, a delicate Lady, the Head-dress of Antiquity, Three Modern Head-dresses, a Billingsgate, an Old Maid, an Old Batchelor, Ancient and Modern Oratory, a Lady in a Good and Bad Temper, a Matrimonial Tete-a-Tete, and a Drunken Buck."[2]

July 28. "George Alexander Stevens, A Scheme to pay off the National Debt, A Wise Man in his own Conceit, A Frenchman, A British Tar, A Dialogue between two Sailors, Bullem versus Boatum, a Proud Man, and a Methodist Preacher."[3]

July 30. "George Alexander Stevens, Wigs. A Brace of Knowing Ones. A Comical Half-foolish Fellow. Every Body, No Body, Some Body. Flattery. A Dutchman. A Spaniard. A Frenchman. A British Tar. And a Mock musical Cantata."[4]

August 4. "George Alexander Stevens, Sir Whiskey Whiffle, Mama's Darling. A Female Nimrod, A Half-foolish Fellow, Two Connoisseurs. A Freeholder. A Specimen of Bar Elocution and Oratory. A Female Moderator, A Buck, And a Drunken Blood."[5]

August 27. Benefit for Bannister. "To Conclude with the Heads of Three Managers."[6]

September 3. Benefit for Lewes. "In which will be given the Favourite Dialogue between Sam Stern and Tom Grog."[7]

December 15. Announces forthcoming performance on December 20. "A part of the Lecture upon Heads which has not been delivered for some months. The characters all new dressed."[8]

December 20. Benefit for Lewes. "And the last Time of his performing in England."[9]

September 10, 1788. "Mr. Arrowsmith's Night . . . Mr. ARROWSMITH will (for this night only) make an Humble Attempt to deliver several Comick Subjects as spoken by Mr. LEE LEWES from the LECTURE on HEADS Amongst the Heads intended for this Evening's Entertainment, will be introduced A comical half-foolish Face. Wooden Heads and Paper Skulls. Head of an Old Maid. Head of an Old Batchelor. Head of a Fine Lady. Head of a Billingsgate Queen. The Joys of Matrimony. Busts of the Laughing and Crying Philosophers. Bullum versus Boatum. Head of a Politician. Head of a British Sailor, with a new Song, ponting out to his Shipmates, a way to take care of their wages and prize-money. Head of an Ancient Buck—to conclude with the Head of a Modern Drunken Buck. The Heads are entirely new."[10]

1. *Morning Chronicle and London Advertiser*, July 23, 1787.
2. Ibid., July 25, 1787.
3. Ibid., July 28, 1787.
4. Ibid., July 30, 1787.
5. Ibid., August 4, 1787.
6. Ibid., August 27, 1787.
7. Ibid., September 3, 1787.
8. Ibid., December 15, 1787.
9. Ibid., December 20, 1787.
10. Ibid., September 6, 1788.

The following story is of special interest. "While at the Royalty Theatre he [Lewes] recited the famous ballad of Johnny Gilpin, but not having created that merriment among his audience which he expected, he came off the stage disgusted with Gilpin, declaring he would give his Lecture on Heads the next night instead of it. A friend observed to him, that if he had worn a comical citizen's wig and thrown it off when he was describing Gilpin's fall from his horse, he would have made the people laugh. 'My dear Sir (replied Lee Lewes), 'it is not *wigs* that people want now-a-days, but heads.'" From Thomas Gilleland, *The Dramatic Mirror* (London, 1808), vol. 2, p. 828.

PHILADELPHIA, PA.: VARIOUS LOCATIONS.

January 26, 30, February 2, 6, 13, 19, 23, 25, 29, March 7, 10, 14, 26, 29, April 2, 1788 (6 perfs.).

During the first four months of 1788, Mr. Smith entertained Philadelphia audiences fifteen times under the general title of *Moral Lectures*. These programs included a large variety of acts frequently interspersed with music and singing. There are occasional faint echoes of the *Lecture on Heads* as noted below. The general impression of the run is that Smith tried to vary the program as much as possible and to present material that would be least likely to offend the city officials. He moved from one locale to another and during the last month was, in effect, alternating with Mr. Pursell, who was doing a variation of the *Lecture on Heads* at the Long Room. The only Smith programs cited are those which suggest the use of the *Heads* format.

January 26. "At . . . the Bunch of Grapes . . . *will be delivered a series of moral* LECTURES: *New and celebrated—consisting of serious, philosophic, comic and entertaining Prologues, Epilogues, Soliloquies, &c. . . . Each discourse will be dressed in proper character.*"[1]

February 25. "THIS EVENING . . . at Mr. Figel's commodious Room . . . that very agreeable Contrast Lecture on the Heads of Captain *Flash*, and Little Billy *Fribble*, by three Persons—Also, a satyrical Lecture on the Head of the celebrated Dr. *Emanuel Last* . . ."[2]

March 7. "Part 6th. A Lecture (By Desire) on the Heads of Captain Flash and little Billy Fribble, by Mr. Smith, Mr. D——g, [Durang] and Mrs. Harriet Foy . . . Part 12th. Epilogue, in Character of Nobody, by Mr. Smith . . ."[3]

March 14. "For the last time before Easter, at the large Room in Church-Alley . . . PART 3d. A Comic Lecture on the Heads of Major Sturgeon and Mrs. Sneak . . ."[4]

March 29. "PART 1st. A Lecture on the Heads of Henry, Tressel, and Gloster . . . PART 8. A Lecture on the Heads of Young Philpot, Old Philpot, and Marla. CITIZEN . . ."[5]

April 2. "PART 12th. A favorite Epilogue in Character of Nobody, by Somebody, not aimed at any Body, and addressed to everybody."[6]

1. *Independent Gazetteer*, January 25, 1788.
2. Ibid., February 25, 1788.
3. Ibid., March 7, 1788.
4. Ibid., March 14, 1788.
5. Ibid., March 29, 1788.
6. Ibid., April 2, 1788.

PHILADELPHIA, PA.: LONG ROOM.

March 11, 17, 25, 28, April 11, 1788 (5 perfs.).

Following are the Pursell performances mentioned above which alternated with Mr. Smith.

March 11. "This Evening. At the request of a number of Friends to a Family in Distress; Mr. Pursel another course of *Lectures on Heads and Manners*, with alterations and additions; At the Long Room, Corner of South and Front-streets. The PAINTINGS and CARVINGS are ENTIRELY NEW INVENTIONS, and EXECUTED In a MASTERLY MANNER. Between the parts of the Performance, VOCAL and INSTRUMENTAL MUSIC. LECTURES, MORAL, SATYRIC and COMIC, with DRESSES suited to each CHARACTER. And Conclude with an HUMOROUS RHAPSODY DRAWN from a WELL KNOWN CHARACTER, and never in PRINT. Tickets at one Quarter of a Dollar each . . . The Door will be opened at half past 6, and the Curtain drawn at a quarter past 7 o'clock. * * *Mr. Pursel flatters himself that from the general applause he met with on his first appearance he will be able to give equal if not greater satisfaction on this his second. * * * As their [*sic*] are but few Tickets will be disposed of, the more speedy application for them, will be the more certain for such Ladies and Gentlemen as may be pleased to honor Mr. Pursel with their company."[1]

March 17. "THIS EVENING" the same with the addition of "Adventures of a Blood."[2]

March 25. "THIS EVENING" the same with the addition of "A Burlesque on Politics" and "The SCOTCH PEDLAR."[3]

March 28. "THIS EVENING" the same with the addition of "A MILITARY FOP, AND A Laughable Dialogue."[4]

April 11. "THIS EVENING" the same with variations.[5]

The last three advertisements also indicated that "Mr. PURSEL would be happy in entertaining a private company at his room,—one day's previous notice being given at his house."

1. *Independent Gazetteer*, March 11, 1788.
2. Ibid., March 17, 1788.
3. Ibid., March 25, 1788.
4. Ibid., March 28, 1788.
5. Ibid., April 11, 1788.

LONDON: THE GREAT ROOM IN CHAPEL COURT.

February 5, 1788 (at least 1 perf.).

"City Academy At the Great Room in Chapel Court, Batholomew Lane, opposite the Bank This Present evening and every succeeding Tuesday will be delivered a Course of Lectures, Serious and Comic . . . by a society of Gentlemen . . ."[1] The *Lectures* were in three parts; the opening of part three was an "Extract from the Lecture on Heads."

1. *Morning Chronicle*, February 5, 1788. No additional advertisements have been located.

SAVANNAH, GA.: MR. GORDON'S ASSEMBLY ROOM, MR. COPP'S ASSEMBLY ROOM.

July 8, 15, December 9, 11, 1788 (4 perfs.).

Mrs. Gardner, a prominent actress from the Theatre Royal, Covent Garden, made her first appearance in Savannah in 1788. Her performance included the *Lecture* and various recitations and was repeated the following week.

"ASSEMBLY ROOM. For One Night Only. ***On TUESDAY the 8th of JULY will be exhibited, *The Lecture on Heads*, by Mrs. GARDNER, From the Theatre Royal, Covent Garden, Being her first Appearance in this Town. With a new INTRODUCTORY ADDRESS . . . In the second part will be introduced a humourous specimen of SCOTCH and IRISH ORATORY . . . Admittance One Dollar . . . ***Mrs. GARDNER most respectfully informs the Publick, that the Lecture she intends to have the honour of performing before them is a copy from the original manuscript of Mr. G. A. Stevens, and not the surreptitious one which has appeared in print; that the apparatus was prepared in London by that celebrated artist Mr. Milburne; and that the greatest care will be taken to render the room cool and commodious; nor will any attention on her part be neglected to display the evening's entertainment in such a style as shall merit the approbation of a generous community, whose countenance and patronage on the occasion she most humbly solicits."[1]

The actress did not advertise the contents of her *Lecture* for any of the four performances, but it is almost certain that the material was based on one of Lewes-Pilon editions, first published in 1785. Mrs. Gardner's version was surely emended in some way, through cutting or the addition of topical material, a practice engaged in by almost every other performer of the *Lecture*.

July 5. "By particular Desire" . . . "Mrs. Gardner having been informed that some inconvenience was complained of by those Ladies and Gentlemen who honoured her with their company on Tuesday last, on account of the disposition of the seats, begs leave to assure the public, that that defect will be removed, by raising the back seats, so that those in front may not obstruct the view." "She delivered the *Lecture* with an infinity of true *comick* humour."[2]

Later that year Mrs. Gardner opened a "school of elocution" in Mr. Copp's Assembly Room and there revived the *Lecture* on two occasions.

December 11. "BY PERMISSION . . . This Present Evening. Being THURSDAY the 11th of DECEMBER, will be exhibited, for the last time, *The Lecture on Heads* . . . Mrs. Gardner most respectfully informs the public, that, as printed bills are not of the same utility for an Oratorical Performance as they are for a Dramatic one, there will be *none* delivered; and that they will please to accept of notice from the *Newspaper alone*. Mrs. G. farther informs them, that nothing shall be wanting, on her part, to render the performance such as shall merit their approbation, and care shall be taken, also, to have the Ball Room commodious and agreeable."[3]

1. *Georgia Gazette*, July 3, 1788.
2. Ibid., July 10, 1788.
3. Ibid., December 11, 1788.

NEW YORK, N.Y.: CITY TAVERN.

July 15, 1788 (1 perf.?).

"And poor M'Pherson, of the Old American Company, detained, we are told, in the city for debt, made heroic efforts to extricate himself. 'For one Night Only,' we read in the Journal of June 16, 1788, 'at the City Tavern, June 19th, Mr. McPherson (previous to his joining the Company at Philadelphia) Proposes to Deliver the celebrated Lecture on Heads with Alterations and Additions.' There were to be also a Prologue in the Character of a Drunken Sailor, and the Picture of a Play-house. The lecture was deferred to June 21st; but, on June 23rd (Monday) we read, 'Mr. M'Pherson, Having been disappointed in his expectations on *Saturday Evening*, is induced to make another attempt'—on June 25th. Then came 'the last attempt'—so advertised—on July 15th. I include the record for its value as evidence in the hardships of a player's life."[1] The chronology and details follow:

June 16. "Positively for one NIGHT only, At the CITY TAVERN, On THURSDAY Evening, June 19, Mr M'PHERSON (previous to his joining the Company at Philadelphia) Proposes to deliver the celebrated LECTURE ON HEADS, With Alterations and Additions. Occasional Prologue. Among a variety of HEADS the following will be exhibited, viz. *American Soldier & Patriot*, Contrasted with *Alexander the Great. An American Married Lady*. With a Dissertation on Courtship and Matrimony. OLD MAID. Old BACHELOR. Master JACKY the Tea table Critic, and *The Head of a Young Lady Contrasted*. Young Female Quaker. *Modern Fine Gentleman*. A LONDON ALDERMAN, or CITY POLITICIAN, Humourously described. FREEHOLDERS HEAD, in a State of Innoculation. A LAWYER. With a HUMOUROUS ORATION, in praise of the Law, exemplified in the Case of *Daniel* against *Dishclout*. A London Blood, With a Description of his 'KEEPING IT UP.' The whole interspersed with Dissertation on the Five Sciences, and Esteem, Gratitude, Friendship, Public Spirit, and Common Sense, &c. &c. &c. Between the First and Second Parts, A PROLOGUE, in the Character of A DRUNKEN SAILOR. The whole to conclude with *The Picture of a Play-House*. TICKETS at Four Shillings each may be had of Mr. HUGH GAINE, at his Book-Store in Hanover-Square, at Mr. GREENLEAF's Printing-Office, and of Mr. BARDIN, at the CITY TAVERN. *** *To begin precisely at half past* SEVEN *o'Clock*. VIVAT RESPUBLICA."[2]

The ad was repeated June 17, 18, 19, 20, and 21, but the following was appended to the notice of the twentieth: "* * * M'PHERSON *begs leave respectfully to inform the* Public, *that (not being able to get the full compliment of* Heads *compleated* yesterday) the Exhibition was unavoidably postponed *to Saturday Evening, June 21*."[3] And then on June 23: "Mr. M'PHERSON, having been disappointed in his expectations on *Saturday Evening* last, is induced to make another attempt— and *On Wednesday* Evening,—The 25th Instant—. . . *To begin precisely at* EIGHT *o'Clock*. N.B. CHILDREN *will be admitted at half price*."[4]

The notice was repeated on June 24 and 25, and since nothing further is announced until July 14 it would have been logical to assume that the *Lecture* had taken place. On that date, however, we read: *"The* LAST ATTEMPT. On TUESDAY EVENING . . . In the course of the LECTURE, Twenty-two Heads will be exhibited."[5] And on the following day:

*"To the Public in general. and the Patrons of the Theatre in particular. As nothing but the extreme necessity to which I am reduced, ould [sic] force from me an address of this kind—to feeling minds (and to such only I appeal) the cause from which it proceeds must plead powerfully in my favor.—I believe it is unnecessary to observe, that I belonged to the Old American Company of Comedians, whose ill success (previous to the benefits) the last season, is as generally known; and to the impartial and unprejudiced patrons of the theatre, I trust I shall stand excused, if in justice to my behavior (which, in the opinion of my creditors must seem reprehensible) I am compelled to declare, That as the company did not perform more than half the time they continued here, and as the salaries were discontinued those weeks we did not play, I have, on an average, received but half salary.—the extra properties wanting for the stage (and which cannot be dispensed with) required great part of this, and the remainder was inadequate to the maintenance of myself and daughter. This circumstance, joined to the small advantage derived from a benefit, conjointly with Mr. Biddle, (an accompt of which will prove, that our shares were only £5) rendered me unable to discharge the few debts I had unavoidably contracted. Therefore, when the company left the place, I had determined to remain, in hopes of extricating myself by delivering the "*LECTURE ON HEADS;*' but as I have unfortunately failed in every attempt hitherto, the consequence must be obvious. I cannot, however, refrain from making one effort more—as, after this declaration, it would be an ungenerous reflection on the worthy citizens of New-York—(whose beneficence has too often shone conspicuously) not to hope for success.* ROBERT F. M'PHERSON *New-York, July 15, 1788."*[6] Let us be sanguine and credit him with the performance at last.

1. George C. D. Odell, *Annals of the New York Stage* (New York, 1927), vol. I, p. 270.
2. *The New York Journal and Daily Patriotic Register,* June 16, 1788.
3. Ibid., June 20, 1788.
4. Ibid., June 23, 1788.
5. Ibid., July 14, 1788.
6. Ibid., July 15, 1788.

LONDON: HAYMARKET, THEATRE ROYAL.

August 22, 1788 (1 perf.).

The *Lecture* was presented by John Palmer after *The Catch Club,* which was the first piece on the program. The evening was a benefit for Mr. Bannister: "G. A. Steven's Original *Lecture on Heads* Head of Alexander the Great—Head of a Cherokee Chief—Head of a Quack Doctor—Cuckold's Head—Nobody's Head—The laughing and crying Philosopher's Heads—And the Head of

Flattery—A fine Lady's Head—The Head of an Old Maid—Cleopatra's Head—Plain Moll's Head—And the Head of a Married Lady."[1]

1. *Public Advertiser*, August 22, 1788.

PHILADELPHIA, PA.: SOUTHWARK THEATRE.

January 31, February 2, 1789 (not performed).

Still at the height of the controversy, this was very shortly before the repeal of the antitheatre laws. Hallam and Wignell did some extensive advertising in two newspapers announcing a five-part benefit entertainment to be done at the Southwark. The performances were never given, but the details are included here since Stevens's material was intended to form a substantial part of the program.

January 31. "The Public are respectfully informed, that at the influence of many Friends of the Drama, a few Nights will be appropriated for the Benefit of the Individual Performers of—The *Old American Company.* For Messrs. Hallam and Wignell. TO-MORROW EVENING, the 31st Instant, will be presented—The following *Miscellaneous Entertainments.* . . . PART THIRD. A Comic and Satiric Lecture on HEADS, Will be attempted, for the first time, by Mrs *Morris* . . . PART FOURTH. Sketches and Caracature, From *Stevens*'s Lecture, with Variations—By Mr. *Wignell*. . . . The doors to be opened at five, and the curtain drawn up precisely a quarter past six o'clock . . . Boxes seven shillings and six pence, Pit five shillings, Gallery three shillings and nine pence."[1]

"MESSRS. HALLUM & WIGNELL respectfully acquaints the Public, that the Entertainments advertised for This Evening, are unavoidably postponed until MONDAY NEXT, when they will positively be Performed."[2] The ad is repeated.

February 2. "MESSRS. HALLAM & WIGNELL respectfully inform the Public, that the Miscellaneous Entertainments intended to have been exhibited at the Theatre, are unavoidably postponed. They therefore request the favor of those who have purchases Tickets, to apply to Mr. Bradford, in Front-street, for a return of their Money; and to accept the sincerest thanks for the encouragement given upon this occasion."[3]

1. *Pennsylvania Packet*, January 30, 1789.
2. *Federal Gazette*, January 31, 1789.
3. *Pennsylvania Packet*, February 2, 1789.

CHARLESTON, S.C.: GREAT ROOM, TRADD STREET.

March 25, 28, 1789 (2 perfs.).

March 25. "THIS EVENING, *Will be* EXHIBITED, At the Great Room, Tradd-street, (*late* Williams's coffee house,) A SATIRICAL Lecture on Hearts. Interspersed with singing, and other Entertainments. . . ."[1]

March 28. The second, and last, announcement gives the full inventory.

"This Evening, The 28th instant, (*For the last time,*) . . . It is sufficient to remark, that the variety and elegance of these entertainments are agreeably calculated to the taste of the grave, the gay, & the polite. PART I. A Great Patriot's Heart—An Agent's Heart—The Heart of a real Captain—A Miser's Heart—A Sailor's Heart—A Coward's Heart. PART II. FEMALE HEARTS. Lover's Heart—Heart of a Good Hussive—Heart of a Scold—Proud Heart—Hard Heart—The Amiable Heart. PART III. Coquett's Heart—Heart of an old Maid—Beaux's Heart—Physician's Heart—Epicure's Heart—The Pious Heart. With several new and favourite Songs, by Miss *Wall.* DUETS by Master *Ryan* and Miss *Charlotte Wall.* To begin at SEVEN o'clock. In order to prevent the place of performance from being crowded, a calculation has been made of the number which it will properly contain, and a proportionate number of tickets struck off, without one of which no person whatever can be admitted. Tickets, at 5s each, to be had at Markland & M'Iver's printing office, No. 47, Bay, and at the place of performance."[2]

Master Ryan, who apparently gave the *Lecture* while Miss Wall did the singing, was "undoubtedly the son of Dennis Ryan."[3]

1. *City Gazette, or The Daily Advertiser*, March 25, 1789.
2. Ibid., March 28, 1789.
3. Mary Julia Curtis, "The Early Charleston Stage, 1703–1798" (Ph.D diss., Indiana University, 1968), pp. 167–8.

LONDON: DRURY LANE.

May 22, 1789 (1 perf.).

"For the Benefit of Mr. R. Palmer . . . Mr. Palmer will (for this Night only) deliver The LECTURE on HEADS after which . . ."[1] The *Lecture* opened this bill followed by the mainpiece, *The Heiress*, and various other entertainments.

1. *Public Advertiser*, May 22, 1789.

LONDON: ROYAL CIRCUS.

August 5, 12, 14, 18, 21, 22, 24, 26–29, October 26, 28–30, November 6, 7, 9, 1789 (18 perfs.).

The Royalty Theatre had closed, and Palmer moved to the Royal Circus on August 1, 1789, where he continued to perform comic lectures and other entertainments. He drew on the Humphreys-Mendoza boxing matches which had captured the public's attention earlier that year. They were bloody, violent, and controversial bouts and received considerable newspaper space. Mendoza, at the time, was giving private boxing lessons at his academy in the Grand Saloon at the Lyceum and claimed that he had gotten rid of all brutality and thus "rendered it neat" so the ladies would enjoy watching it. On August 5 Palmer satirized the pugilists for the first of ten performances that month.

August 5. "By Particular desire Mr. Palmer . . . will deliver a Lecture on the Heads of Hector and Achilles, contrasted with Humphreys and Mendoza."[1]

Palmer continued to perform at the Circus but dropped the minilectures in favor of other entertainments. On October 26 he resumed them by satirizing two other boxers.

October 26. "In the Lecture on Heads Mr. PALMER will contrast the Heads of Hector and Achilles with those of JOHNSON and PERRINS."[2]

On November 6 Palmer switched back to Humphreys and Mendoza for three more performances as the season came to an end.

1. *The Diary; or, Woodfall's Register*, August 5, 1789.
2. Ibid., October 26, 1789.

LONDON: SADLER'S WELLS.

September 29, 1789 (1 perf.).

This *Lecture*, part of a larger bill, was very similar to the one Mr. Arrowsmith gave at the Royalty Theatre on September 6, 1788 (q.v.): "For the Benefit of Mr. ARROWSMITH SADLER'S WELLS . . . Mr. Arrowsmith will (for that night only) make an humble attempt to deliver several comic subjects from the LECTURE ON HEADS. Amongst the HEADS intended for this evening's entertainment will be introduced A Comical half-foolish Face—Wooden Heads and Paper Skulls— Head of an Old Maid—Head of an Old Batchelor—Head of a Fine Lady— Head of a Billingsgate Girl—The Joys of Matrimony—Queen Bess, with the Ladies favourite Song of her Golden Days—Busts of the Laughing and Crying

Philosophers—Head of a Politician—Head of Poor Jack, with the favourite Song written by Mr. Dibdin—Head of an Ancient Buck—to conclude with the Head of a Modern Drunken Buck. The Heads are entirely new . . . Boxes 3s. 6d. Pit 2s. Gallery 1s."[1]

1. *The Diary; or, Woodfall's Register*, September 29, 1789.

LONDON: COVENT GARDEN.

April 7, 1790 (1 perf.).

"End of the 2nd piece [*The Englishman in Paris*] a *Dissertation upon Law* (from the Lecture on Heads) by Lee Lewes."[1] The *Public Advertiser* of April 5, however, announced that Lewes was to perform Hippesley's *Drunken Man*.

1. *The London Stage*, ed. Charles Beecher Hogan (Carbondale, 1968), pt. 5, no. 2., p. 1242.

AUGUSTA, GA.: COURT HOUSE.

June 17, 23, 1790 (2 perfs.).

Mrs. Robinson and Miss Wall performed excerpts and variations of the *Lecture* with Miss Wall primarily engaged in singing. It was their first appearance in Augusta.

June 17. "On Thursday evening last, Mrs. Robinson and Miss Wall performed in this town (for the first time) a variety of theatrical exhibitions, before a numerous and respectable audience.—The sketch of *Fashionable Raillery*, delivered by Mrs. Robinson, was performed in a most humorous and spirited manner; and her comic powers in the *Touch on the Times* could not be more fully evinced than by the repeated plaudits which she universally received from her audience.—The curious expoundations of the law, in the action of *Bullum versus Boatum* kept the house in a continual laughter. Exclusive of the pointed and genuine wit with which this learned cause abounds, it was delivered in a style that did infinite honor to Mr. [*sic*] Robinson's abilities,—and perhaps nothing could be chosen better adapted to the present times. . . .

"Without commenting any farther upon the different parts, we have only to observe that the whole audience, to a single person, were so highly pleased with the whole of the exhibition, that we hope those ladies and gentlemen who did not then attend, will not deny themselves the pleasure of being there on next Wednesday night.—After the exhibition had ended, some gentlemen favored us with a few traits of their theatrical abilities, which did not a little contribute to the entertainment of the evening."[1]

June 23. "By Permission * * * *On Wednesday Evening next,* Will be performed at the Courthouse, The Satirical Lecture on Hearts, With other entertainments."[2]

The following notice is devoted exclusively to Miss Wall and rhapsodizes on her abilities as a singer and her personal attributes. She is also eulogized for her contribution to the *Lecture on Hearts.*

"*From a Correspondent.*—Merit, in whatever shape it may appear, is always entitled to encouragement and applause. Every man of feeling, every man of uncorrupted taste, will then join with me in paying the just tribute of praise to the musical talents of Miss Wall. . . . The elegant simplicity of her dress, the beautiful symmetry of her form, and sweet melody of her voice, are calculated, in an eminent degree, to delight the eye, charm the ear, and render her an object highly interesting. . . .

"The manner in which Miss Wall acted the part assigned to her in the satirical lecture on hearts, was wonderfully easy, and chastly correct. A person accustomed to the grimace, affectations, and forced gesture of the British stage, would, perhaps, condemn the simple and natural movements of this graceful actress. But it is in acting and singing, as it is in speaking, the nearer we approach to nature, the more happy the effect. Miss Wall's unaffected manner of singing and acting, together with the union of so lovely a person, and so sweet a voice, will always produce the most engaging effects, and passionately interest the affections of every man of real feeling . . ."[3]

1. *Augusta Chronicle,* June 19, 1790.
2. Ibid.
3. Ibid., June 26, 1790.

PHILADELPHIA, PA.: SOUTHWARK THEATRE.

July 12, 1790 (1 perf.).

"Mr. MORRIS and Mrs. HARPER's NIGHT. *By the Old American Company* . . . will be Presented, . . . After the Play, [The Merchant of Venice] a COMIC OLIO, chiefly selected from—The Lecture on Heads, With a Word, or two, about HEARTS. And (by particular desire)—The remarkable LAW CASE, "Bullum versus Boatum," Will be delivered by Mr. WIGNELL. . . . With other entertainments as will be expressed in the bills. The Public are respectfully informed, that the emoluments of Mr. Morris and Mrs. Harper's former nights, having fallen considerably short of the expectations of their Friends, they are induced once more jointly to solicit their patronage . . . Places in the Boxes may be had at Mr. North's next door to the Theatre, where also tickets may be had, and at Mr. Bradford's book-store. The managers respectfully request that their Friends and Patrons will supply themselves with Tickets, as the Door-keepers are in the most particular Manner prohibited from receiving Money. Box, 7/6 Pit 5/ Gallery 3/9."[1]

1. *Pennsylvania Packet*, July 12, 1790.

HALIFAX, NOVA SCOTIA: THEATRE.

September 14, 21, October 12, 1790 (3 perfs.).

McPherson keeps trying.

September 14. "THIS EVENING, the 14th Instant, *Mr. M'Pherson* Proposes to Deliver the Celebrated Lecture on Heads. With an Occasional Prologue. *Part 1st.* The HEAD OF ALEXANDER the GREAT, A CHEROKEE CHIEF, A QUACK DOCTOR, NOBODY, SOMEBODY & ANYBODY, A MODERN FINE GENTLEMAN, LAUGHING and CRYING PHILOSOPHERS. Interspersed with Dissertations on the Five Sciences. On Friendship, Gratitude, Generosity, Esteem, Public Spirit, and Common Sense, Wit Judgment and Genius. . . . *Part 2d.* HEAD of a MARRIED LADY, (with a Dissertation on Courtship and Matrimony.) An old MAID, An old Bachelor, A LAWYER, (with Orations in Praise of the Law, exemplified in the Case of Daniel vs. Dishclout.) HEAD of a LONDON BLOOD, (with the droll Description of his 'Keeping it Up') . . ."[1]

September 21. ". . . LECTURE ON HEADS . . . After which, in Addition to the most pleasing Part of the last Entertainment, will be presented the following: Head of Flattery; Statue of Honesty; a Freeholder; a Worldly Wise Man, a Connoisseur; A Female Politician (or President of the Ladies' Debating Society in London) A Male Politician; Master Jackey; the Tea-Table Critic; Diana, the Huntress; Sir Domini Full-Fed Double Chin (or the City Politician humourously described) Squire Groom (with an Account of his Courtship) The Case of BULLUM *vs.* Boatum. . . ."[2]

October 12. ". . . LECTURE ON HEADS . . . After which . . . Head of a British Hero, An ornamented Head, An English Valet, and a New-England Waiter, . . . Head of a British Tar, A Frenchman, and a Spaniard. Nobody's Somebody's Anybody's and Every-body's Coat of Arms. . . . A TABERNACLE HARANGUE . . ."[3]

1. *Royal Gazette and Nova Scotia Advertiser*, September 14, 1790.
2. Ibid., September 21, 1790.
3. Ibid., October 12, 1790.

LONDON: HAYMARKET, THEATRE ROYAL.

October 13, 1790 (1 perf.).

"On Wednesday next, The 13th instant . . . End of the Opera, Mr. Palmer will (for that Night only) deliver THE LECTURE UPON HEADS . . . Tickets to be had of Mr. Palmer, No. 3, London-road, St. George's Fields; and of Mr. Rice; at the Theatre, Where places for the boxes may be taken."[1] The evening was by permission of the Lord Chamberlain and was a benefit for Mr. Palmer. The opera referred to was *The Spanish Barber.*

1. *Gazetteer and New Daily Advertiser*, October 11, 1790.

HALIFAX, NOVA SCOTIA: THEATRE.

December 3, 1790 (1 perf.).

December 3. "On FRIDAY Evening the 3d December. Will be delivered a Few Select Subjects From The Lecture on Heads. With a New Prologue. After Which Will Be Presented a Dramatic Medley. . . . The whole to conclude with An EPILOGUE, (In Honour of Masonary,) By Mrs. MECHTLER . . ."[1] Mrs. Mechtler sang a number of songs during the program and was a soloist at other times during the season. Although the performer for the *Lecture* is not specified, I would assume it to be M'Pherson. Part of the announcement in the *Royal Gazette* for a March 8, 1791, performance reads, "Mrs. Mechtler and Mr. M'Pherson are engaged as before."

1. *Royal Gazette and Nova Scotia Advertiser*, November 30, 1790.

LONDON: HAYMARKET, THEATRE ROYAL.

March 7, 1791 (1 perf.).

"UNDER THE PATRONAGE OF HIS ROYAL HIGHNESS THE PRINCE OF WALES, THE DUKE OF YORK, AND THE DUKE OF CLARENCE At the Theatre Royal in the Haymarket, on Monday next . . . End of the Play, [*The Busy Body*] A WHIMSICAL DISSERTATION UPON LAW, By Mr. LEE LEWES . . . Tickets and Places for the Boxes to be had of Mr. Rice, at his Office, Haymarket; and of Mr. Lee Lewis, at Mr. Brough's, No. 18, Portland-street, Soho."[1]

1. *Public Advertiser*, March 5, 1791.

AUGUSTA, GA.: THE THEATRE.

May 21, 1791 (1 perf.).

"This Evening. *A Mental Evening's Amusement.* * * * Mr. *Wall* (of Amherst county, Virginia, and formerly an actor in the Richmond theatre) will exhibit this Evening, at the Theatre in Augusta, a moral, satirical, and instructive *Lecture on Heads* Interspersed with quotations from the Dramatic Poets. Between the parts of the Lecture, some pieces of Music will be played on the GUITAR. To which will be added, a critical dissertation on NOSES. Mrs. *Robinson* will also join with her theatrical talents, in a scene taken from Shakespeare's Catherine and Petruchio; or *The Taming of the Shrew.* An Epilogue addressed to every body, not aimed at any body, will be spoken by Lawrence Ryan, in the character of Nobody. The whole to conclude with a poetical Oration by a Master Mason. To begin at 7 o'Clock. * * *Tickets for admittance may be had at Mrs. Robinson's, for 3s. 6d. each. Mr. Wall proposes, during his stay in town, to teach Ladies to play on the Guitar."[1]

1. *Augusta Chronicle*, May 21, 1791.

HALIFAX, NOVA SCOTIA: THEATRE.

July 21, 1791 (1 perf.).

July 21. "For the Benefit of Mr. M'Pherson. (*His* LAST *attempt in this Town.*) On THURSDAY Evening, the 21st Instant, will be presented. *An Attic Entertainment.* Comprising a Concert *Of* VOCAL *and* INSTRUMENTAL MUSIC: AND A LECTURE ON HEADS. . . . *Part 1st* . . . LECTURE on Eight HEADS; *Part 2d* . . . LECTURE on ten HEADS; *Part 3d* . . . LECTURE on eight HEADS. . . . An EPILOGUE by Mr. M'Pherson. To conclude with a GRAND MILITARY SYMPHONY, by Shaffer. Doors to be open'd at half past 7, and to begin precisely at 8 o'clock.—Tickets and places for the Boxes, may be taken of Mr. Howe on Wednesday, the 20th inst. Tickets for the 1st and 2d pit, may be had at the British Tavern, at the Coffee House, and at the different Printing Offices. Box 3s6.—First Pit 2s.—Second Pit 1s6. *Vivant Rex et Regina!* The Band, will consist of 20 Performers—selected from the three Bands."[1]

1. *Royal Gazette and Nova Scotia Advertiser*, July 19, 1791.

HARTFORD, CONN.: MR. BULL'S LONG ROOM.

November 22, 1791 (1 perf.).

"*By permission.* Mr. ASHTON, Begs leave to inform his friends in particular, and the Pub-[lic] in general, that on Tuesday Evening, will be perform'd at Mr.

Frede[r]ick Bull's Long Room, the first part of George Alex. Stevens Lectures on Heads with other amusements as will be specified in the bills of the day, with Vocal and Instrumental Music. The Scenery and the Heads are entirely new: the Painting performed by a young Man of this City. Tickets at 1/6 may be had of Capt. Frederic Bull."[1]

1. *Connecticut Courant* (Hartford), November 21, 1791.

BALTIMORE, MD.: MR. STARCK'S LONG ROOM.

March 31, April 3, 1792 (2 perfs.).

"*A Theatrical Boquet* [by Mr. Godwin]. With an ADDRESS to the Audience, relative to his performing in this town, some Years ago. The celebrated HEADS, OR BUSTS (selected from STEVEN'S LECTURES) . . . Quack-Doctor—Humorous Oration in Praise of Law; The Trial of Daniel versus dishcloth; The Four Parts of Law; Venus's Girdle; Jealousy, from Doctor Young; and two Heads from Dryden and Lee, With an EPILOGUE, characteristic of a Spaniard, Italian, Frenchman, Dutchman, and Englishman. Twelve other Heads, with 'Bucks have at ye all.' With an ELOGIUM on GENERAL WASHINGTON, &c."[1] Three weeks later Godwin was in Philadelphia.

1. David Ritchey, *A Guide to the Baltimore Stage in the Eighteenth Century* (Westport, Conn., 1982), p. 122.

PHILADELPHIA, PA.: THEATRE-NORTHERN LIBERTIES.

April 23, 1792 (1 perf.).

"This Evening, April the 23rd, Mr. GODWIN will Present his Theatrical Evening Brush, With Lectures on a Variety of Heads, as large as Life. . . . On this occasion Mr. *Godwin* respectfully solicits the Presence of the 'Friends to his Endeavours.'"[1]

1. *Dunlap's American Daily Advertiser* (Philadelphia), April 23, 1792.

CHARLESTON, S.C.: MR. WILLIAMS' COFFEE HOUSE.

June 4, 1795 (1 perf.).

"Mrs. Kenna and Mrs. Robinson, because 'the vicissitudes of the stage have placed them in a disagreeable situation,' prepared a 'Lecture on Hearts' which they gave at Mr. Williams' Coffee House on June 4."[1]

1. Mary Julia Curtis, "The Early Charleston Stage, 1703–1798" (Ph.D. diss., Indiana University, 1968), p. 307–8.

HALIFAX, NOVA SCOTIA: THEATRE ROYAL.

November 8, 1797 (1 perf.).

The performer remains anonymous. "Under the Patronage of his Royal Highness Prince Edward, and his Excellency the Governor. On Wednesday, the 8th Nov. Will be Presented AN OLIO, or Attick Evening's Entertainment. Composed of the Sublime, the Pathetic, the Humorous and the Musical—Part I. A PROLOGUE Written for the occasion. A LECTURE on HEARTS, compiled from the works of the late celebrated *George Alexander Stevens*. [*sic*] Consisting of A Royal Heart, A Tender Heart, The Heart of a Sailor, The Heart of an Old Maid, A Usurer's Heart, The Heart of an amiable Woman, The Heart of a Miser, The Heart of a Soldier. These Hearts, with their proper emblems, will be exhibited to the Audience elegantly painted by an eminent Artist. After the LECTURE, a Song . . . The whole to conclude with an Epilogue to be spoken in the Character of Harlequin, who will leap through the Jaws of a Fiery Dragon."[1] Note that the *Lecture on Hearts* is here attributed to Stevens!

1. *Royal Gazette and Nova Scotia Advertiser*, November 7, 1797.

LONDON: COVENT GARDEN.

May 23, 1798 (1 perf.).

"By Particular Desire—For the Benefit of Mrs. Mountain . . . on Wednesday next will be performed [*The Widow of Malabar*] . . . End of the Tragedy (by Desire of Several Persons of Distinction, and positively for that Night only) a humorous, satirical Recitation, called KRAINIOGRAPHON, selected from G. A. Stevens's Lecture on Heads—in which: The Head of Alexander the Great, The Head of a Lawyer, The Head of a Cherokee, Every Body's Coat of Arms, The Head of a Quack Doctor, The Head of Flattery—Girdle of Venus; The Quack Doctor's Coat of Arms; The Head of Nobody, exhibited by Mrs. Mountain in the Character of a Student."[1] Mrs. Mountain was the former Miss Wilkinson, who performed the *Lecture* with such success at Hull in 1784 (q.v.).

1. *Morning Chronicle*, May 17, 1798.

HALIFAX, NOVA SCOTIA: GALLAGHER'S LONG ROOM.

January 14, 17, February 6, 18, April 9, 1799 (5 perfs.).

January 14. "Will be delivered by Mr. Powell, COLLINS's Celebrated Evening Brush . . . After the Brush, A Satirical, Humorous and Critical Dissertation on Noses, According to Lavater."[1]

January 17. ". . . After the Brush a Satirical, Humorous and Critical Dissertation on Noses, According to Lavater. The Roman Nose, The Blunt Nose, The Ruby Nose, The Hook'd Prognosticating Nose of Goody Screech Owl."[2]

February 6. Same as above.[3]

February 18. The Evening Brush "With a variety of other Entertainments" which almost certainly included the "Dissertation on Noses."[4]

April 9. "Mr. POWELL, will give An OLLA PODRIDA or Entertaining PASTICCIO. To which will be added a Critical, Satyrical and Moral Lecture upon Human Hearts. Veluti in Speculum. *Syllabus.* An upright Royal Heart. A warp'd Royal Heart. The Heart of a Pretended Captain. Heart of a Real Captain. The Heart of a British Soldier. Heart of Monsieur Jean Babtist L'Volage. By Desire. The dissertation on Noses, According to Lavater, will be repeated."[5]

1. *Royal Gazette and Nova Scotia Advertiser*, January 8, 1799.
2. Ibid., January 15, 1799.
3. Ibid., January 29, 1799.
4. Ibid., February 12, 1799.
5. Ibid., April 9, 1799.

BATH: GREAT ROOM FACING MR. HAZARD'S LIBRARY.

February 28, 1800 (1 perf.).

The Daniel/Dishclout and Bullam/Boatum continue to be popular.

"At the GREAT ROOM facing Mr. HAZARD'S LIBRARY, CHEAP-STREET, BATH (THE ENTRANCE AT THE SECOND DOOR IN UNION-PASSAGE.) For One Night, At the particular Request of several Ladies and Gentlemen, On FRIDAY EVENING, Feb, 28, 1800, Mr. PINDAR FROM THE THEATRES ROYAL HAYMARKET, BATH &C. &C. WILL GIVE THE FOLLOWING RECITATIONS (INTERSPERSED WITH THE INIMITABLE PERFORMANCES OF SIGNIOR ROSSIGNOL.) VIZ: Tom, Dick and Will's Critical Observations on Modern Dramatists, Novel Writers, &c.—The Newcastle

Apothecary,—The Razor Grinder,—Daniel *versus* Dishclout, a whimsical Law Case,—The Pilgrims and Peace,—Bullam *v.* Boatum, &c. . . . Front Seats, 2s. 6d.—Back Seats 1s. To begin at Half past Seven o'Clock Tickets to be had of MRS. PINDAR, at her Shop in the Abbey Church-Yard."[1]

1. From the Playbill Collection, vol. 177, British Library.

HALIFAX, NOVA SCOTIA: THEATRE, GOLDEN BALL.

March 27, 1800 (1 perf.).

The performer remains anonymous. "By Permission, On Thursday March 27th, will be performed a variety of Entertainments properly *selected* and *adapted* for rational Amusement; viz. . . . A Humorous TRIAL, selected from the late famous George Alexander Stevens's *Lecture on Heads*, viz. Daniel against Dishclout, or, The Cook in the Dripping Pan . . . Front Seats 3s. Back do. 2s. *No money taken at the Door.*—Doors open at six, and begin precisely at seven.—N.B. The Ladies and Gentlemen of Halifax may depend on the utmost regularity, and punctuality of Performance, as every Attention has been paid to render the entertainment *agreeable.*"[1]

1. *Royal Gazette and Nova Scotia Advertiser*, March 25, 1800.

MT. VERNON, N.Y.: A FEW DOORS ABOVE THE HOSPITAL, BROADWAY.

September 10, 1800 (1 perf.).

"Mr. HODGKINSON'S NIGHT. On WEDNESDAY EVENING, Sept. 10, will be presented, a Comedy, in 3 acts, called, The Columbian Daughter, Or, AMERICANS IN ENGLAND . . . After the Comedy, Mr. [Giles?] BARRETT will deliver select parts of the celebrated LECTURE ON HEADS, *Interspersed with Songs, Recitations, Glees, &c.* 1st—1 Head of a Quack Doctor—2 Pretty Fellow—3 Nobody's Head—4 Dissertation on Nothing—5 No-body's Some-body's, or Any-body's Coat of Arms—6 Illustration of Law, Bullum versus Boatum, Mr. BARRETT . . . 5th—Dissertation on Architecture, Painting, Poetry, Music and Astronomy—Head of a Swindler—Head of an Old Maid—Head of an Old Batchelor—Dissertation how every Lady will or may possess the Beauties of Venus. Mr. BARRETT.*** The performance will begin at HALF PAST SEVEN, precisely."[1]

1. *Commercial Advertiser*, September 10, 1800.

WALES: LLANFYLLIN TOWN HALL.

November 1, 1800 (1 perf.).

"AN ENTERTAINMENT AT LLANFYLLIN.—The following is a copy of a bill of an entertainment held at LLanfyllin in the year 1800. The original was lent me by Mrs. Bibby of Brynaber, to whom I am indebted for a variety of interesting 'bye-gone' matters for my note book. T.W.H.

". . . By Desire of several of his Friends, whom it is his pleasure to oblige, Mr. DAVIS Takes the liberty of laying before them the following Entertainment for Saturday evening, November 1st, 1800, called The EVENING BRUSH For rubbing off the Rust of Care, Selected from the Works of G. A. Stephens, [*sic*] Collins, Dibdin, &c. with Transparent Paintings of the Characters; And a variety of SONGS by Miss SMITH. In the Course of the Entertainment the following COMIC SONGS Will be introduced by Mr. Davis; The Brush, Captain Wattle and Miss Roe, The Seven Ages, The Medley of Beggars, The Medley of Lovers, The Whirligig, The golden Days we now possess, Nobody, &c. Front Seats, 2/–; Back Seats, 1/– To begin at Seven o'Clock."[1]

1. *Bye-Gones, relating to Wales and the Border Counties* (Oswestry, 1880–1), vol. 5, p. 234.

PHILADELPHIA: MR. WHALE'S BALL ROOM.

December 19, 1809 (1 perf.).

"Mr. WEBSTER, Respectfully informs his friends and the public, that on THIS EVENING, he will deliver (at Mr. Whale's Ball Room back of the Pennsylvania Bank, Dock Street) *George Alexander Stevens's Lectures on Heads, interspersed with Songs.* IN TWO PARTS. The number of Heads to be lectured on the above evening, will amount to eighteen . . . Tickets 1 dollar, to be had at Blake's Music store, and at the door on the night of performance. The performance to commence at 7 o'clock precisely."[1]

1. *Poulson's American Daily Advertiser* (Philadelphia), December 19, 1809.

NEW YORK, N.Y.: ASSEMBLY ROOM, CITY HOTEL.

March 20, 1810 (1 perf.).

"On March 20 . . . [Mr. Webster] delivered Stevens's long disused lecture on Heads. But perpend: 'These Lectures, in their original state, contain much *gross and offensive language.* Mr. Webster assures the ladies and gentlemen of this city, that he has entirely expunged every offensive passage, and arranged them in such a manner as not to offend the most delicate ear.' "[1]

1. George C. D. Odell, *Annals of the New York Stage* (New York, 1927), vol. 2, p. 344; *New York Evening Post*, March 20, 1810.

SAVANNAH, GA.: EXCHANGE COFFEE HOUSE.

March 20, 24, 1810 (2 perfs.).

March 20. A dramatic olio by Mr. H. W. Prigmore including "Part Second. An oration in praise of law, with the pleadings of counsellor Smiffle and counsellor Plausible in the humorous trial of Daniel against Dish-Clout; An essay on nothing; on face painting; On flattery . . . Part Third. The girdle of Venus; Matrimonial tumult; matrimonial tranquility . . ."[1]

March 24. "Part Second. The Head of Alexander the Great; An Indian Chief; The Head of Bonaparte; The Quack Doctor; The Old Bachelor and an Old Maid . . . Part Third. On Law—with the Trial of Boatum, versus Bullum, and Bullum, versus Boatum . . ."[2]

1. *Columbian Museum*, March 19, 1810.
2. *Savannah Republican*, March 22, 1810.

ST. JOHN, NEW BRUNSWICK: THEATRE, DRURY LANE.

May 16, 1810 (1 perf.).

"For One Night Only Theatre, Drury-Lane, Saint John on Wed. May 16th Mr. Powell will give his Attick Entertainment . . . To which will be added a Whimsical and Critical Dissertation on Noses: The Ruby Nose, Roman Nose of old Ben Blunderbuss, The Prognosticating Snout of Goody Screech Owl, Etc. Etc. . . . Tickets and places for the Boxes to be taken of Mr. McCarthy at Mr. Powell's Lodgings, on Monday next; and as the number of tickets will be limited, if they should be sold, no more will be issued nor any money admitted at the door. Boxes 5/ Gallery 2/6."[1]

1. J. Russell Harper, "The Theatre in St. John," *Dalhousie Review* 34, no. 3 (Autumn 1954): 267–68.

SAVANNAH, GA.: THE EXCHANGE.

August 27, 1812 (1 perf.).

Recitations by Mr. Knox including "Description of a Storm" by Stevens (probably a reading of the song).[1]

1. *Savannah Republican*, August 15, 1812.

SAVANNAH, GA.: PLACE UNKNOWN.

January 15, 1818 (1 perf.).

Recitations by Mr. Judah including "Daniel versus Dish-Clout, a law case" and "Bullum versus Boatum, a law case."[1]

1. *Columbian Museum*, January 15, 1818.

SAVANNAH, GA.: EXCHANGE LONG ROOM.

May 1, 4, 1818 (2 perfs.).

Mr. Dwyer on the road does "A Lecture on Heads" and "Daniel versus Dish-Clout."[1]

1. *Columbian Museum*, May 1, 4, 1818.

AUGUSTA, GA.: THE THEATRE.

May 9, 1818 (1 perf.).

Dwyer reached Augusta several days later and continued his tour with the *Lecture*: "*Mr. Dwyer's* First appearance in Augusta. This evening, (Saturday) May 9th, At the Theatre, Mr. Dwyer, from the Theatre Drury Lane, London will deliver (entirely from memory) George Alexander Stevens celebrated *Lecture on Heads*, Localized and rendered suitable to an American audience . . . Tickets at $1 each . . . Doors to open at half past 6—Performance to commence at half past seven."[1] [For the syllabus, see entry for July performances in New York.]

1. *Augusta Chronicle and Georgia Gazette*, May 9, 1818.

NEW YORK, N.Y.: BANK COFFEE HOUSE.

July 22, 25, 1818 (2 perfs.).

". . . the elegant [John] Dwyer . . . after an absence of four years, came, on July 22nd, to the Bank Coffee House, where he delivered that never-dying lecture on Heads. And he did it again on the 25th! He had an evening on August 12th at Washington Hall; but the advertisement in the Columbian provides no clue to the programme."[1]

"MR. DWYER respectfully informs his friends and the public that he will deliver entirely from memory, George Alexander Stevens' celebrated LECTURE ON HEADS, rendered suitable to an American audience. The exhibition of the above Lecture in Great Britain gave independence to its author, and general satisfaction to its auditors; it satirically lashes the vices and follies of that country and forms a source of rational and elegant amusement—The following Heads, painted by an eminent artist will be displayed and personified or described.

PART 1st.

Prefatory Address	
Sir Tandem Whiffle	Head of
Foolishly Comical Fellow	do
Master Jackey Mama's Darling	do
London Blood going to keep it up	do
London Blood after he has kept it up	do

PART 2d.

St. James's Lady	Head of
St. Giles' do	do
Old Maid	do
Old Batchelor	do
Jonas the card playing conjuring Jew	do
The Laughing Philosopher	do
The Crying do	do

PART 3d.

The Apothecary	Head of
Conoisseur	do
Materialist	do
Culinary Politician	do
Lawyer	do

"In the course of the evening the following recitations. A head of GENERAL WASHINGTON, and a sketch of his character, in which a comparison will be drawn between Cincinnatus and Lime, written by Mr. Dwyer. . . . The whole to conclude with the burlesque law case of 'Daniel versus Dish-Clout.' Tickets at 75 cents each . . . Doors to open at 7, and the performance to commence at 8 o'clock."[2]

1. George C. D. Odell, *Annals of the New York Stage* (New York, 1927), vol. 2, p. 514.
2. *New York Evening Post*, July 20, 1818.

PHILADELPHIA, PA.: THE MANSION HOUSE.

October 14, 1818 (1 perf.).

"*Mr. Dwyer's 1st appearance these 4 years.* AT THE MANSION HOUSE, (Next to the Washington Hall) *On Wednesday Evening*, Oct. 14. Mr. Dwyer respectfully informs his friends and the Public that he will deliver (entirely from memory) G. A. Stevens' celebrated Lecture on Heads, rendered suitable to an American audience. The exhibition of the above lecture in Great Britain, gave independence to its author, and general satisfaction to its auditors, it satirically lashes the vices and follies of that country, and forms a source of comic, rational, and elegant amusement. The heads are painted by an eminent artist. In addition to the Lecture the following recitations: . . . The whole to conclude with the burlesque law case of 'Daniel versus Dishcloth.' Doors to open at 7, and the performance to commence at half past 7 o'clock. Tickets at 1 dollar each. . . ."[1]

1. *Poulson's American Daily Advertiser* (Philadelphia), October 13, 1818.

NEW YORK, N.Y.: WASHINGTON HALL, MR. DWYER'S ROOM, TAMMANY HALL.

May 10, 16, 17, 18, 19, 20, 26, 29, June 28, 1820 (9 perfs.).

May 10. "*Lecture on Heads.* At Washington Hall, on Wednesday Evening, May 10th. MR. DWYER, RESPECTFULLY informs his friends and the public, that he will deliver G. A. Stevens' celebrated Lecture on Heads, in which he will introduce the HEAD OF A CLINTONIAN and THAT OF A BUCK-TAIL—and a full length portrait of a Broadway DANDY. In addition to the Lecture, Mr. Dwyer will Recite the Battle of Hohenlinden . . . Performance to commence at half past 7 o'clock. Tickets at 50 cts. each to be had at the bar."[1]

May 16–20. "Sans Souci, or DWYER'S AMULET TO DISPEL CARE. On TUESDAY EVENING, May 16. Mr. Dwyer, respectfully informs his friends and the public, that he will on that Evening, and every succeeding one till further notice, Sundays excepted, give an Entertainment under the above head, at the commodious Room next door to Mr. Longworth's Shakespeare Gallery, Chatham Row. In the course of the Evening he will introduce the following American Heads—The Clintonian and Bucktail—The American Cicero, Patrick Henry—Gen. Washington—The Broadway Dandy. For particulars see small bills. Performance to commence a quarter before eight. Tickets 50 cents. Each ticket will admit a Lady and Gentleman, or two Children."[2]

The following day: "We omitted to mention, that the tribute, so justly merited, to the memory of our great orator, Patrick Henry, in yesterday's paper, was from the pen of Mr. Dwyer, and is introduced by him into his entertainment of *San Souci*."[3]

A drop in attendance may have induced Dwyer to prepare an *Oration and Lecture on Oratory*, which he advertised during the latter part of May and early June. Meanwhile, he gave two additional performances of the *Lecture* before the end of May.

May 26, 29. Dwyer advertised the *Lecture* for May 30, but it was actually given four days earlier. "DWYER'S LECTURE ON *American Heads*. At his Room. No. 7 Chatham-row, next to Mr. Longworth's Shakespeare Gallery, on TUESDAY EVENING, May 30th. As novelty is always acceptable, Mr. DWYER, avails himself of its claim, by offering to the public a species of Entertainment never attempted but by him in this country, i.e. a LECTURE on NATIVE MANNERS and CHARACTER, written by a gentleman of New York, in the style of G. A. Stevens. The Lecture will be interspersed with Recitations and Songs. A professor will preside at the piano forte . . ."[4]

A month later Dwyer tried again.

June 28. "Mr. Dwyer respectfully informs his friends and the public, that he will this *evening* at Tammany Hall, deliver *G. A. Stevens' celebrated Lecture on* Heads, accompanied with the Drama, recitations, by one of his pupils, viz Brutus Harangue on the Death of Caesar . . . Performance to commence at 8 o'clock. Tickets, (which will admit a lady and gentleman), 50 cents each to be had at the bar."[5]

1. *New York Columbian*, May 10, 1820.
2. Ibid., May 13, 15–20, 1820.
3. Ibid., May 17, 1820.
4. Ibid., May 24–6, 29, 1820.
5. *New York Evening Post*, June 28, 1820.

NEW YORK, N.Y.: THEATRE, SPRUCE STREET.

May 23, 1820 (1 perf.).

During Mr. Dwyer's run: "THEATRE. No. 11 SPRUCE STREET. For the Benefit of Mr. ELLISTON . . . On Tuesday Evening, May 23, . . . [*The Tragedy of Barbarassa*, the last act of *Macbeth*] after which . . . Mr. Simpson will give the comic Recitation of Daniel vs Dishclout . . ."[1]

1. *New York Columbian*, May 20, 1821.

Bibliography of the Works
of George Alexander Stevens

Abbreviations

The abbreviations listed below are used in the bibliographical information that follows.

AAP	Auburn University
BL	British Library, London
CLU	University of California, Los Angeles
CSmH	Henry E. Huntington Library, San Marino, Calif.
CSt	Stanford University
CtY	Yale University
CtY-M	Yale University, Medical School Library
CU	University of California, Berkeley
CU-A	University of California, Davis
DeU	University of Delaware
DFo	Folger Shakespeare Library
EST	Evans Short Title
EAI-SS	Early American Imprints. American Antiquarian Society (Shaw & Shoemaker)
GU	University of Georgia
ICN	Newberry Library, Chicago
ICU	University of Chicago
IEN-D	Northwestern University Dental School, Chicago
InU	Indiana University
IU	University of Illinois
KU	University of Kansas
KyU	University of Kentucky
LC	Library of Congress
LNT	Tulane University
LU	Louisiana State University
MB	Boston Public Library
MdBJ	Johns Hopkins University
MH	Harvard University
MiU	University of Michigan
MiU-C	University of Michigan, William L. Clements Library
MnU	University of Minnesota
MoSU	St. Louis University
MWA	American Antiquarian Society, Worcester, Mass.
NjP	Princeton University

NjR	Rutgers University
N	New York State Library, Albany
NBu	Buffalo and Erie County Public Library
NBuG	Buffalo and Erie County Public Library, Grosvenor Reference Division
NIC	Cornell University
NN	New York Public Library
NNC	Columbia University
NNNAM	New York Academy of Medicine
NNR	Russell Sage Foundation Library, City College of New York
NNU	New York University
NcD	Duke University
NcGU	University of North Carolina, Greensboro
NcU	University of North Carolina, Chapel Hill
OC	Public Library of Cincinnati and Hamilton County
OCU	University of Cincinnati
OClW	Case Western Reserve University
OU	Ohio State University
OrCS	Oregon State University
OrU	University of Oregon
PP	Free Library of Philadelphia
PPL	Library Company of Philadelphia
PPWI	Wistar Institute of Anatomy and Biology, Philadelphia
PSt	Pennsylvania State University
PU	University of Pennsylvania
PU-F	University of Pennsylvania, H. H. Furness Memorial Library
RPB	Brown University
RPJCB	John Carter Brown Library, Providence, R.I.
TxU	University of Texas
VU	University of Virginia
WaU	University of Washington
WU	University of Wisconsin

I. *The Lecture on Heads*

"LECTURE UPON HEADS In Number II of *The Court Miscellany; or, Lady's New Magazine*, which is published This Day, Price only Six-pence, is given, among a great Variety of Original and Interesting Articles in Prose and Verse. 1. The Whole of the celebrated Lecture upon Heads . . . Printed for Richardson and Urquhart, under the Royal Exchange . . ." Adv. in *Public Advertiser*, September 2, 1765.

"THE LECTURE UPON HEADS, that has been lately read near Islington, has just been published; it is not without humor, as the reader will see by the following Extracts, the whole being too much for our purpose." In *Gentleman's Magazine*, September, 1765, pp. 403–4. The extracts consist of the Lawyer and Sir Full Fed Domine Double Chin. The Islington performance was given at the Long Room in Sadler's Wells by Gibson, not Stevens.

The *Lecture* printed in the *Public Ledger*, September 4, 5, 6, 7, 1765, in three installments: "That the reader may the better understand the following celebrated LECTURE, it will be necessary to observe, that the person who recites the Lecture has all the different Heads by him, either painted on pasteboard, or cut in wood; which are, one by one, exhibited to the audience during the recital."

The *Lecture* printed in *Lloyd's Evening Post*, September 2–4, 3–5, 4–6, 6–9, 1765. Same as above.

The *Lecture* printed in *London Magazine*, September 1765, pp. 482–85. Extracts only. Printed for R. Baldwin in Pater-noster Row. Adv. in *Public Advertiser*, October 3, 1765.

"This Day is published, Price only 6 pence (Embellished with a large Half Sheet Copper-Plate, representing the several humorous Heads exhibited in the Lecture on Heads, lately delivered with uncommon Applause, very neatly etched in Caricatura, by which the true Meaning of that excellent Satire is fully explained . . . *The Universal Museum and Complete Magazine of Knowledge and Pleasure*. For SEPTEMBER, 1765. [pp. 455–65] Containing, among many other Articles, The Lecture on Heads entire, and carefully corrected which is the only correct Copy yet printed of that popular Performance . . . Printed for J. Payne, at the Feathers, in Pater noster-Row; and sold by Mr. Hoey, run in Dublin; and by all the Booksellers and News-Carriers in Great Britain and Ireland." Adv. in *Public Advertiser*, October 3, 1765.

"The most striking Passages of the celebrated Lecture on Heads." Printed in *The Universal Magazine of Knowledge and Pleasure*, September 1765, pp. 149–54. Printed for J. Hinton, at the Kings-Arms, in Newgate Street. Adv. in *Public Advertiser*, October 3, 1765.

"This Day at Noon will be published, Price only Three-pence THE celebrated LECTURE on HEADS. Which has been exhibited upwards of one hundred Times with the most universal Applause. Printed for J. Pridden, at the Feathers in Fleet Street; and sold by all Booksellers in Town and Country." Adv. in *Public Advertiser*, September 2, 1765. During the next few years Pridden advertised and issued a number of editions and printings of the *Lecture*, several of which are extant. The following entries are an attempt to identify and place them in a coherent sequence. On September 3, the *Public Ledger* announced "This day is published . . . a new edition," which perhaps was an additional advertisement for the first edition. There must have been a second and third edition, one of which probably sold for four pence and may be the subject of the following entry in the *Critical Review; or, Annals of Literature*, September 1765, p. 235.

> 22. The celebrated Lecture on Heads. Fol. Pr. 4d. Pridden. When Milo read the speech that his friend Tully pronounced in his favour, 'Cicero (said he) must have been in a terrible fright when he spoke this fine oration, otherwise I should not now be eating oysters in exile.' He meant, that if the orator had spoke it with his usual emphasis, it must have had such an effect upon the people, that they would have recalled him (Milo) from banishment. As the oration for Milo miscarried for want of those graces of elocution; so these orations of Mr. George Alexander Stevens have, in our opinion, owed their success chiefly to certain oratorical arts of gesticulation, of which the composition itself gives us no idea.

The fourth edition was then announced in the *Gazetteer and New Daily Advertiser* on September 16: "This day is published . . . 6d . . . A new edition being the 4th. To this edition is now added, a curious frontispiece of all the heads, coats of arms, &c. &c. designed by Mr. O'NEALE . . . N.B. Such gentlemen who have had the former editions of the Lectures of Heads, may have the frontispiece separate, price only 3d."

An early announcement for the next edition (the fifth?) in the September 20 issue of the *Gazetteer* with the O'Neale illustrations: "New edition . . . printed on fine paper . . . This print clearly explains the whole of the Lecture, and is necessary to be had with the book, to illustrate the subject." A fifth edition is confirmed at six pence in the September 26 *Gazetteer*.

Then from the *London Chronicle*, January 7–9, 1766: "On Thursday next will be published, A New Edition, being the Sixth, Price only 6d. The Celebrated LECTURE on Heads, &c which has been exhibited upwards of Two Hundred Nights, with universal Applause. To this Edition is given an entire new Frontispiece of all the Heads, Arms, &c." Note that the number of performances has doubled. A copy at MH.

Then: "George Steven's Celebrated Lecture on Heads; Which has been exhibited upwards of Two Hundred and Fifty successive Nights, to crowded Audiences and met with the most universal Applause . . . The Seventh Edition. With an entire new Frontispiece, representing all the various Heads, &c. Printed for J. Pridden . . . 1766. Price *only* Six-pence." A boxed copy at BL (1484.m.35.) Folio.

Then a curious announcement in the *Public Advertiser*, October 30, 1766: "This day is published Price six-pence A New satirical, political anatomical Lecture on HEADS and no Heads, as performed by SAWNEY MAC STEWART, at St. J——s. 'When Caps, among a Croud are thrown, / What fits you best, take for your own.' Sold by J. Pridden."

Then probably the eighth edition: "A Lecture on Heads by the Celebrated George Stevens; Which has been exhibited upwards of Three Hundred successive Nights to crowded Audiences, and met with the most universal Applause. London. Printed for J. Pridden at No. 100 in Fleet-Street." 8°. 18 pp. With the 51 heads, etc. (BL 12330.dd.13.[3] with frontispiece closely trimmed, top legend missing, bound in after p. 18; and BL T. 192.[1.] bound in with ten unrelated tracts; and BL 1609/43.[1.] bound with Dodd's *Lecture on Hearts* and *Dissertation on Noses*.)

". . . The only correct Copy in small size in Octavo, Price only Four-pence THAT celebrated Piece of Wit and Humour called A LECTURE on HEADS, with a curious Frontispiece, representing the exact Manner it was exhibited, with the Disposition of the Heads as performed in the Haymarket, and at the Long Room opposite to Sadler's Wells. Sold by R. Bond, near Bartlet's Buildings, Holborn, at the Pamphlet Shops at the Royal Exchange, the Book-seller's Shops in Exeter Exchange, in the Strand, and the Corner of the Piazza, Covent Garden." Advertised in the *Gazetteer*, September 24, 1765, and the *Public Advertiser*, October 1, 1765. [See "Fawcett's Collection of Eighteenth- and Nineteenth-Century English Drama," vol. 5, no. 9.] VU/ICU/NN/MB/CtY.

And in the *Public Advertiser*, October 15, 1765: "This Day is published, A new Edition, with the Whole of the Introduction and the Head of a Conjurer, never before printed . . . Take Care to have this new Edition, with the Head of a Conjuror, never before printed."

"The Celebrated Lecture on Heads: Which has been exhibited upwards of one hundred successive Nights, to crowded Audiences, and met with the most universal Applause. By. G. Alexander Stevens. Dublin: Printed for J. Hoey, sen. in Skinner-row, J. Hoey, jun. in Parliament-street, and J. Williams, in Skinner-row, 1765." 12°. 60 pp. (BL 12332.ee.41.), also CtY.

"The Celebrated Lecture on Heads; Which has been exhibited upwards of one Hundred successive Nights, to crowded Audiences, and met with the most universal Applause. New-York: Re-printed by John Holt, at the Exchange." 1767. 32 pp. (LC AC901/.H3/ #23 bound in with other items). Also listed in EST with note that only known copy at LC could not be reproduced. The *Lecture* was also published over a period of three weeks beginning August 7 in Holt's *New York Gazette, or, Post Boy.*

"An Essay on Satirical entertainments. To which is added Stevens' new Lecture on Heads, now delivering at the Theatre Royal, Hay-Market. With Critical observations." Printed and sold by J. Bell 8°. pp. viii, 87. Four editions were published in 1772. 1st edition (BL 12330.e.7). (DFo PR/3717/S2/L4/E7), also RPB. 2 edition at NN. 4th edition at CtY/MH. The following review was published in *Critical Review; or, Annals of Literature* (July 1772), p. 70: "The short Essay in the beginning of this pamphlet is to be considered only as introductory to the Observations which follow. Concerning the latter it is difficult to say, that they are sometimes just, sometimes frivolous, and generally dictated with candour. But how far the author is justifiable for publishing Mr. Steven's Lectures, we shall not determine, as the matter is now in litigation."

"NEW LECTURE ON HEADS, BY GEORGE ALEXANDER STEVENS . . . LONDON, Printed: BOSTON: Reprinted for Henry Knox, in Cornhill. 1772." 8°. 56 pp. NN/MiU-C/MB/N/CtY/RPJCB/MH/MWA. Also, EST #12568.

By 1780, Lee Lewes had appropriated the *Lecture* and performed it with some frequency. He, with the assistance of Frederick Pilon, altered the original text, in several cases adding new, contemporary material. The manuscript submitted to the Lord Chamberlain's office is noted in the Larpent Catalogue, #527. The title page to the first published edition of this version reads: "A LECTURE ON HEADS, by G. A. STEVENS: As DELIVERED BY That Celebrated Comedian Mr. Lewes, at the THEATRES ROYAL of LONDON, DUBLIN, and EDINBURGH, and As performed by him with universal APPLAUSE at different capital Cities on the Continent. LONDON: Printed for T. Moore, No. 33, Pater-noster-Row. 1784." 4°. Frontispiece with 63 heads, 2 pp. of "Advertisement" (i.e., a preface), followed by 31 pp. of text. (BL 793. 1. 40.[g.]). The advertisement is quoted in full:

> The LECTURE on HEADS was an undertaking which we need not here to recommend; since in the first instances it recommended itself:—It received the patronage of the Public, as we presume, because deserving of it.
>
> Almost everyone knows, how often its original author, Mr. G. Stevens, delivered his Lecture in various parts, which succeeded to his wish, in gaining him both Fame and Advantage.
>
> Some others have, indeed, attempted an exhibition of this sort, without meeting with the like success; but we have reason to conclude the fault lay in the Lecturer, not in the Lecture; as every man is not born with the talents of an Humorist, any more than abilities requisite to form an Orator.
>
> At present Mr. Stevens's Lecture is delivered on the Continent by Mr. Lewes, in whose Hands, it was, from the first, pretty apparent that it would succeed. He has fulfilled every expectation that could be framed upon it; and he exhibits it at present, to crowded and most respectable audiences.
>
> As it is obvious that many of the brightest strokes, and most striking allusions in the Lectures on Heads, originally related to temporary matters; so it appeared proper now for the Lecturer to add some new subjects, and to make other improvements, such as it was judged might be most agreeable to his hearers.
>
> In this dress, we here present the performance to the Reader; not doubting but it

may prove an agreeable companion in the closet, as affording food for laughter, and the means of enjoying an innocent and rational amusement.

Among the new heads are, "Pr[ime] M[iniste]r's Head," "Fox and North; or the Coalition," "Tristam Shandy," "B[re]sl[a]w" (who replaces Jonas, the conjuror), and "The S[a]r[a]t[o]ga General."

The so-called "first authentic edition" appeared in 1785. It was the Lewes text with the Pilon additions and an added "Essay on Satire." This version comprised a large number of variants which are treated here as a group. The earliest edition begins with a folded frontispiece showing, at left, a lecturer at a table holding a head with a long wig and some fifteen people watching at right. "FRONTISPIECE to the LECTURE on HEADS. Publish'd as the act directs, August 2d 1785 ... Designed by Charles Fox. Engraved by Thomas Trotter." Title page reads: "A Lecture on Heads written by George Alexander Stevens, with additions by Mr. Pilon; as delivered by Mr. Charles Lee Lewes, at the Theatre Royal in Covent Garden, and in various parts of the Kingdom. To which is added an Essay on Satire. London: Printed (by Assignment from Mr. Lewes) for G. Kearsley, at Johnson's Head, No. 46, in Fleet-Street 1785. Price Two Shillings sewed. Entered at Stationers-hall." 8°. Includes Address to the Public, errata, Pilon prologue for the June 24, 1780, performance, Mr. Pratt's prologue for the Bath performance, September 11, 1780, the Newbury prologue, the text of the Lecture and the Essay on Satire. (BL 1080.i.53), (DFo PR3717/S2/L4/1785), also NNNAM. Two errors occur in this edition which are repeated for a number of years: the section on the Freeholder's Head reads "in a state of inoculation" instead of "intoxication" (p. 22), and in the Essay on Satire we find "Conscious, therefore, of the entertainment" instead of "consciousness" (p. 114). The errors are corrected many years later but are included here as an interesting sidelight on the publishing history of the text.

Then similar to the first edition, the title page reads "A New Edition, Corrected." 1787. 12°. On p. ix in an advertisement for the Lecture we find "Mr. Stevens never disposed of the Copy-Right of this celebrated Lecture till he sold it to Mr. Lewes for a valuable consideration, who afterwards consigned it to Mr. Kearsley [PP]. It is thought necessary to mention this circumstance, as spurious editions, both incorrect and mutilated, are in circulation." (BL 12316.f.8.), (DFO PR3717/S2/L4/1787, an excellent copy with a hand colored frontispiece), also ICU/OrU/CSmH/MB.

Then similar to the first edition with title page variants: "A New Genuine Edition Corrected. The Public are requested to observe that there are two spurious Editions of this Lecture, which are not only inelegant but very inaccurate." And ". . . at the Theatre-Royal, Covent-Garden, The Royalty-Theatre, Well-Close Square, and in various Parts of the Kingdom; also in the East Indies . . . Price only One-Shilling, Sewed. With the genuine Edition of G. A. Steven's Songs, Half-a-Crown, sewed; of Three-Shillings bound—The Lecture, or Songs may be had separate. 1788." 8°. (BL 12331.b.44.[1.] songs not included), also ICU/NN/CSt/MH/InU/PSt/MdBJ/NNC/MB/ICN/CSmH/MiU-C/VU/PPL/CU.

Also (same as?) "WIT AND HARMONY A Cheap and Correct Edition of the Works of George Alexander Stevens, is published this day containing A Complete Collection of his Songs, published verbatim from his last corrections, also his celebrated LECTURE upon HEADS as delivered originally by himself, with additions as spoken by Mr. Lee Lewes . . . To which is added, an ESSAY on SATIRE by Mr. Pilon . . . N.B. There are spurious and incorrect Editions of STEVENS's works, in circulation, against which it is necessary to caution the publick. The Songs may be had separate, price 1s 6d. and the Lecture on

Heads price 1s or bound together 3s." For Kearsley. 1788. Advertised in the *Morning Chronicle*, January 2, 1788. I know of no extant copy and cannot determine if this edition contains the three prologues, etc.

Also a Dublin printing similar to above with the songs: "Dublin: Printed by William Porter, for Mess. Byrne, Wogan, Jones, Moore, and Dornin. 1788." 12°. (BL 1079.g.20.).

Then "A New Genuine Edition Corrected. The Public are requested to observe that there are . . . A LECTURE ON HEADS written by George Alexander Stevens, Esq. with additions by Mr. Pilon, as delivered by Mr. Charles Lee Lewis, At the Theatre Royal Covent Garden . . . Also in the East Indies. To which is Added AN ESSAY ON SATIRE. London: Printed and sold by William Lane, Leadenhall-Street. 1795." Contains the three prologues. CtY/PU-F/MH/MWA/PPL/NNC/WU.

Then another edition similar to the first. With oval-shaped frontispiece containing 8 to 10 figures, one looking through small spy-glass (or kaleidoscope?). Title page: "A Lecture on Heads by Geo. Alex. Stevens . . . Pilon . . . Lewes . . . Essay on Satire . . . With Twenty-four heads by Nesbit, from designs by Thurston. London: Printed by T. Bensley, Bolt Court, Fleet Street; for Vernor and Hood, Poultry; J. Cuthell, Holborn; and J. Walker, Paternoster Row. 1799." 8°. There are actually 26 heads. The designs are imaginative and well done but are artist's conceptions, often 3/4 length and in action but do not represent actual heads used in performance. (BL T.450.[6]), (LC PR3717/.S2L4/ 1799), also CtY/PP/NcD/CtY-M/MH/OCU/MB.

Then similar to 1799 edition with oval frontispiece but contains 47 heads by Nesbit. Title page: ". . . London: Printed for . . . Otridge and Son, Strand . . . 1802." (BL 1607/210), also NjR/VU/NNR/ICN/PU.

Then similar to the 1802 edition. Title page: "With forty-seven Heads by Nesbit, from designed by Thurston—London: Printed for Vernor, Hood, and Sharpe, Poultry; J. Cuthell and Martin, Holborn; J. Walker, Paternoster-Row; and Otridge and Son, Strand, At the Union Printing-Office, St. John's Square, by W. Wilson.—1806." 12°. Does not include the Bath prologue. Text has now been corrected to read "intoxicated" and "consciousness." (BL 1079. g. 21; this copy has incorrect signature at bottom of p. 101 that reads H3 for H2), also CtY/MoSU/NcU/CSmH/MH/CtY-M/PPL.

Then similar to the 1799 edition: "A Lecture on Heads . . . With twenty-four Heads. Belfast: Printed and Sold by Samuel Archer, 22, High-Street. 1807." With the older errors. (BL 1493.1.7).

Then "Woodward's Edition." With folded frontispiece by Rowlandson depicting performer on stage holding a head, other heads on table, part of stage right, proscenium door and box, etc. Hand colored in some copies. Title page: "A Lecture on Heads . . . Embellished with Twenty-Five Humorous Characteristic Prints. From Drawings by G. M. Woodward, Esq.—London. Printed for Vernor, Hood, and Sharpe; Cuthell and Martin; J. Walker; Otridge and Son; and Longman, Hurst, Rees, and Orme; By W. Wilson . . . 1808." 12°. Does not include the Bath prologue. Several of the prints are identified as published by Thomas Tegg, No. 111, Cheapside, on March 30 and April 20, 1808. Apparently the prints were also available separately. (BL C116.b.27), (LC PR3717/ S2L4 with the prints bound as a group preceding first page of the text), also PPWl/ CtY-M/TxU/CSt/NIC/GU/OU/MH/OClW.

Then similar to 1806 edition. The type has been reset but the placement of the text and pictures almost identical. Same signatures. Title page. "Printed by W. Wilson, 4, Greville-Street, Hatton-Garden, for J. Cuthell; J. Walker; Otridge and Son; Longman, Hurst, Rees, Orme, and Browne; R. Scholey; Newman and Co.; Cradock and Joy; Sherwood, Neely, and Jones; and Gale, Curtis, and Fenner. 1812." 8°. (BL 012331.e.136), also IEN-D/NcU/OCU/NNC/CtY-M/NNNAM.

Then another American edition. Title page: "A Lecture on Heads . . . [then a small cut of the Laughing and Crying Philosophers, which is repeated on p. 63]. Embellished with forty-five heads, illustrative of the subject. Baltimore: F. Lucas, Jr. 138 Market Street." Ca. 1820. Does not include the Bath prologue. With the Nesbit/Thurston illustrations. With "intoxication" and "consciousness." 16°. (BL 12330.aa.29.), also NN (listed as 24°.) NcD/MH/MB/MdBJ.

Then the last of the Lewes-Pilon versions. Title page: ". . . With forty-seven heads by Nesbit from Designs by Thurston. A New Edition. London: Printed for Longman, Hurst, Rees, Orme, and Brown; Baldwin, Cradock, and Joy; R. Scholey; Newman and Co.; Sherwood, Neeley, and Jones; G. and W. B. Whittaker; and C. Taylor. 1821." Verso "Printed by T. C. Hansard, Peterborough Court, Fleet Street, London." 12°. Does not include the Bath prologue. With "intoxication" and "consciousness." (BL 12350.aaa.2.), also NcD/ICN/CSmH.

Evans (EST) #12567 lists an edition: "Just published (price 1 shilling) by Samuel Dellap and to be sold at his shop in Front Street between Market and Arch Streets"/ Philadelphia/ on the basis of an advertisement in the September 11 and 14, 1772, issues of the *Evening Chronicle*. The same edition was advertised in the *New York Gazette*, September 21, 1772, "to be sold by Thomas Nixon at his Shop at the Fly Market." No dated copy of this edition has been located. Evans subsequently claimed this entry was erroneous and reentered it as #20728 for the year 1787.

The Evans reentry (#20728) is undated. The title page reads: "THE CELEBRATED LECTURE ON HEADS: By George Alexander Stevens. Which has been exhibited upwards of one Hundred successive Nights, to crowded Audiences, and met with the most universal Applause. Printed for SAMUEL DELLAP, in Philadelphia." 8°. 28 pp. (LC PR3717/.S2L4/ 1787), also PPL/MiU-C/MB/RPJCB. I cannot trace the source of this uncertainty about the dating; perhaps it is based on the date used for the LC entry card, but I am reasonably convinced that the original Dellap edition came out in 1772. Perhaps there were later printings.

This version is in a bound volume which includes most of the catches, glees, duets, pantomimes, and various entertainments presented at the Royalty Theatre between 1787 and 1788 but most are undated. It includes the *Lecture* as delivered by Mr. Palmer. Title page in its entirety reads "Lecture on Heads as delivered by Mr. Palmer, at the Royalty Theatre. A Picture of the Playhouse; or Bucks Have at Ye All. By Mr. Palmer. The Golden Days of Good Queen Bess! Written by Mr. Collins, Author of the Brush." No date, place, or publisher. Ca. 1787? 8°. The text of the *Lecture* is only eight pages long. (BL 11779.c.88.[10.]), also MH.

A version entered by Evans (EAI-SS) #27742. "George Alexander Stevens' Celebrated Lecture on Heads; Revised, Corrected and Enlarged" (Boston, 1794). "Imprint assumed by Evans from advs." The so-called "ghost" (?).

Title page "The Lecture on Heads by the Celebrated George-Alexander Stevens. With Additions. Cooke's Edition. London: Printed for C. Cooke, No. 17, Paternoster-Row, by WM Calvert, Great Shire-Lane; and sold by all Booksellers in the United Kingdom." 1800? but perhaps earlier. 12°. Some interesting material in the Address to the Reader:

We present the following improved Edition of the "Lecture on Heads," by George-Alexander Stevens, in the fullest confidence that it will prove an acceptable present to the Public; there having been hitherto no copy of this celebrated work of humour printed either under the care of the Author, or with any particular attention to the original composition: for we cannot admit the pretensions of the late Mr. Lee Lewis upon this subject, or grant that his Edition published in 1785 is in any respect superior to those he affects to treat with so much contempt. On the contrary, we candidly confess we prefer the copy published by Pridden, in Fleet-street, insomuch as it approaches nearer the work of Mr. Stevens. . . .

We have taken care to add to the original Lecture all the improvements and additions it received from the hints and suggestions of the most celebrated wits of the day, Churchill, Shuter, &c. and have omitted nothing that might tend to elucidate and exhibit in higher colours the various characters lectured upon!

(BL 12352.aa.45.[1.]), also MH (listed as 24°).

"The Humourist's Miscellany: containing original and select articles of Poetry, on Mirth, Humour, Wit, Gaiety, and Entertainment. To which is prefixed, the Celebrated Lecture on Heads; by the late G. A. Stevens, Esq. . . . Second edition with considerable additions.—London: Printed by James Cundee, Ivy Lane; for B. Crosby and Co. Stationers'-Court, 1804." Preface includes "We have given this whimsical Lecture in its *native* dress; for however ingeniously it was altered by the late Mr. Pilon, it must be observed, he adapted it to his *own* time, and such are the revolutions which have happened, that *his* edition would be found *equally* unfit for the *present*." The text is in five parts and based largely on the Lewes editions. Has "inoculation" for "intoxication." (BL 11602.c.26.)

Another Lewes-Pilon variant without the *Essay on Satire*. Title page: "MIRTH AND SONG: Consisting of a *Lecture on Heads*, Written by GEORGE ALEXANDER STEVENS, Esq. and THE COURTSHIP, with a collection of APPROVED SONGS. BOSTON: Printed by E. Lincoln, For John Whiting, of Lancaster 1804." 24°. The *Lecture* in five parts is 58 pp. Has "inoculation" for "intoxication." MH/CtY/RPB/MWA/NN/OC/EAI-SS Supplement S7308.

Title page: "A LECTURE ON HEADS. *For the Amusement of all Ages. First American, from the Third London Edition.*

> This attempt you will see's to succeed the Projector,
> In an humble abridgement of Steven's Lecture:
> And since for mere Mirth I exhibit this plan,
> Condemn if you please, but Approve if you can.

—PHILADELPHIA. Published by Wm. Charles. No. 32 South Third-street. 1817." Extremely abridged. Only 12 pp. Six lectures. Lecture Five, e.g., only 33 words. With occasional, unrelated decorations. NN/EAI-SS #42217.

Title page: "The Works of the late G. A. Stevens, Esq. Consisting of his celebrated Lecture on Heads, and Songs.—A New and Improved Edition, to which is prefixed A Life of the Author.—By W.H. Badham, Esq.—Risum teneatis, Amici? *Hor.*—London: Printed for Washburn and Son, Gloucester; G. Williams, Cheltenham; and Knibb and Langbridge, Worcester. 1823." 12°. (BL 11661.e.8. The title page of this copy is preceded by an additional title page with an engraving of a domestic scene dated 1824 by "Witherington, del and Waren sc.") Also (CtY Im/St47/B 824. Same as BL copy except "By C. Tolley, Esq." instead of "W. H. Badham, Esq." Verso of title page reads: "London:

Printed by Thomas Davison, Whitefriars.") Also (LC PR/3717/.S2/1823. Same as CtY copy but contains the Badham title page, then half title, then the Tolly title page.)

Also a reissue. Front wrapper adds: "Printed for Edward Edwards, 53 Newgate Street; [London] and the other proprietors.—1825. Printed by W. Sears, Gutter Lane." (BL 11622.aa.55.)

Allibone's Dictionary of Authors (p. 2247) lists an 1860 edition. This has not been located and is probably a misprint for 1806.

II. Other Works by (or Attributed to) Stevens.
Individual or in Collection.

Religion; or, The Libertine Repentant. A Rhapsody (London, 1751), printed and sold by W. Reeve and F. Noble. 8°. (BL T. 1057. 3.), also NjP/OrU/CtY/MnU.

A Week's Adventure; or, an Epistle from England. Advertised in *The Covent-Garden Journal* (Dublin), vol. I, no. 37 (Thursday, August 27, 1752), p. 147. "On *Monday* next will be published, at the *Mercury* in *Skinner-Row, Dublin* . . . Price a penny" [by James Hoey]. Also a second edition entitled *A Week's Adventures in England: An Epistle from George Alexander Stevens to His Friend in Dublin.* Advertised *CGJ*, vol. 1, no. 42 (October 12, 1752), p. 167.

Distress upon Distress; or, Tragedy in True Taste. A Heroi-Comi-Parodi-Tragedi-Farcical Burlesque in Two Acts . . . with Annotations . . . by Sir Henry Humm. And Notes Critical . . . by Paulus Purgantius Pedasculus . . . (Dublin, 1752), printed for the author by James Esdall on Cork Hill. 8°. (BL 11777.d.83), (LC PR1241/.L6/vol. 48), also OrU/LU/ICU/NNC/CSmH. Also (London, 1752), reprinted from the Dublin Edition, for R. Griffiths in St. Paul's Church-yard . . . Price 1s. 6d. 8°. (BL 163.i.49.), (DFo PR/3717/S2/D6), also KU/IU/MiU/NBuG/NN/MH/TxU/CtY/ICN.

The Choice Spirit's Feast: A Comic Ode (London, 1754), printed by J. Towers, in Picadilly. 4°. (BL 11632.g.52), (DFo PR/3717/S2/C2).

The Birth-Day of Folly, an Heroi-Comical Poem, by Peter: With Notes Variorum, for the Illustration of Historical Passages Relating to the Hero of the Poem, and Other Remarkable Personages (London, 1755), printed for M. Cooper, at the Globe in Paternoster Row. (DFo PR/3717/S2/B3), also CtY/IU/MH/NIC/PU/ICN.

Albion Restored; or, Time Turned Occultist [a masque] (London, 1758), J. Seymour. 8°. CtY/NjP/CSmH/CU. [Nicoll (p. 396) attributes this work to Stevens. According to the *Biographia Dramatica* (1782, vol. 2, p. 6) it was never acted.]

The Polite Songster: A Collection of Three Hundred of the Most Celebrated English and Scots Songs . . . The Humorous and Much-Admir'd Burlesque Burletta, by G. A. Stevens . . . (London, 1758), J. Ross. (NIC M/1738/P76). [Without music.]

A Collection of New Comic Songs. To Which Is Added, the Swadler's Harangue. To a Crowded Audience at the Marlborough Green (Dublin, 1759). H. Saunders, at the corner of Christ-Church-Lane. (DFo 151002).

The History of Tom Fool [Novel] (London, 1760), 2 vols., printed for T. Waller, opposite Fetter-Lane, Fleet Street. 12° (BL 12614.bb.12.), (LC PR/3717/.S2/H5), (DFo PR3717/S2/H4), also CSmH/LU. Also *Tom Fool's History; or, Modern Taste Displayed* (London, 1761), T. Waller, 2d ed. CLU/InU.

The Beauties of All the Magazines Selected (London, 1762, 1763, 1764), 3 vols. 8°. (BL P.P.5659). [These volumes were edited by Stevens but apparently contain some of his own material.]

The Dramatic History of Master Edward, Miss Ann, and Others, the Extraordinaries of These Times (London, 1763). 12°. NNC/InU/ICU/NBuG/CtY/MH/MoSU/NIC. Also (London, 1785). 12°. (BL 10825.b.40), also CLU/InU/NN/IU/CSmH/ICU/MiU/MH/ICN/LU/NNC/WaU. Also (London, 1786). 12°. (BL 1079.g.19. and G.14244), (DFo PR 3717/S2/D7 and 193467), also InU/MB/MH/RPB/CtY/NcU.

The French Flogged; or, British Sailors in America, a Farce of Two Acts as It Was Performed at the Theatre Royal, Covent-Garden (London, 1767), printed for J. Williams at no. 38, Fleet-street. 8°. (BL 161.e.26), (LC PR/1241/.L6/vol. 214), (DFo PR/3717/S2/F7), also CtY/MiU/CSmH/MiU-C. See also Larpent MS 6.L. or #172.

The Court of Alexander. An Opera in Two Acts. As It Is Performed at the Theatre Royal in Covent-Garden. . . . (London, [1770]), printed for T. Waller, in Fleet-Street. 8°. (BL 161.e.2.), (LC PR1241/.L6/vol. 37), (DFo PR/1241/06), also CSmH/LNT/MiU/LU/NcD/ICU/CtY/NN/MH/TxU. Also second edition (London, 1770). (BL 11775.g.11.); also NBu/NBuG/DeU/NcGU/NNU. Also third edition (London, 1770). (LC PR1241/.P55 incomplete); also InU. Also (Dublin, 1770), printed by J. Exshaw. 12°. (BL 1346.b.27.), (DFo PR3717/S2/C7).

The Storm; or, Dangers of the Sea [song] (London, 1770?), (BL Rox. III. 401.); also as *Storm at Sea*, single sheet. 4°. (BL 11630.f.7. [138]).

Once the Gods of the Greeks [song] (London, 1770?); also published as *The Origin of English Liberty.* IU/CtY.

The Humours of London, a Choice Collection of Songs . . . a Choice Variety by Geo. Alex. Stevens . . . And Other Celebrated Geniuses. . . . (London, [1770?]), printed for J. Cooke, in *Paul's Alley, St. Paul's Church-yard.* (LC PR/1215/.H8).

The Choice Spirit's Chaplet; or, A Poesy from Parnassus. Being a Select Collection of Songs, from the Most Approved Authors: Many of Them Written and the Whole Compiled by George Alexander Stevens, Esq. (Whitehaven, 1771), printed by and for John Dunn and sold by Messrs. Hawes, Clarke, and Collins in Pater-noster Row. 8°. (BL 11621.aaa.21.), (LC PR/1187/.S8 incomplete), also MH.

The Fair Orphan [comic opera] ([London], 1771). 8°. [Nicoll (p. 326) attributes authorship and performance to Stevens.]

Songs, Comic and Satyrical (Oxford, 1772). 12°. (BL 239.h.2. and 11621.aaa.20. imperfect copy, and 11633.de.45. in 8°.), (DFo PR/3717/S2/S6/1772), also ICU/NBuG/WU/CtY/NjP/NcD/NcU/PPL/IU/MH/InU/CSt/MiU/PU; also (Dublin, 1778). Also (Oxford, 1782), the second edition . . . printed for the author; sold by G. Robinson and J. Bew, in Paternoster-Row; and E. Newberry, the Corner of St. Paul's Church-Yard. (LC PR3717/.S2/S6), also VU/CtY/OrCS. Also (London, 1788). 12°. (BL 1078.f.10.), also MB/PP/ICU/PSt/MH. Also (London, 1801), printed by J. Cundee, Ivy Lane, 12°. (BL 11621.bbb.12.), (DFo PR3717/S2/S6/1801), also AAP/InU/CU-A/PP/MH/NN/MdBJ/KyU. Also as *Songs, Comic, Satyrical, and Sentimental. By George Alexander Stevens . . .* (Philadelphia, [1778]), printed by R. Bell, Third Street. MiU-C/MH. [These editions were Stevens's answer to the pirated *The Choice Spirit's Chaplet* (supra.). See also *Critical Review; or, Annals of Literature* (July 1772), p. 70, for comments on the earliest edition.]

The Trip to Portsmouth: A Comic Sketch of One Act, with Songs. (London, [1773]), printed for T. Waller, in *Fleet-Street*; T. Becket, in the *Strand*; and G. Robinson, in *Paternoster Row.* 8°. (BL 841.d.37.), (LC PR/1241/.L6/vol. 40), (DFo PR/3717/S2/T8), also CtY/WU/MH/PPL/MB/NN/CSmH/MH; also (Belfast, 1774), printed by James Magee.

Songs in the Trip to Portsmouth (London, 1773), 8°. See Larpent MS 11.L.

The Songster's Horn Book: Written by Geo. Alex. Stevens (London, [177?]), by R. Falkener. IU.

The Songs, &C. in the Cabinet of Fancy; or, Evening's Exhibition (London, 1780), printed for

R. Snagge, no. 186, in Fleet Street. 8°. (DFo PR3717/S2/S5). See also Larpent MS 15. L OR #533.

The Vicar and Moses: A New Song (London, 1780). (BL Rox. III. 313 Broadside folio and Rox. III. 875 Slip folio).

The Adventures of a Speculist; or, A Journey through London. Compiled from Papers Written by George Alexander Stevens. . . . [a novel] (London, 1788), 2 vols. in 1. Printed for the Editor and sold by S. Bladon, No. 13 Paternoster Row. 12°. (BL 1079.h.17. and G.16084–85.), (DFo PR/3717/S2/A2), also NN/ICN/MH/IU.

Gay Bacchus, As Sung by Mr. Dighton at the Anacreontic Society (London, 178?), J. Fentum. (LC M1621/.G/Case); also *Gay Bacchus, a Favorite Song, Sung at the Anacreontic Society, Written by G. A. Stevens, Set by T. Smart* (London, [178?]), Preston. (LC M1621/.S).

New Roast Beef Song, by G. A. Stevens (London, 178?). (LC M1621/.L/Case.) [The tune by Leveridge adapted to new words by Stevens, with continued accompaniment and part for guitar at end.]

Management: A Dramatic Satire by Humphrey Hum Esq, Dedicated without Permission to a Mighty Lessee from the Unpublished MS of the Late G. A. Stevens (London, [1820?]). NIC/OC/MH/MB.

No Magic Like Gold; or, The True Stockwell Conjurer. (This, This and This Only Is True Conjuration.) Sung by Mr. Bannister in the Interlude at Mr. Weston's Benefit: Words by G. A. Stevens. [n.p., n.d.] [Voice and bass; also flute solo.]

The Wine Vault [a song.]. Published as late as 1845 in Thomas Campbell's *Specimens of the British Poets.*

III. Unpublished Works.

St. George for England. A droll. (ca. 1760). Authority for this work comes from the George Downing entry in the *Biographical Dictionary of Actors* . . . vol. 4, p. 464.

Hearts of Oak. A musical interlude comprising a song and dance by sailors. ". . . being a mere temporary affair on the declaration of war with Spain, met with good success." BD, (1782), vol. 2, p. 146. Larpent MS 7.L. (#205) January 13, 1762.

The Mad Captain. An opera? Probably an adaptation of Robert Drury's opera which was acted at Goodman's Fields in 1733. Nicoll attributes the work to Stevens (p. 334), stating that it was performed at Yarmouth in 1769. It may have been done in 1771 with Snagge.

IV. Attributed

The Humours of an Irish Court of Justice: A Dramatic Satyr . . . "Written by an exil'd Freedman of that Country for his Amusement during his Retirement and dedicated to the Lovers of Truth and Liberty." (London, [1750]). Printed and sold without *Temple-Bar*, and at the *Royal Exchange*. (Price Six-pence.) Dedication signed, "A Freeman Barber." (LC PR1241/.L6/vol. 104. p. 30 is misnumbered p. 36), also CtY. This work is ascribed to Stevens in Stephen J. Brown, ed., *A Guide to Books on Ireland* (New York, 1970), p. 165. The dating, contents, and style all render this attribution suspect.